Increasing Service User
Participation in Local Planning

Related books of interest

Empowering Workers and Clients for Organizational Change
Marcia B. Cohen and Cheryl A. Hyde

The Community Needs Assessment Workbook
Rodney A. Wambeam

A Practical Guide to Evaluation, Second Edition
Carl F. Brun

Social Work Evaluation: Enhancing What We Do, Second Edition
James R. Dudley

**Writing Clearly for Clients and Colleagues:
The Human Service Practitioner's Guide**
Natalie Ames and Katy FitzGerald

**Using Statistical Methods in Social Science Research with a
Complete SPSS Guide, Second Edition**
Soleman H. Abu-Bader

**Evidence-Based Practices for Social Workers:
An Interdisciplinary Approach, Second Edition**
Thomas O'Hare

Using Evidence to Inform Practice for Organizational Change
Maria Roberts-DeGennaro and Sondra J. Fogel

Social Service Workplace Bullying: A Betrayal of Good Intentions
Kathryn Brohl

Increasing Service User Participation in Local Planning

A How-To Manual for Macro Practitioners

JUDITH M. DUNLOP
Kings University College at Western University, Canada

MICHAEL J. HOLOSKO
University of Georgia, United States

LYCEUM
BOOKS, INC.

5758 South Blackstone Avenue
Chicago, Illinois 60637

© 2016 by Lyceum Books, Inc.

Published by

LYCEUM BOOKS, INC.
5758 S. Blackstone Avenue
Chicago, Illinois 60637
773-643-1903 fax
773-643-1902 phone
lyceum@lyceumbooks.com
www.lyceumbooks.com

6 5 4 3 2 1   16 17 18 19 20

ISBN 978-1-935871-77-4

Printed in the United States of America.

Library of Congress Cataloging-in-Publication Data

Names: Dunlop, Judith M., author. | Holosko, Michael J., author.
Title: Increasing service user participation in local planning : a how-to manual for
    macro practitioners / Judith M. Dunlop, Western University, Ontario, Michael J. Holosko,
    University of Georgia.
Description: Chicago, Ill. : Lyceum Books, Inc., [2016] | Includes bibliographical
    references and index.
Identifiers: LCCN 2015050784 | ISBN 9781935871774 (pbk. : alk. paper)
Subjects: LCSH: Community-based social services. | Social service—Citizen participation. |
    Community development.
Classification: LCC HV40 .D825 2016 | DDC 307.1/2—dc23
LC record available at http://lccn.loc.gov/2015050784

Contents

List of Figures

List of Activity Sheets

Acknowledgments

This book would not have been written if I had not had the privilege of having my MSW thesis on interorganizational collaboration supervised by Michael Holosko in 1987. My MSW experience led to the completion of a PhD based on research on collaborative networks at Memorial University of Newfoundland. Over the past twenty-eight years, Michael and I have continued to collaborate on a number of research projects, books, book chapters, and articles devoted to the development of collaboration theory. With this book, thanks to you, Michael, we have experienced another creative and intellectually fulfilling journey.

I join with Michael in acknowledging the contributions of all our students both Canadian and American who supported us through their expertise with research, knowledge of APA requirements, and computer skills. In Canada, thanks to Derek Chechak and Sara Morrison, Kings University College at Western University, who were with us from the very beginning. Special thanks to Graham Fawcett at the University of Windsor for his superior IT skills. We had a great team to work with and were supported wholeheartedly and expertly throughout the journey. Much appreciation is extended to all of you!

—Judith M. Dunlop

I would like to formally thank my oh-so-visionary professors at the Universities of Toronto and Pittsburgh where I completed my MSW and PhD degrees, respectively. Some thirty-five plus years ago, you taught me that macro practice and micro practice was a false dichotomy, and these were actually two domains of practice that were overlapping circles. The eclipsed shaded area of these circles is where I have spent my entire academic career—and this text is a testimony to that reality.

Also, a special thanks in the preparation of this text goes to Joelle Pettus, Trasie Topple, Anna Ramminger, J. Lloyd Allen, and Ching Nga Poon. I thank each of you for your unequivocal support, masterful research and typing, critical thinking, editing, and giving "student voice" to this practical hands-on planning manual. It was much appreciated!!!

—Michael J. Holosko

Preface

We wrote *Increasing Service User Participation in Local Planning: A How-To Manual for Macro Practitioners* as a sequential and instructional approach demonstrating how service users can become more meaningfully involved in planning for local community service system reform using a community development planning model (CDPM).

Other countries all over the world—Ireland, Scotland, Wales, England, Sweden, Australia, New Zealand, and Ghana, to name a few—have either developed, mandated, and/or legislated the voices of service users in local community development planning initiatives. Although the United States and Canada have started to incorporate service users into community processes, we contend that in most cases, service users have been merely placated and the importance of their voice has been minimized, more so than in the countries noted above, where service users are a necessary element for any responsible planning activity.

The backbone of the text is an eight-step, field-tested planning model illustrating how service users join with service providers to conduct a local needs assessment and gap analysis and to identify a priority community need and specific intervention model to meet that need. The planning process culminates with a funding proposal submitted to procure funding to bring new resources to the local community. Written as a recipe for successful social planning, the eight-step model could be used in many other community initiatives such as strategic planning, visioning, mission development, assessing community problems or assets, locality development, developing healthy communities, resource procurement and mobilization, community priority establishment, promoting community advocacy, community capacity building, and developing or improving new service structures. Thus, the proposed model could be used educationally, politically, economically, and/or environmentally.

The primary market for this text is graduate students in social work foremost, followed by students in public health, public administration, nursing, medicine, community psychology, business, education, recreation and culture studies, environmental studies, and tourism planning. The secondary market is practitioners in local governments, businesses, politics, and health and human services who are required to incorporate service users meaningfully with other community stakeholders and partners in planning more effectively.

Using evidence-informed data and a community development empowerment approach, this manual is specifically designed to promote service user/provider partnerships, creating a pathway for leadership in planning local community initiatives. To do this, each step in the model offers three sequential action steps to be achieved by using various additional activity sheets completed by both service users and providers. Upon completion of each planning step, service users and providers complete individual and group evaluations to collaboratively discuss and assess their achievements before proceeding to the next step. Thus, transparency, empowering voices, identifying successes or improvements, and planning effectiveness evolve as the eight-step empowerment planning model unfolds.

The introduction has two main sections entitled "Service User Participation" and "The CDPM." The first relates the history and context of service user voice in community development planning. It describes how service users have been generally trivialized and placated in such planning endeavors, and as such, it provides the rationale for the manual. The second section presents the core assumptions of the community development planning model (CDPM). It contextualizes the model both in broader neoliberalism trends and also more local empowerment concerns of individuals, organizations, and communities. This part of the introduction addresses the purpose and aims of the manual.

Following this contextual scaffolding, the eight-step model is unpacked in sequential chapters 1–8. Chapter 1, "Planning Step 1: Define Stakeholder Participation," describes how community stakeholders, including service users and providers, are sought out and how to begin the collaborative process of the community planning activity. Chapter 2, "Planning Step 2: Build Mission and Purpose," presents the essential planning steps in joint mission-building. Chapter 3, "Planning Step 3: Identify Community Strengths," describes how the identification and tapping of community assets is integral to this planning process. Chapter 4, "Planning Step 4: Identify Community Needs Using EID," makes a foray into the newly uncharted area of not only pinpointing real community needs but illustrating how evidence-informed data (EID) are used to achieve this purpose. Chapter 5, "Planning Step 5: Identify Services and Set Priorities Using EID," demonstrates how collaborative discussions are used to carefully sift and sort through EID and to set priorities for the needs of the community. Chapter 6, "Planning Step 6: Plan Service Using EID," describes how needs become transformed from priorities, previously identified in chapter 5, to actual service provision. Chapter 7, "Planning Step 7: Decide on Intervention and Sponsors," begins the dovetailing of the planned intervention and community sponsors. Finally chapter 8, "Develop Joint Proposal," culminates with how a funding proposal is written and submitted to include an EID needs assessment, service gap analysis, and identification of priority community need and a priority intervention model to meet the community need using a detailed work plan for all joint and individualized activities.

In the interests of simplicity and pragmatism, we formatted each of the eight-step planning chapters in the same way, defined each planning step with three accompanying action steps, and for each action step used field-tested activity sheets to navigate the step. Upon the completion of each planning step we included a selected case vignette drawn from our experiences to illustrate the activities of the step, a process evaluation form designed to achieve mastery in each step both individually and in group form, at least four current web-related resources, and a sample of the PowerPoint presentation summarizing the step. A glossary of community development planning terms is presented at the end of the text. When these terms are used in the text they are bolded. (A supplementary digital package including reusable versions of all planning activity sheets, full PowerPoint presentations, and the glossary is available for purchase.)

We hope that the content and style of this manual provides readers with the rationale, structure, and means showing how service users and providers may simply and effectively use this planning process in the way it was conceived, field-tested, and written.

JMD
MJH

Introduction

PART I. SERVICE USER PARTICIPATION

Separating Myth from Reality

In the introduction to this manual we want to be controversial as we explore why service user participation (SUP) has not been more widely implemented around the world. Our experience has informed us that SUP works but there are definite parameters around how it works; we discuss the "how" in part II of this introduction, when we present the community development planning model (CDPM). In the remaining chapters of the manual (chapters 1 to 8), we introduce readers to an eight-step **planning process** that is pragmatic and highly committed to a joint planning process for **service users (SUs)** and **service providers (SPs).** (That said, the parallel planning process was designed to increase SU knowledge and expertise in community planning before SUs participate in the joint SU/SP planning process.)

In introducing the **eight-step model of evidence informed planning** that is the foundation of this manual, it is important for us to highlight the participatory nature of this local SU/SP planning process. While the model follows a step-wise pathway as outlined in part II of this introduction, the model is firmly rooted in the CDPM. We understand that each local community and context is unique. In addition, each local SU/SP planning group is unique; how the participants find their way to jointly owned decisions about services for their local community is the main theme of this manual.

This planning manual contains a large number of planning activity sheets that have been designed to increase dialogue and **collaboration** among the SU/SP **local planning** group. In no way are they prescriptive, however. Instead, they are mechanisms of collaboration designed to be used, or not used, or amended, or eliminated, or added to, or in any other way changed to meet the needs of the unique local SU/SP planning group. Our experience has taught us, though, that having structured exercises is helpful to facilitate conversation and discussion among planning group members. The parallel planning process introduced in this manual seeks to level the playing field by having both SUs and SPs complete the planning exercises separately, after which SUs and SPs will review them together to search out their common objectives. There are also a number of consultants who are important to this SU/SP planning process, notably those with expertise in (1) research and group decision-making, (2) **budgeting,** (3) geographical information systems (GIS) mapping, and (4) information technology. While the technical expertise of these consultants is helpful to the successful completion of the planning steps, it is not expected that the SU/SP planning group will automatically have resources to hire consultants to take on these tasks.

Such consultants may come to the SU/SP planning process in a number of ways. First, the research and group facilitation skills can be expected to be part of the macro practitioner's role in working with the planning group. Second, the organizations that compose the SU/SP planning group may have budget expertise within their agencies that could be offered as a donation in kind. Third, the GIS mapping expertise could come from students or faculty at local universities or colleges who would be willing to volunteer their services as part of their service learning or graduate course work. Fourth, the information technology skills required for the Web-based reporting system in this planning process may be donated by any of the local agencies that are participating or through the local university or college student or faculty complement. The approach used by each local SU/SP planning group will be different and will rest on that group's decisions about what type of consultation is needed. In this SU/SP planning model, the macro practitioner will engage in local **community development** (CD) to recruit and engage local technical expertise in the required areas to support the SU/SP planning process.

The planning process outlined herein with its eight sequential steps does allow for the planning group members to go back and retrace their steps if there is a lack of understanding or consensus on decisions. It is important to note that the planning process is step-wise and participatory and focuses on the planning process itself, and not on a predetermined **outcome.** Each of the eight planning steps contains three **action steps,** and within each of these action steps there are a number of possible planning activity sheets designed to assist both SUs and SPs with their joint decision-making on what will work best for their unique local community. The specific planning model is outlined in part II of this introduction.

Although there is much controversy over the use of terms used to describe the relationships between those who provide and those who receive service, we are using the terms *service user* (or SU) and *service provider* (or SP) in this manual. Terms that others have used include *client, customer,* and *expert by experience* (McLaughlin, 2009). While the ideological debate about the marketization of welfare services is an important discourse (Dunlop, 2006; Holosko & Barner, 2014; Mooney & Neal, 2010), the idea that the **client** is primarily a customer who exercises choice in a free market system is not the central focus of this manual; this primer is about the relative merits of voluntary/mandatory SUP. Where the proverbial rubber hits the road for SUP is how SUP can work effectively in the right conditions, with the right people, at the right time.

SUP: Separating Myth from Reality

While this how-to manual is not the place to introduce an in-depth historical or political analysis of the extent of SUP, it is true that there has been a shift in thinking about SUP worldwide, as well as in thinking about the issues that surround it. In fact, there has been a change not only in thinking, but in doing. Increasingly, many government reforms promote if not mandate SUP (Dunlop, 2007). While government rhetoric may highlight SUP, there are few instances where SUs have equal decision-making power with SPs. It is evident that policy-makers need to develop new strategies to legislate SUP in order to overcome what is mainly ad hoc and marginalized SUP in local planning for services. This lack of implementation of SUP is in many ways why we have written this how-to manual.

Our collective experience in teaching, research, and practice in community planning has been characterized by both the light and dark sides of the history of SUP. We have discovered there is a somewhat mythological aura surrounding SUP in community planning. The assumption that no SU/SP planning process can ever be successful is challenged by this manual that outlines a field-tested and sequential parallel and joint planning process designed to increase collaboration between SUs and SPs. A wide range of issues compose the mythology surrounding SU/SP relationships. We hope to take you on a journey in this land of SUP and introduce you to its voluntary/mandatory landscape riddled with power issues, SP resistance, lack of authentic voice, decision-making, and other quandaries about the real meaning of SUP.

We have an interest in challenging the proverbial mythology that SUP is difficult, or impossible. Our experience has taught us that, in fact, it is not. But effective SUP does take receptiveness to change and willingness to overcome a resistance to sharing power. Once SUs and SPs come together in a planning process that does not pander to or privilege SP knowledge, negative stereotypes or myths about the contributions of SUs can be shifted. Authentic SU/SP participation can be mostly about proximity; as the song goes, "Getting to know you, getting to know all about you." While we know that joint SU/SP planning processes are difficult to implement, the problem may simply be a case of SUs and SPs working in a vacuum, where myths take root and minds close to the possibilities of true **partnerships.** Whatever your belief system, we need to grow our knowledge of the history and context surrounding SU participation so we can explore the delicate questions surrounding barriers to SU participation, such as tokenism, lack of voice, lack of decision-making power, and SP resistance. The remainder of this part of the introduction is devoted to examining the complex myths and realities that surround SUP and begs the question: Why does it work sometimes with some people in some places, but not with other people in other places? We suggest that the sequential parallel joint planning process developed for this manual is a step that aims to equalize power and **democratic decision-making** and create myth-busting community planning realities.

History of SUP

Increasingly, government policy reforms lead one to naïvely believe that SUs and SPs have joined in mutually rewarding partnerships, but nothing could be farther from the truth. While government rhetoric may highlight SUP, in reality there are few instances where SUs have equal decision-making power. We contend that policy-makers need to develop new strategies to legislate SUP, in order to overcome what is mainly ad hoc and marginalized participation in local planning for services.

In the past three decades, governments in Australia, Canada, New Zealand, Sweden, the United Kingdom, and the United States have placed increased emphasis on SU involvement and its role in community planning and the delivery of health and human services. The World Health Organization has promoted SU involvement, and several countries have developed legislation strengthening the influence of SUs and giving them greater control over the services they receive (Omeni, Barnes, MacDonald, Crawford, & Rose, 2014). Since the 1960s government policies in a number of countries, previously identified, have promoted active involvement in planning, implementation, and evaluation by SUs (Arnstein, 1969; Friedman, 1977). This includes the promotion of SU voices and visions at the policy/planning table (Fleischer & Zames, 2001). Furthermore, privatization and other government actions and efforts have been encouraging the use of a market model, which provides increased competition among SPs (see introduction part II). This model in turn, limits the role of the government, which further facilitates the emphasis of consumer choice (Savas, 2000). This model creates the space for SU voice and choice to be incorporated into expectations of social welfare **programs** through government mandates and performance indicators around the world; and through various SU groups, nongovernmental entities, and nonprofits (Aronson, 1993; Lammers & Happell, 2003; Mizrahi, 1992).

For example, in the past twenty years UK health policy has continued to encourage SU involvement. **Advocacy** efforts have pushed successive governments to highlight SUP as a means of increasing the acceptability and value of services (UK Department of Health, 1990, 1999). The National Health Service and Community Care Act

(UK Department of Health, 1990) established formal requirements for SUP in government planning of services (Omeni et al., 2014). The New Labor government in the United Kingdom continued these developments with the National Service Framework for Mental Health (UK Department of Health, 1999), which positioned SU involvement as one of its central beliefs. Developments such as the Health and Social Care Act of 2001 further consolidated increased focus on SU involvement by setting out requirements for all National Health Service (NHS) organizations to ensure active SUP in treatment decision-making, as well as the planning and evaluation of services (UK Department of Health, 2001). In recent years, the government has continued to make changes to the structure of the NHS through the Health and Social Care Act of 2012, emphasizing strategies that may give people more choices and control over how their support needs are met (UK Department of Health, 2012).

One such change was the implementation of the UK Local Government and Public Involvement in Health Act that was drafted in 2007 (Government of United Kingdom, 2007). This legislation was created with the government's plans to abolish the Commission for Patient and Public Involvement in Health and the patient forums that had been established in 2001. Local Involvement Networks were to replace patient forums, with the intention of promoting public and community influence in health and social care. These arrangements purportedly would make NHS organizations in the United Kingdom more accountable to their local populations so that patient and SU voice would be strengthened through the creation of these new mechanisms (Healthcare Quality Improvement Partnership, n.d.). Despite all of the proposed legislation and policy changes that were created to increase SUP, as of this writing the United Kingdom still has a lag in SUP in community planning (Healthcare Quality Improvement Partnership, n.d.). The real story behind this lack of inclusion of SUs in local community planning is based on the historical resistance of SPs to the democratic inclusion of SUs as necessary partners in decision-making.

Current Context of SUP

The UK example outlined above, which includes mandatory SUP, raises some interesting questions about what is happening across the ocean in Canada and the United States. While there are pockets of noteworthy examples in these two countries, the absence of American or Canadian legislation and funded SUP initiatives demonstrates that there is a long way to go before SUP is of much importance in these domains. It is noteworthy that in both countries there has been a counter-shift in support for SUP. During the 1970s and 1980s in Canada, there were various jurisdictions where SUP was of great importance, namely the Children's Services Coordinating Committees and District Health Councils in the Province of Ontario, but these have been disbanded and not replaced. The same situation has occurred in the United States with two exceptions: (1) federally funded Community Health Centers that are mandated to have 51 percent of SUs as board members, and (2) federal Healthy Start Programs that mandated SUP and dedicated specific funding to facilitate SUP. One can speculate that the resurgence of interest in SUP in other countries may have an impact on the adoption of SUP in both Canada and the United States. That being said, research suggests that without a legislative mandate for SUP very little happens (Dunlop, 2002, 2006, 2007; Dunlop & Holosko, 2005). It has been suggested that, in the United States, the role of nonprofits is to engage their SUs in planning for local services. To date, however, it appears that such initiatives have been legislated. For example, the previously mentioned Community Health Centers and Healthy Start Programs are two federal U.S. initiatives that have successfully implemented SUP. That said, there seems to be in the United States, much like in Canada, a dilution of genuine interest in SUP in favor of more-technical and more-professional planning approaches. A certain equilibrium, therefore, exists in these two countries where the status quo of non-SUP appears unchallenged. Given the controversy surrounding SUP in the United Kingdom, one can conjecture that it is only a matter of time before the reforms from the United Kingdom and Europe, namely the raising of SU voice and power, will shift to North America. The recent nationalization of health care and the unfolding of the Patient Protection and Affordable Care Act (2010) in the United States may spur SUP as this model is one that is oriented to a community-centered approach.

The 2000 U.S. Healthy Start Program sites had mandatory SUP with dedicated funding exclusively for SUs. Whether it was legislative mandate for SUP and/or the commitment to SUP by Healthy Start managers, SUs were recruited, trained, brought into the decision-making arena, and helped to become SU advocates. In turn, the development of SUP was facilitated by program managers who were committed to building strong families and communities through democratic decision-making and advocacy training. The Healthy Start staff were trained specifically about how to work with SUs, and various protocols and learning experiences were developed to build SU confidence and democratic involvement in the entire planning process (Dunlop, 2006, 2007). Collaboration between SUs and SPs in these sites was successful despite the presence of the issues that complicate successful SUP such as (1) built-in SP resistance to SUP and (2) lack of authentic voice for SUs.

Built-in SP Resistance to SUP

The success of SUP depends on whether SPs are willing to become true partners with SUs. Integral to the success of these partnerships is the capacity of SPs to change their perceptions about SU expertise. In addition, it has been recognized that SPs can refocus their values and ideas by engaging in reflective practice that questions their status positions, relationships, and capacity for transformation in SU/SP partnerships (Morrow, Ross, Grocott, & Bennett, 2010). This transformation in the provider role requires unlearning and abandoning traditional paternalistic approaches and substituting them with more-democratic **participatory relationships** (Adams & Drake, 2006). However, there is a difference between rhetoric and reality when SPs continue to control what types of SU knowledge will be valued (Wilson & Beresford, 2000). The minimizing of SU knowledge and voice by SPs also requires examination. A study by Beresford on user-controlled research emphasized four critical areas in the development of SU voice: (1) the capacity to be useful, (2) the identification of new issues, (3) the ability to be more inclusive, and (4) personal benefits for the participants (2007).

Notwithstanding the identified problems with SUP, there is growing research interest in exploring SUP and its impact on health- and social-care research and education (Barber, Beresford, Boote, Cooper, & Faulkner, 2011; Carey 2009; Smith, Gallagher, Wosu, Stewart, Cree, Hunter, & Wilkinson, 2011). This has recently been strengthened by studies that seek to explore and describe SUs' conceptions of actual participation (Carey, 2009; Hernandez, Robson, & Sampson, 2010; Kvarnström, Willumsen, Andersson-Gare, & Hedberg, 2012; Ryan-Nicholls & Haggarty, 2007; Smith et al., 2011). In addition, there has been support for SU-initiated awareness training for SPs that would ideally improve partnership development (Carr, 2007). Finally, research on systems of care has identified strategies for developing SUP that support educator and consultant roles for SUs in their work with SPs. Training curriculum has been developed to increase SU/SP collaboration where "family members serve as trainers, educators and consultants to the same systems that were treating their child" (McCammon, Spencer, & Friesen, 2001, p. 12). Dowding and John (2011) stated clearly that anything that reduces SU voice in planning for health and human services is not likely to improve care at all. The devaluing of SUs in interprofessional community planning groups inhibits full participation and decision-making in the collaborative partnership. SPs who cannot listen, or do not "hear" the voices of experience and knowledge that SUs bring to the group, can destroy the goodwill and trust that is necessary for successful collaboration between SUs and SPs.

Research on the active involvement of SUs working collaboratively with SPs identifies the need for genuine mutuality in identifying needs and developing services (McCammon et al., 2001). This shift in the roles of SPs is a phenomenon that researchers are increasingly exploring, albeit mostly from an SP perspective. There is much research suggesting that SUs are inclined to participate in shaping the formation, implementation, and execution of direct care programs (Forest, Risk, Masters, & Brown, 2000; Fudge, Wolfe, & McKevitt, 2008; Holosko, 1997; McLaughlin, 2009). These same research studies also suggest that SUs, while willing to participate, were often hesitant to do so because SPs rarely take their suggestions seriously. Research on SUP suggests that, while SUs willingly shared their opinions regarding how to improve a program's quality or the quality of care being received, program administrators often failed to recognize these contributions when making decisions (Fudge et al., 2008). Consequently, SUs gave their opinion on program improvement but SPs did not incorporate their views in recommended program changes. This lapse in recognition of SU contributions is often based on a level of bias and stigmatization by SPs (McLaughlin, 2009). Consequently, this turning away from SU knowledge and expertise means that services may not improve for clients and be less than acceptable (Holosko, 1997). Forest et al. (2000) reported that SPs in their interactions with SUs tended to rely on their textbook knowledge and expert role rather than their interpersonal and communication skills. As Forest et al., noted, this SP distancing approach toward SUs resulted in SUs reporting that they thought SPs lacked **self-awareness** and competence (Forest et al., 2000). Historically, SPs' relationships with SUs have been characterized by a lack of recognition of the importance of SU knowledge and experience in the development of local services (Beresford & Croft, 2008).

What is needed is a stronger voice for SUs in the planning and development of services. Many studies have shown that closer proximity and working directly with SUs has contributed to changes in SP attitudes, views, and beliefs about the value of SU voice (Mockford, Staniszewska, Griffiths, & Herron-Marx, 2012). Research also strongly suggests that mandated SUP is necessary for meaningful involvement in local community planning, and that successful SUP must be built one step at a time (Staniszewska et al., 2011). Some research suggests that proximity creates partnerships (Mockford et al., 2012) because SPs, through reflective practice, must challenge themselves to explore the socially constructed meaning of SUs as outsiders to the process (Morrow et al., 2010). Macro practitioners must learn to deal with the dynamic tensions that occur when diverse points of view are brought together. The nontraditional relationship building between SPs and SUs requires a comprehensive understanding of **practice guidelines** for working with local SU/SP planning groups and a reengineering of identification with a specific professional role (Dunlop & Angell, 2001).

At the end of the day, there are a number of nuanced, historical, and contextual interpretations of SP resistance to SUP. While we have looked at a number of different lenses that characterize SP resistance, reflecting on these lenses leads us to two primary themes: (1) SP avoidance of getting to know you (SU), and getting to know all about you (SU), and (2) SP resistance to giving up the role of expert. This manual is designed to incrementally help SUs and SPs to get to know each other better and to ultimately help SPs change their interpretations of SU expertise. As the SUs and SPs work together throughout the eight planning steps, it is hoped that the balance between valuing professional knowledge over experiential knowledge will be shifted and the proximity that brings "getting to know you, getting to know all about you" will transform SU/SP power relationships.

Lack of Authentic Voice for SUs

Previous research has shown clearly that SPs silence the voice of SUs by discounting their experiential knowledge (Levin, 2004). Despite increasing political commitment and legislation that seeks to bring SU expertise and contributions to the forefront of planning for services, the voices of SUs are often muted when they are incorporated into interprofessional planning entities. Increasingly, top-down directives for SUP result in tokenism with its subsequent minimal or nonvoice (Holosko, Leslie, & Cassano, 2001). These directives represent an add-on rather than a true recognition of SU voice (Beresford, 2007). SU voice can be classified in two categories: (1) individual voice and (2) collective voice and action (Dowding & John, 2011). Individual voice is specific to complaints related to service. Collective voice and action require individuals to be involved in some advocacy or pressure group directed at specific collective actions. This notion of voice as collective action provides an important framework for understanding SUP in all health and human service agencies. The rhetoric of SUP can cloak underlying power dynamics, where SPs support SU voice only as SU tokenism. The influence of SPs on SU voice cannot be underestimated. When the voice of SUs is trivialized by SPs, new knowledge based on lived experience is avoided and interpreted as not important to the planning process (Beresford, 2007). When SU voice is missing or watered down, the likelihood of improving service quality is inevitably compromised. While there has been commitment and legislation that seeks to bring SU expertise more to the forefront of planning for services, SU voice remains quiet or silent in most interprofessional planning entities in many countries. As such, SU voice is missing or diluted and the likelihood of improving service quality is compromised. SU voice can be amplified only by a joint chorus of SUs and SPs. It appears that more evidence is needed to convince SPs that SU voice leads to better service outcomes overall (Mockford et al., 2012).

Increasing SU voice within health and human services can be achieved by expanding the network of SPs who are engaged with SUs. If SUs can engage with multiple professionals face to face and be listened to and respected, then the process may eventually lead to joint decision-making and negotiation regarding service provision (Kvarnström, 2011; Kvarnström, Hedberg, & Cedersund, 2013). Voice is thus solidified when SUs and SPs enter into a transparent dialogue and agreements that move toward a more equitable collaboration with power sharing of the role of the alleged expert. Giving up the expert role within interprofessional relationships requires SPs to change their interpretations of SU expertise. Furthermore, it requires that SPs restrain from devaluing or controlling their SU partners.

Perhaps the most obvious point to make about SU voice is that of silencing. SUs enter a planning process with SPs, often for the first time, with no knowledge of the planning terrain or its language. Like a traveler who does not speak the local language, the first defense is to be quiet. Primarily, we do not wish to offend; secondarily, we do not know how to talk in this new environment. There is no sense of continuity for SUs when they enter a planning process with SPs. Most SPs are familiar with both the planning environment and its language, and usually rush in to talk up the planning goal, as if they were handling a crisis. It is well known that the only way we can understand another language initially is if the person speaking does so very slowly. Thus, SUs are immediately forced to the backbench before the game even starts. Historically, this may be why SPs tend to report that SUs are not interested without assessing first how their own communication patterns may hinder or help the planning process.

The raising of authentic voice, then, is just one of the reforms that is needed in successful SU/SP local planning initiatives. There are others, too numerous to mention, but let's have a look back at how SP resistance inhibits authentic SU voice. First, the lack of experience working with SUs is a known barrier because this lack of experience leads to paralysis as SPs try to control the process, and SUs retreat as if they were on enemy territory. Second, research suggests that proximity creates better partnerships (Mockford et al., 2012). This may be the case, but if SUs' conversational or decision-making styles contrast widely with the technical style of the SPs, then they are not even on the same planning level. The usual decision-making dynamic consists of SPs overpowering SUs. This usually results in SUs withdrawing from the planning process, leaving no mechanism for the SUs and SPs to reframe their experience, discuss what has happened, and seek a resolution.

A strong case can be made that SPs, through reflective practice, must challenge themselves to explore their perceptions of SUs as outsiders to their well-entrenched SP planning process. The onus then is on SPs to challenge their own interpretations of the importance of SU voice and acknowledge their discomfort and resistance to the experiential knowledge of SUs. SPs must challenge their own perceptions of privilege and accept, once and for all, that they are not the only agents of potential change in their community. SUs need an equal place at the planning table. SUs are increasingly seen as agents of change who are actively participating in democratic decision-making (Kvarnström et al., 2013). SU voice can only be amplified by a joint chorus of SUs and SPs with strong desires to work toward improving services for their shared local community.

Part I of this introduction has set the contextual stage for the planning model that we describe in part II, and for the more pragmatic down-to-earth chapters that follow (chapters 1–8). We have tried to explain the growing demand for increased SU participation worldwide, and why macro practitioners should care about the emergence of SUP, not the least of which is our concern for individual autonomy and choice, improved social policy, and **social justice.** The landscape for macro practice has shifted to become more politicized, which requires us to be aware of the linkages between policy development and community planning. Arguably, SUP reflects emerging participatory approaches to planning. Part I of this introduction has set the stage for understanding SUP with its discussion of SUP history, SUP context, SP power and resistance, and SU authentic voice.

Finally, part I of the introduction allows us to be fully open about why engaging in SUP is critical and why the eight-step SU/SP planning model in the subsequent chapters is driven by an understanding of the positive and negative experiences of SUs and SPs in local communities. Part II presents the planning model that SUs/SPs will engage in throughout the eight-step planning process, and provides the scaffolding for the eight-step planning process. The ensuing planning chapters 1 through 8 are designed to allow for the sequential SU/SP parallel and joint planning process to unfold. They contain a number of important planning components, not the least of which are the field-tested activity sheets for each planning step that may be used in this approach. We hope that as you work your way through this how-to manual you will find the steps useful—not only for successful planning outcomes, but as a guide for how to promote the free exchange of ideas and decisions between SUs and SPs, resulting in a joint decision that demonstrates unanimity, and the beginning of new SU/SP relationships based on ongoing respect, trust, and the valuing of diverse kinds of knowledge and experience.

PART II. THE CDPM

In part I of this introduction we provided the **rationale** or why we wrote this how-to manual. Part II describes the what and how of the content and its context. It has five subsections: (1) a field-tested CDPM, (2) an eight-step CDPM process, (3) a **work plan** for the CDPM planning process, (4) an evaluation of the CDPM planning process, and (5) a brief note on writing style.

Subsection 1 is the main content part of part II of this introduction. Both authors developed and field tested a joint SU and SP model derived primarily from the fifty-some years of extant CD literature, as it is referred to in Australia, New Zealand, and the United Kingdom; and the parallel community empowerment and program development literature, as it is referred to in Canada and the United States. The purpose of the proposed planning model is to build a collaborative planning group between SUs and SPs based on mutual respect and trust, and to encourage democratic decision-making at the local level.

Each of the eight sequential planning steps in chapters 1–8 is anchored in this scaffolding model that itself is a defined process of acquiring skills and knowledge, learning problem-solving skills, increasing personal and professional confidence, and building community capacity through SUs and SPs working together over time. Subsection 2 presents the eight-step CDPM process; this is the planning process that is the planning framework for the CDPM of community planning. Subsection 3 is a work plan for the CDPM planning process; this work plan outlines the action steps and timelines that compose the year-long planning process and the responsibilities of SUs and SPs throughout their joint SU/SP planning process.

Subsection 4 presents an evaluation of the CDPM planning model; it is used to assess each planning step component and, if done properly, can result in both individual and community **empowerments**. Finally, subsection 5 is a brief note on the writing style we use in this manual. We wanted to inform readers about the conversational tone for the manual, which seeks to provide a structure for understanding the principles of the CDPM and the pragmatics of the eight-step planning process that characterizes the CDPM.

Subsection 1. A Field-Tested CDPM

The Context: External Trends Shaping Today's Health, Social Policies, and Services

Often, health and human service employees who toil for long hours with their clients or patients work under stressful conditions; they can be rather naïve about how broader state, national, and international trends shape their day-to-day practice (Feit

& Holosko, 2013; Holosko & Barner, 2014; Holosko & Pettus, 2014). Indeed, their well-intended altruistic and mission-driven orientation to moving clients through systems of care creates somewhat of a tunnel vision, in which many cannot look beyond the immediate needs of their clients, or how they implement **interventions** for them (Holosko & Leslie, 1998). Two of the more pervasive external trends that have been apparent for some forty years all over the world are (1) **neoliberalism** and (2) **globalization.** These trends trickle down daily to the doorsteps of the health and human service organizations in which we implement policies and services for clients/patients (Dunlop, 2006, 2009; Feit & Holosko, 2013; Holosko, 2009).

Neoliberal globalization is a blending of two terms that are now more conceptually interrelated than they were a decade or so ago (Holosko & Barner, 2014). Unfortunately, this widesweeping conservative political and economic agenda that started with Prime Minister Margaret Thatcher in the United Kingdom and President Ronald Reagan in the United States has not fared well at all for health and social welfare services. Neoliberalism's main elements as described by Martinez and Garcia (1997) include these:

1. The rule of market drives services not government.
2. There are annual reductions of expenditures for health and social services.
3. There is increasing deregulation from government authority and responsibility.
4. Governments turn to privatization as a means of providing health and human services.
5. Governments eliminate the concept of public good or community and replace them with individual responsibility, at any cost (p. 100).

Under neoliberal globalization we have witnessed more worldwide poverty than ever before, more disparities between economic and social groups, more income inequalities between the rich and the poor, less security and rights, less social justice, decreased environmental health, and poorer worker safety standards and employment policies (SUNY Levin Institute, 2013). If we drill down a bit farther to hone in on our federal, state, or regional and local health and human service organizations levels, we see how these trends have influenced the ways we have developed and implemented social policies and services much more than one may realize.

Holosko (2013) in Feit and Holosko (2013) cited ten such pervasive neoliberal globalization trends. However, for this introduction, and for this manual, we will discuss only three trends and their back stories in this section on external trends shaping today's health, social policies, and services. These trends are (1) increased demands for services, coupled with fewer resources; (2) a community **devolution** from federal→state→local levels; and (3) integrative approaches to **service delivery.**

In regard to the first trend, every day around the world more and more people need more and more services, often just to survive let alone to thrive. The story behind this first trend also has two messages: As many developed countries increase their health and human service budgets annually due to the increased number of people needing services, actual per capita expenditure on health and social welfare decreases each year (Holosko & Barner, 2014). As a result, health and human service workers already employed in very stressful and regulatory environments are expected to do more with less daily—and often they simply are not able to do so. In addition, health and human service organizations have responded to this pressing need to serve more people by developing waiting lists, tightening eligibility criteria, reducing budgets annually, offering compressed and shortened time frames for treatment, increasing their fees for services, and promoting privatization of government-administered services, which is now becoming the norm in many countries in the world.

The second trend has to do with the shifting of responsibilities and authority downward from federal→state→local levels in many countries. Called a **devolution** revolution by Nathan (1996), a term then used by Dunlop (2009) and Holosko (2009), this trend results in communities having abruptly dropped on their laps greater responsibilities for the funding and administration of local services and policies. The story behind this trend is also two-fold. First is the YTI-YOI syndrome (you touch it—you own it), so that now local communities are far more accountable for the disposition and administration of their health and human services than they ever were before. Coupled with this is that many communities have not developed their own infrastructures and/or care capacities that are often fragmented and underresourced, which undermines their ability to build effective **communities of care** to assume these new additional responsibilities (Holosko & Pettus, 2014).

Finally, the third trend is that communities are now increasingly encouraged to build their local integrative systems of care (Pires, 1996) by bundling together multiple agencies in cross-sectional collaborations—or networks, alliances, or partnerships—among public, secular, and faith-based nonprofit and for-profit community organizations. Indeed, funders prioritize integrative **service coordination** in efforts to meet community-identified needs through partnerships that both empower and engage community residents and SUs in decision-making, and that maximize community resources, preclude **service duplication,** and ideally facilitate more-efficient service delivery (Parrish, Harris, & Pritzker, 2013, p. 362). This trend resonates with the raison d'être for the writing of this collaborative planning manual.

These three trends, as well as others not mentioned here, set the organizational context to better understand both the proximal general environment and the **task environment** (Hasenfeld, 1983) of the health and human service organizations in which we ply our daily and altruistic craft. The more we are aware of these trends, and, more importantly, of their potential impacts, the better we will be able to ethically practice with our clients and build better communities of care, communities of collaboration, and communities of compassion. After all, isn't this what we are really trying to achieve?

Empowering Individuals, Organizations, and Communities

A simple yet poignant definition of empowerment is "the act of giving somebody the power or authority to do something" (Oxford Dictionary Online, 2015). This serves as a conceptual starting point to define this rather evasive concept because, in our experiences with many communities, we have come to realize that (1) empowerment is differentially interpreted by both those who are empowering others, and those who receive the empowerment to do something; (2) empowerment is a process that implies that through planned activities or behaviors people can become empowered; this is often a positive thing for many groups and individuals; and (3) empowerment is also an outcome; individual self-esteem, self-efficacy, locus of control, self-awareness, goal achievement, skill development and knowledge, decision-making, and personal confidence are all noted in the literature on empowerment.

Although empowerment has historically been differentially defined by many disciplines, like medicine, nursing, social work, criminology, education, and business, it has also been defined by **vulnerable populations** such as persons in poverty or who are sick, the elderly, individuals who are homeless, persons with mental health problems, persons with addictions, and individuals who are incarcerated. Since the overarching framework for this manual is one that uses a social planning model to achieve a collaborative community goal, we will frame our definition of empowerment from a CD lens, which has been around for some forty years in most of the developing world. The CD definition of empowerment expands on the abbreviated one, previously cited.

The Community Empowerment Action Plan defines community empowerment as a process where people work together to make change happen in their communities by having more power and influence over what matters to them (Scottish Government, 2009, 8). The Community Empowerment Action Plan is the name of a government planning process used in the United Kingdom, in this case in Scotland, as the planning process for neighborhood regeneration. Laverack and Labonte (2000, p. 260) identified the operational domains of community empowerment as (1) participation, (2) **leadership**, (3) organizational structures, (4) problem assessment, (5) resource mobilization, (6) asking why, (7) links with others, (8) the role of outside agents, and (9) program **management**.

Assumptions of the CDPM

There are many different strategies used in CD. Eight of the more common are:

1. Locality development
2. Social action
3. Social planning
4. Social reform
5. Community relations
6. Social capital formation
7. Capacity building
8. Asset-based development

This manual focuses on social planning (#3), which includes three main features: (1) a problem-solving planning process to address social problems; (2) involvement of **needs assessments** and analyses of service delivery mechanisms, systems coordination, and other technical expertise; and (3) involvement of community members in consultation, interpretation of results, and service planning (Ontario Healthy Communities Coalition, 2015; Rothman, 1996; Twelvetrees, 2008).

One of the main rationales for the inclusion of the open and collaborative planning process described in this manual was our experience in thinking about a major downside of empowerment—which is **disempowerment,** a subject rarely addressed in models of CD (Dunlop & Holosko, 2005; Holosko, 1997; Holosko et al., 2001). We were also concerned about offsetting the historic placating that always goes on in CD strategies toward the recipients of services or SUs. We therefore offer some core assumptions about SUs from our own experiences working with groups in various communities in Australia, Canada, New Zealand, Sweden, the United Kingdom, and the United States. These assumptions make the model presented herein work; they have been adapted from the SU approach earlier noted by Holosko et al. (2001). In a sense, these almost read like a **code of ethics** (COE) for SUs.

Core SU Assumptions of the CDPM

1. SUs have a basic right and, in turn, an obligation to actively participate in community planning activities that affect their lives and communities.

2. This planning process is a deliberate one in which SUs are allowed to obtain respect, legitimacy, and resources.

3. The CDPM has a number of distinct features, minimally including (a) active solicitation of SU voice and promotion of ongoing dialogue, (b) full **transparency** and accountability, (c) a defined process with a beginning and an end, (d) a focus on the interactions between SUs and various community **stakeholders,** (e) the development of collaborative partnerships and alliances between SUs and all identified SPs and other community stakeholders, (f) the means to securing and valuing SU knowledge and incorporating such feedback into the defined planning process, and (g) a correct implementation of the CDPM to empower SUs (incorrect implementation of the model disempowers SUs) (Holosko et al., 2001, 128–129).

The Building Blocks of the CDPM

As indicated in part I of this introduction, the current trend in many governments around the world is to enable people to play more-active roles in their community's futures. This echoes the trend previously noted in this introduction called a devolution revolution. As such, it has been shown that authentic community engagement occurs when people in communities create structures and processes that are empowering for themselves, and at the same time people in public agencies create structures and processes that are empowering for themselves and others (Community Development Exchange [CDX], 2008). Figure 0.1 presents the interrelated building blocks of our CDPM which anchors the planning process outlined in chapters 1–8 of this manual. As indicated in figure 0.1, the CDPM is cyclic and dynamic, with each element contributing to the next one in the circle; when completed, the cycle contributes to the eventual individual community empowerment. We summarize each element in this cycle in figures 0.2 through 0.6; each element is referenced and fairly self-explanatory.

Figure 0.1. The CDPM

The first step in figure 0.1 identifies a community-based **strengths perspective.** Often we use the term *strengths-based perspective* as an umbrella concept for strengths, which we frequently do not clearly delineate. Figure 0.2 presents the eight selected principles of the community-based strengths perspectives of our model.

Figure 0.2. Selected Strengths-based Perspectives of the CDPM

1. A conscious effort to incorporate a positive and optimistic view of SUs and communities' capacity needs.
2. A focus on individual and community strengths and assets, and not on deficits or problems.
3. Seeking and valuing SU and community voice and decision-making ability, in all instances.
4. Viewing the community as a potential goldmine of resources that need to be tapped.
5. Acceptance that a transparent and trusting relationship between all community stakeholders is essential.
6. Understanding that the community of care needs constant **outreach** and relationship-building to ensure effective SU navigation with available service providers.
7. Realization that realistic benchmarks for the achievement of outputs and outcomes require strengths reframing.
8. Reframing all barriers, concerns, and obstacles as challenges.

Source: Based on Modrcin, Rapp, & Chamberlain (1985); and Holosko (in press).

CD is about building active and sustainable communities based on platforms of social justice and mutual respect. The core CD values of our model articulated in figure 0.3 refer to actively changing power structures to remove barriers that prevent people from participating in issues that may affect their lives, a distinct element of the CDPM illustrated in figure 0.1.

Figure 0.3. Core CD Values

1. Learning: Recognizing skills, knowledge, and expertise that people contribute and building on these.
2. Equality: Challenging discrimination and oppressive practices within organizations and communities.
3. Participation: Facilitating democratic involvement by people and issues which affect their lives based on full citizenship, autonomy, and shared power.
4. Cooperation: Working together to identify and implement action behaviors, encourage networking, and connecting between communities and organizations.
5. Social Justice: Enabling people to claim their human rights and meet their needs and have greater control over decision-making processes which affect their lives.
6. Advocacy: Developing strategies for the identification of individuals and communities to advocate for themselves in partnership with other stakeholders.

Source: Based on CDX (2008).

Also, we often think of empowering individuals and sometimes forget that people who work in healthy organizations can be empowered within and by their respective agencies and workplaces. Figure 0.4 identifies selected characteristics of empowerment organizations, the third element in figure 0.1.

Figure 0.4. Selected Characteristics of Empowerment-Oriented Organizations
1. Includes SUs/consumers in organizational decision-making.
2. Creates partnerships to design and evaluate programs.
3. Delivers culturally appropriate services.
4. Minimizes power differential between SUs and SPs.
5. Promotes psychological empowerment of workers by giving them more autonomy to make decisions that affect their work.
6. Creates administrative leadership structures ideologically committed to empowering SUs and staff members.
7. Encourages staff to advocate for improvement in service delivery and SU resources.
8. Increases the political power of the organization and its **constituents.**

Source: Based on Hardina (2005).

The CD literature has many examples of successful and unsuccessful collaborations occurring in a variety of healthy human service organizations. Figure 0.5 identifies selected factors thought to be contributing to successful community collaborations, another element of the CDPM.

Figure 0.5. Factors Contributing to Successful Community Collaborations
1. People: Make sure the chemistry and commitment of people who work together is positive.
2. Vision: Create a shared vision and common goals that incorporate members' perspectives and identifies mutual needs that cannot be met by one organization alone.
3. Trust: Build trust through mutual respect for each person's life experience, knowledge, and contribution.
4. Time: Prepare adequately for planning, implementation, and follow-up.
5. Planning: Consider, agree on, and commit to all aspects of the community collaborative, including purpose, function, decision-making processes, risks and benefits to each member, and anticipated results.
6. Communication: Establish a transparent flow of information among members and mechanisms to ensure that all members are kept current on matters related to the collaboration and create clear means of voicing concerns and suggestions.
7. Learning Together: Make sure participants can learn about each other, about the issues or needs that are being discussed, and about how to work together.
8. Decision-Making: All partners must negotiate and understand the decision-making and the problem resolution process.
9. Leadership: Shared leadership should constantly renew energy and increase commitment in collaborations.
10. Technology: Use electronic communication to enhance and support the work of the partnership by facilitating connections and opportunities for innovation.
11. Flexibility: Make adjustments as needed as circumstances change: one or more members may not be able to contribute to the extent originally intended or may not be able to remain involved.

Note. Based on Ontario Healthy Communities Coalition (2015); and Dunlop & Holosko (2005).

Next, the five dimensions of community empowerment in figure 0.6 provide a framework for the planning work presented later in this manual that is empowering for communities. These dimensions can also be used for identifying elements of planning and evaluating the work process and outcomes that lead to community empowerment.

Figure 0.6. Dimensions of Community Empowerment

1. Confidence: Working in ways that teach people skills and knowledge; and instilling hope in them that they can make a difference.
2. Inclusiveness: Working in ways that recognize and promote the equality of opportunity and good relations between groups and that challenge inequality and exclusion.
3. Organization: Working in ways that bring people together around common concerns and issues in organizations and groups that are open, democratic, and accountable.
4. Cooperative: Working in ways that build positive relationships across groups, that develop and maintain links to national bodies, and that promote partnerships that work.
5. Influence: Working in ways that encourage and equip communities to take an active part and influence community decisions, services, and activities.

Source: Based on CDX (2008).

Our collective experiences using the field-tested collaborative planning approach presented in this manual demonstrate that it is important to understand that (1) the CDPM approach is anchored in a CD perspective, (2) it is built on a sound and checkable conceptual model, and (3) it is anchored in the concept of empowerment. The information presented in this introduction has been adapted and tweaked for its relevance and contextualization to today's neoliberal social and political reality. It is also the rationale behind why we use the term *evidence-informed practice* (or EIP) throughout this manual: the model is based not only on tried-and-true concepts, but also on **empirical** evidence that SUs have imputed, literature has informed, and SUs and SPs have implemented.

Subsection 2. The Eight-Step CDPM Process

Each of the following planning steps corresponds to the chapter with the same number. Thus, for a discussion of step 4, please see chapter 4.

Step 1. Define Stakeholder Participation. This planning step is designed to select those stakeholders who are necessary to ensure a representative community group, and whose participation is necessary to ensure a successful planning process.

Step 2. Build Mission and Purpose. This step is designed to help the SU/SP planning group develop a cohesive identity, and to clearly articulate who they are, what they hope to achieve, and how they will achieve their stated objectives.

Step 3. Identify Community Strengths. This step is designed to help the SU/SP planning group engage in a planning process that mobilizes existing community resources and encourages planning members to focus on community strengths, rather than on deficits.

Step 4. Identify Community Needs Using EID. This planning step involves working together to collect evidence-informed data (EID) to provide a foundation for their joint SU/SP decision-making about potential priority needs and interventions.

Step 5. Identify Services and Set Priorities Using EID. This step allows the SU/SP planning group to use EID in their decision-making activities to select priority needs and interventions previously identified in the local community.

Step 6. Plan Service Using EID. This step involves the development of intervention model rating criteria that the SU/SP planning group uses to examine specific intervention models and to further explore their suitability for meeting the identified local priority needs.

Step 7. Decide on Intervention and Sponsors. This step requires the SU/SP planning group to review the EID they have already collected and to agree on a priority intervention model to meet the specific local needs they have identified in previous planning steps.

Step 8. Develop Joint Proposals. Finally, this planning step delineates the activities that the SU/SP planning group must undertake in order to develop the culminating proposal and budget for funding. This step also requires the SU/SP planning group to review available funding and select the most feasible opportunity from funding available for their specific target group and intervention.

Subsection 3. A Work Plan for the CDPM Planning Process

We now present the comprehensive CDPM work plan for the eight-step planning process that gives the concrete details and time frames for completing the planning activities within it. This work plan lists the planning tasks required, places them in sequential order, shows whose responsibility it is to complete the planning task, and gives the approximate timing of each planning activity. These twenty-six planning activities and their time frames are illustrated in figure 0.7. The figure also includes a column for designation of responsibility for completion.

The work plan is designed to limit confusion about what planning activities need to take place, who needs to be responsible, and what amount of time is needed to complete the activity. That said, the time frames are not carved in stone. The activity sheets chosen by the SUs and SPs in the CDPM planning groups must reflect their unique local planning processes, so some may be used and others not used, or some may be amended in a way that works for their specific local context. Since we know that each community is unique and each planning group contains a unique group of stakeholders, it is not expected that SUs and SPs will adhere strictly to these time frames or use all of the activity sheets. In our experiences, mission development can take a very long time when there are competing interests. Likewise, engaging stakeholders is not a task that can be done quickly because it is dependent on stakeholders wanting to be part of the SU/SP planning group initiative. Thus, we present the work plan in figure 0.7 as a guideline, and not as a prescription.

Perhaps of most interest is that the work plan sets the agenda for the eventual planning group meetings: since the planning task, time line, and responsibility are clearly outlined, the agenda for meetings is preset to follow this outline. For SUs and SPs, this is an important element of the work plan element because it can prevent meeting after meeting where nothing really happens. The work plan can also serve as an important recruitment strategy because it clearly sets out in writing (1) this is

Figure 0.7. Sample Work Plan for the CDPM

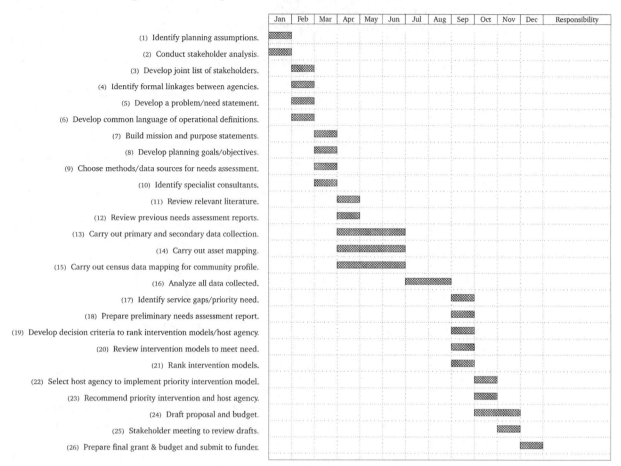

	Jan	Feb	Mar	Apr	May	Jun	Jul	Aug	Sep	Oct	Nov	Dec	Responsibility
(1) Identify planning assumptions.	▓												
(2) Conduct stakeholder analysis.	▓												
(3) Develop joint list of stakeholders.		▓											
(4) Identify formal linkages between agencies.		▓											
(5) Develop a problem/need statement.		▓											
(6) Develop common language of operational definitions.		▓											
(7) Build mission and purpose statements.			▓										
(8) Develop planning goals/objectives.			▓										
(9) Choose methods/data sources for needs assessment.			▓										
(10) Identify specialist consultants.			▓										
(11) Review relevant literature.				▓									
(12) Review previous needs assessment reports.				▓									
(13) Carry out primary and secondary data collection.				▓▓▓									
(14) Carry out asset mapping.				▓▓▓									
(15) Carry out census data mapping for community profile.				▓▓▓									
(16) Analyze all data collected.							▓						
(17) Identify service gaps/priority need.									▓				
(18) Prepare preliminary needs assessment report.									▓				
(19) Develop decision criteria to rank intervention models/host agency.									▓				
(20) Review intervention models to meet need.									▓				
(21) Rank intervention models.									▓				
(22) Select host agency to implement priority intervention model.										▓			
(23) Recommend priority intervention and host agency.										▓			
(24) Draft proposal and budget.										▓▓			
(25) Stakeholder meeting to review drafts.											▓		
(26) Prepare final grant & budget and submit to funder.												▓	

what we plan to do, (2) this is how long it is going to take us to do it, and (3) this is who is responsible to do it. The graphic representation of the defined process of planning lets people know that this is a competently managed process. Furthermore, the work plan acts as a guide to implementation and monitoring, and promotes confidence for SUs and SPs that they will not just be spinning their wheels at endless meetings, but will always be working toward the goal of joint proposal development to add new resources to their local communities.

Subsection 4. Evaluation of the CDPM Planning Process

Since the eight planning steps are sequential and build on each other to culminate in a tangible product and outcome, the evaluation model selected was a process evaluation. Holosko and Thyer (2011) defined this as "called a Level 1 evaluation, it is typically required for evaluation and demonstration projects conducted to understand *what* [our italics] was learned during implementation of the project. These evaluations seek to understand what happened to whom and how, in the program. They *inform* [our italics] others about what they might expect if they were to launch a similar project. They typically include program descriptions, program monitoring, and quality assurance" (p. 93).

As Holosko and Thyer (2011) indicate, two main assumptions for using this evaluation type are (1) its emphasis on processes and not on outcomes, and (2) its need to collect information to use **data** on an ongoing basis to direct practice in an evidence-informed (EI) way.

Given the fact that social technology and Web-based resources are becoming more mainstream in the social and behavioral sciences (Dunlop & Fawcett, 2008; Holosko, 2016), we recommend that one of the SPs—normally the SP who was active in this vision and implementation process—dedicate a confidential space on the agency's Web site to keep information about the planning process tracked, and then to monitor it for accountability. One SU and one SP would have coediting privileges. All other SUs and SPs would have read-only privileges. SUs and SPs could then access this Web site, which would be password protected, and all could use the Web site for fingertip information sharing and ongoing process feedback. When such Web sites are used in this way, they typically include a chronology of events, feedback on various steps in the process, lessons learned, challenges confronted, and a descriptive account of the project. For example, if during the planning process the collaborative SU/SP group deems that certain selected information should become known to the community (i.e., when the needs assessment will be conducted and who its funders may be, etc.), that decision should be consensually made, and then appropriately disseminated to the community via the Web site, or through other forms of social technology. When used properly, such social technology platforms can provide timely data to both the group itself and to the community at large (Chan & Holosko, 2016; Leslie, Holosko, & Dunlop, 2006).

This process evaluation anchors and collects parallel sequential data on each of the eight planning steps, in each of the following eight chapters:

Step 1. Define Stakeholder Participation

Step 2. Build Mission and Purpose

Step 3. Identify Community Strengths

Step 4. Identify Community Needs Using EID

Step 5. Identify Services and Set Priorities Using EID

Step 6. Plan Service Using EID

Step 7. Decide on Intervention and Sponsors

Step 8. Develop Joint Proposals

In addition, each of the eight planning steps has three foundational action steps with corresponding work activity sheets. Each chapter has a unique set of steps that require differing numbers of activity sheets, with some chapters using only four or five and others using a larger number, with the largest number being thirteen sheets to complete. Upon completion of all three action steps in each chapter, SUs and SPs will fill out a brief evaluation sheet independent of each other; these sheets ask them to assess each action step in each of the eight chapters. After doing this separately and in a group, they will then meet together for no more than one hour to discuss what was learned in this planning step. An SU and an SP will weekly alternate the chairing of this evaluation meeting. In regard to summarizing what was learned, SUs and SPs as a joint group will summarize three to five main takeaway points of this collaborative learning process for the dedicated Web site previously mentioned.

Subsection 5. A Brief Note on Writing Style

Finally, given the manualized format of this planning guide, we want to share with you some information about its writing style. In our collective sixty years of teaching in schools of social work, nursing, public health, medicine, public administration, and sociology, we both acknowledge that our postmodern and technologically adept students have taught us much about education, information, and knowledge dissemination. With regard to our writing style, we feel compelled to explain why we used it. In this regard, we thank those legions of students whom we have collectively taught for over these many decades, who in all honesty taught us more about how we should think, teach, and write for today's postmodern students in order to be more effective as educators and communicators than we ever imagined possible. In this regard, our main guiding framework was K.I.S.S, which (to us) means "Keep It Simple for Students." Also, we tried to (1) use 5¢ rather than 10¢ words, (2) not get lost in the theoretical forest emphasizing the importance of everything, (3) transform academic rhetoric into more practical thinking, (4) distill the essential takeaway points whenever possible, (5) present current and timely materials supplemented by technology, and (6) write in a single voice. In regard to the latter, we strove for an overall uniform, confident, informative, and conversational tone throughout.

Additionally, we (1) formatted all chapters in the same way, (2) defined each in a single planning step (one per chapter in chapters 1–8) with three accompanying action steps, and (3) made sure each action step had four to thirteen suggested activity sheets students, and macro practitioners can use in order to complete the action step. Each of these activity sheets presented has been field-tested in three different communities, and was then carefully crafted further for its generalizability across various settings and its applicability for use with a variety of cognate disciplines.

After the three action steps in each of the planning process chapters, there are subsections of the chapter that include (1) a selected case vignette that illustrates a real-world experience with the planning step, (2) a brief evaluation sheet designed to assess what was learned both individually and as a group in the planning step, (3) four current Web-related resources with a brief description of the site, and (4) a sample of the PowerPoint presentation to summarize the overall step.

We hope that this stylistic description provides the rationale, structure, and means by which both SUs and SPs may simply and effectively use this manual in the way it was conceived, field-tested, and written. But we prefer that you be the judge of that!

REFERENCES

Adams, J. R., & Drake, R. E. (2006). Shared decision-making and evidence-based practice. *Community Mental Health Journal, 4*(2), 87–103.

Arnstein, S. R. (1969). A ladder of citizen participation. *Journal of the American Institute of Planners, 35*(4), 216–224.

Aronson, J. (1993). Giving consumers a say in policy development: Influencing policy or just being heard. *Canadian Public Policy, 19*(4), 367–378.

Barber, R., Beresford, P., Boote, J., Cooper, D., & Faulkner, A. (2001). Evaluating the impact of service user involvement on research: A prospective case study. *International Journal of Consumer Services, 35*(6), 609–615. doi:10.1111/j.1470-6431.2011.01017.x

Beresford, P. (2007). The role of service user research in generating knowledge-based health and social care: From conflict to contribution. *Evidence & Policy: A Journal of Research, Debate and Practice, 3*(3), 329–341.

Beresford, P., & Croft, S. (2008). Democratising social work: A key element of innovation: From client as object to service user as producer. *Innovation Journal, 13*(1), 3–24.

Carey, M. (2009). Happy shopper? The problem with service user and career participation. *British Journal of Social Work, 39*(1), 179–188. doi:10.1093/bjsw/bcn166

Carr, S. (2007). Participation, power, conflict and change: Theorizing dynamics of service user participation in the social care system of England and Wales. *Critical Social Policy, 27*(2), 266–276.

Chan, C., & Holosko, M. J. (2016). A review of information and communication technology: Enhanced social work interventions. *Research on Social Work Practice* (Special Issue on Intervention Research), *26*(1), 88–100.

Community Development Exchange (CDX). (2008). *What is community empowerment?* National Empowerment Partnership, London.

Dowding, K., & John, P. (2011). Voice and choice in health care in England: Understanding citizen responses to dissatisfaction. *Public Administration, 89*(4), 1403–1418. doi:10.1111/j.1467-9299.2011.01960

Dunlop, J. M. (2002). Managerial perceptions of local collaboration: The Ontario Healthy Babies/ Healthy Children example. *Dissertations Abstracts International, 64*(09), 3478.

Dunlop, J. M. (2006). *Managerial perceptions of collaboration: The Michigan Healthy Start Initiative.* School of Social Work, University of Windsor, Windsor, ON, Canada.

Dunlop, J. M. (2006). Privatization: How government promotes market-based solutions to social problems. *Critical Social Work, 7*(2), 1–21.

Dunlop, J. M. (2007). *Managerial perceptions of collaboration: The Illinois Healthy Start Initiative.* School of Social Work, Kings University College at The University of Western Ontario, London, ON, Canada.

Dunlop, J. (2009). Social policy devolution: An historical review of Canada, United Kingdom and United States (1834–1999). *Social Work in Public Health, 24*(3), 121–209.

Dunlop, J. M., & Angell, G. B. (2001). Inside-outside: Boundary spanning challenges in building rural health coalitions. *Professional Development: The International Journal of Social Work Education, 4*(1), 40–48.

Dunlop J., & Fawcett, G. (2008). Technology-based approaches to social work and social justice. *Journal of Policy Practice, 7*(2–3), 140–153.

Dunlop, J. M., & Holosko, M. (2005). The story behind the story of collaborative networks: Relationships do matter! *Journal of Health and Social Policy, 19*(3), 1–17. doi:10.1300/J045v19n03_01

Feit, M. D., & Holosko, M. J. (2013). *Distinguishing clinical from upper level management in social work.* London: Taylor & Francis.

Fleischer, D. Z., & Zames, F. (2001). *The disabilities rights movement: From charity to confrontation.* Philadelphia: Temple University Press.

Forest, S., Risk, I., Masters, H., & Brown, N. (2000). Mental health service user involvement in nurse education: Exploring the issues. *Journal of Psychiatric and Mental Health Nursing, 7*(1), 51–57. doi:10.1046/j.1365-2850.2000.00262.x

Friedman, J. (1977). The transitive style of planning. In N. Gilbert & H. Specht (Eds.), *Planning for Social Welfare* (pp. 113–118). Englewood Cliffs, NJ: Prentice Hall.

Fudge, N., Wolfe, C. D. A., & McKevitt, C. (2008). Assessing the promise of user involvement in health service development: Ethnographic study. *British Medical Journal, 336*(7639), 313–317. doi:10.1136/bmj.39456.552257.BE

Government of United Kingdom. (2007). *Local government and public involvement in Health Act, c. 28.* London.

Hardina. D. (2005). Ten characteristics of empowerment-oriented social service organizations. *Administration in Social Work, 29*(3), 23–42.

Hasenfeld, Y. (1983). *Human service organizations.* Englewood Cliffs, NJ: Prentice-Hall.

Healthcare Quality Improvement Partnership. (n.d.). *Healthcare quality improvement partnership service user network.* Retrieved from http://www.hqip.org.uk/involving-patients/service-user-network/

Hernandez, L., Robson, P., & Sampson, A. (2010). Towards integrated participation: Involving seldom heard users of social care services. *British Journal of Social Work, 40*(3), 714–736.

Holosko, M. J. (1997). Service user input: Fact or fiction? The evaluation of the Trauma Program, Department of Rehabilitation, Sault Ste. Marie, ON. *The Canadian Journal of Program Evaluation, 11*(2), 111–126.

Holosko, M. J. (2009). Introduction. Special Issue: Global Realities of Social Policy: The Devolution Revolution. *Social Work in Public Health, 24*(3), 189–190.

Holosko, M. J. (2013). Current trends influencing health and human service organizations. In M. D. Feit & M. J. Holosko (Eds.), *Distinguishing clinical from upper level management in social work* (pp. 18–35). London: Taylor & Francis.

Holosko, M. J. (2016). Introduction to the special issue on intervention research. *Research on Social Work Practice, 26*(1), 5–7.

Holosko, M. J. (in press). *Social work case management.* Thousand Oaks, CA: Sage.

Holosko, M. J., & Barner, J. (2014). Neoliberal globalization: Social welfare policy and institutions. In M. Vidal de Haymes, S. Haymes, & R. Miller (Eds.), *The Routledge handbook on poverty in the United States* (pp. 239–248). London: Taylor & Francis.

Holosko, M., & Leslie, D. (1998). Obstacles to conducting empirically based practice. In J. Wodarski & B. Thyer (Eds.), *Handbook of empirical social work* (Vol. 2. *Social problems and practice issues,* pp. 433–453). New York: Wiley and Sons, Inc.

Holosko, M., Leslie, D., & Cassano, D. R. (2001). How service users become empowered in human service organizations: The empowerment model. *International Journal of Health Care Quality Assurance, 14*(3), 126–132.

Holosko, M. J., & Pettus, A. J. (2014, June). *Neoliberalism and globalization: Trends shaping sustainable social work practice.* Invited keynote speaker at the Conference on Social Work and Social Sustainability in Asia, SAR, Hong Kong, China.

Holosko, M. J., & Thyer, B. (2011). *A pocket glossary of research terms.* Thousand Oaks, CA: Sage.

Kvarnström, S. (2011). *Collaboration in health and social care: Service user participation and teamwork in inter-professional clinical microsystems.* (Dissertation Series No. 15, 2011, School of Health Sciences, Jonkoping University, Sweden).

Kvarnström, S., Hedberg, B., & Cedersund, E. (2013). The dual faces of service user participation: Implications for empowerment processes in interprofessional practice. *Journal of Social Work, 13*(3), 287–307.

Kvarnström, S., Willumsen, E., Andersson-Gare, B., & Hedberg, B. (2012). How service users perceive the concept of participation, specifically in interprofessional practice. *British Journal of Social Work, 42*(1), 129–146. doi:10:1093/bjsw/bcr049

Lammers, J., & Happell, B. (2003). Consumer participation in mental health services: Looking from a consumer perspective. *Journal of Psychiatric and Mental Health Nursing, 10*(4), 385–392.

Laverack, G., & Labonte, R. (2000). A planning framework for community empowerment goals within health promotion. *Health Policy and Planning, 15*(3), 255–262.

Leslie, D., Holosko, M. J., & Dunlop, J. (2006). Using information technology in planning program evaluation. *Journal of Evidence-Based Social Work, Special Edition on Information Technology and Evidence-Based Practice, 3*(3/4), 73–90.

Levin, E. (2004). *Involving service users and carers in social work education* (SCIE Guide 4). London: Social Care Institute for Excellence.

Martinez, E., & Garcia, A. (1997). *What is neoliberalism? A brief definition for activists.* CorpWatch: Holding Corporations Accountable.

McCammon, S. L., Spencer, S. A., & Friesen, B. J. (2001). Promoting family empowerment through multiple roles. *Journal of Family Social Work, 5*(3), 1–24.

McLaughlin, H. (2009). What's in a name: "Client," "patient," "customer," "consumer," "expert by experience," "service user"—What's next? *British Journal of Social Work, 39*(6), 1101–1117. doi:10.1093/bjsw/bcm155

Mizrahi, T. (1992). The right to treatment and the treatment of mentally ill people. *Health and Social Work, 17*(1), 7–12.

Mockford, C., Staniszewska, S., Griffiths, F., & Herron-Marx, S. (2012). The impact of patient and public involvement on UK NHS Health Care: A systematic review. *International Journal for Quality in Health Care, 24*(1), 28–38. doi:10.1093/intqhc/mzr066

Modrcin, M., Rapp, C., & Chamberlain, R. (1985). *Case management with psychiatric disabled individuals: Curriculum training guide.* Lawrence: University of Kansas School of Social Welfare.

Mooney, G., & Neal, S. (2010). "Welfare worries": Mapping the directions of welfare futures in the contemporary UK. *Research, Policy and Planning, 27*(3), 141–150.

Morrow, E., Ross, F., Grocott, P., & Bennett, J. (2010). A model and measure for quality service use involvement in health research. *International Journal of Consumer Studies, 34*(5), 532–539. doi:10.111/j.1470-6431.2010.0091

Nathan, R. P. (1996). The devolution revolution: An overview. *Rockefeller Institute Bulletin,* 5–130.

Omeni, E., Barnes, M., MacDonald, D., Crawford, M., & Rose, D. (2014). Service user involvement: Impact and participation: A survey of service user and staff perspectives. *BMC Health Services Research, 14*(1), 120–141. doi:10.1186/s12913-014-0491-7

Ontario Healthy Communities Coalition. (2015). *Inclusive community organizations: A tool kit.* Toronto, ON.

Oxford Dictionary Online. (2015). *Empowerment.*

Parrish, D. E., Harris, D., & Pritzker, S. (2013). Assessment of a service provider method to promote inter-organizational and community collaboration. *Social Work, 58*(4), 354–364.

Patient Protection and Affordable Care Act, Pub. L. No. 111-148, 104 Stat. 119, 119–1025 (2010).

Pires, S. (1996). *Characteristics of systems of care as systems reform initiatives.* Washington, DC: Human Service Collaborative.

Rothman, J. (1996). The interweaving of community intervention approaches. *Journal of Community Practice, 3*(3-4), 69–99.

Ryan-Nicholls, K. D., & Haggarty, J. M. (2007). Collaborative mental health care in rural and isolated Canada: Stakeholder feedback. *Journal of Psychosocial Nursing, 45*(12), 37–45.

Savas, E. S. (2000). *Privatization and public–private partnerships.* New York: Chatham House/Seven Bridges Press.

Scottish Government. (2009). *Scottish Community Empowerment Action Plan. Celebrating success: Inspiring change.* Edinburgh.

Smith, M., Gallagher, M., Wosu, H., Stewart, J., Cree, V. E., Hunter, S., & Wilkinson, H. (2011). Engaging with involuntary service users in social work: Findings from a knowledge exchange project. *British Journal of Social Work, 42*(8), 1460–1477. doi:10.1093/bjsw/bcr162.1-18

Staniszewska, S., Adabajo, A., Barber, R., Beresford, P., Brady, L, Brett, J., & Williamson, T. (2011). Developing the evidence base of patient and public involvement in health and social care research: The case for measuring impact. *International Journal of Consumer Studies, 35*(6), 628–632. doi:10.111/j.1470.6431.2011.01020.x

SUNY Levin Institute. (2013). *What is globalization?* State University of New York.

Twelvetrees, A. (2008). *Community work* (4th ed.). London: Palgrave/Macmillan.

UK Department of Health. (1990). *National Health Service and Community Care Act 1990, Chapter 19.* London.

UK Department of Health. (1999). *National service framework for mental health.* London.

UK Department of Health. (2001). *Health and Social Care Act, Chapter 15.* London.

UK Department of Health. (2012). *Health and Social Care Act,* chapter 7. London.

Wilson, A., & Beresford, P. (2000). Anti-oppressive practice: Emancipation or appropriation? *British Journal of Social Work, 30*(5), 553–573.

Planning Step 1
Define Stakeholder Participation

OVERVIEW AND RATIONALE

This first step in the CDPM planning model is to conduct a comprehensive stakeholder analysis to ensure that all relevant SUs, SPs, community partners, community groups, and resources have been identified. Given the formative nature of this planning step, it is imperative that SUs and SPs elect appropriate stakeholders during this group identification process. The history of planning in the local community should also be explored to determine if there are established groups who should be included in the scan of local stakeholders. In many ways the planning and implementation trajectory hinges on this foundation. Once this is completed, the recruitment process can begin.

Stakeholder analysis or stakeholder participation refers to individuals and groups who should be included in the planning and implementation process since the planning initiative is likely to affect them. According to Brugha and Varvasovszky (2000), the concept of stakeholder analysis "was adapted from the organizational and management literature in the 1970s and 1980s, drawing on the earlier work of policy scientists, who were concerned with the distribution of power and the role of interest groups in the decision-making and policy process" (p. 240). Since the 1970s and 1980s, this planning and implementation process has evolved and taken on a more refined and systematic implementation method. As an overarching activity, a stakeholder analysis today is often used to "generate knowledge about the relevant actors so as to understand their behaviour, intentions, interrelations, agendas, interests, and the influence or resources they have brought—or could bring—to bear on decision-making processes" (Brugha & Varvasovszky, 2000, p. 241).

Because this planning model is centered on the involvement of both SUs and SPs, the stakeholder analysis must equally identify both groups. To aid in the selection process, Maurer and Smith (2008, p. 386) established the following criteria:

1. Persons for whom the **plan** is designed—that is, the consumers (Action Step 1.1);
2. Those who are concerned with the social problem (Action Steps 1.1 and 1.2);
3. Those who appear best able to contribute resources to the plan (Action Step 1.2); and,
4. Those who are most likely to follow through in carrying out the plan (Action Steps 1.1, 1.2, and 1.3).

Ultimately, the goal of this process is to select those stakeholders who will be committed to effectively planning and advocating for funding to secure new resources for the local community. Because of this important role for stakeholders, creating a community group with credibility is essential, and, as Bryson (2004) stated, "Some initial stakeholder analysis work will need to be done—before the 'right' group of people can be found" (p. 73). It can be particularly challenging to select the right group when striving for representative incorporation of SUs, since their perspectives and contributions are often seen as secondary. However, we echo the perspective of Thomas (1993, 1995) who maintained that stakeholders should be involved "either because they have information that cannot be gained otherwise, or because their support is necessary to ensure successful implementation" (as cited in Bryson, 2004, p. 73). Similarly, anyone whose participation is "necessary to ensure a successful strategic planning process" should be included (Bryson, 2004, p. 73; see also Chrislip, 2002; Finn, 1996). This, without a doubt, includes representative SUs. Interestingly, some authors encourage identifying and including those who may potentially oppose the work of the group (Maurer & Smith, 2008). As these authors noted, "Involving opponents in the planning process is much better than waiting until the program is implemented, then facing resistance and program failure" (Maurer & Smith, 2008, p. 386). Maurer and Smith provide a good example of a framework that can be used to assess stakeholder participation in local communities (2008, p. 236). However, it is important to note that their example is only a suggested template. Each local community planning group is responsible for designing the stakeholder analysis that responds to their unique local context and planning process.

Following this initial planning group selection, a more comprehensive stakeholder analysis must occur to ensure a successful participatory planning process. This analysis also affords an opportunity for planning members, likely together as a group for the first time, to ensure that key stakeholders who would be critical to the overall planning group are not absent. This should be completed before any further planning process occurs, as it is critical to have the involvement and support of selected prominent community leaders in addition to SUs and SPs. Taken one step farther, Levin (2004) contended that a separate delineation process specific to SUs themselves may occur. Such delineation can include not only past or current recipients of service, but also those who are eligible for service and not yet accessing it. During the formative stages of launching the planning initiative, SUs can establish a list of potential members for SU involvement before beginning their stakeholder analysis.

The desire to incorporate authentic SU voice is not without its own issues. The illusion of equal partnerships between SUs and SPs conceals the truth that provider knowledge is somehow deemed as privileged within the relationship. Often, SPs placate or treat as peripheral the ideas and opinions of SUs, who have lived experiences in the local community and with local services (Dowding & John, 2011). The language of SPs and the formality of their meetings can lead to intimidation and actual disempowerment of SUs (Holosko, Leslie, & Cassano, 2001).

Increasingly, SU involvement in planning and policy decision-making has become the policy of choice for governments as well as health and social care providers in most democratic countries (Ottman and Laragy, 2010). With the increasing focus and mandate on SU participation in planning, delivery, and evaluation processes, it is generally accepted that complex problem solving requires the concerted efforts of community members, SUs, and SPs.

Indeed, a growing body of research evidence suggests that actively engaging users in the program and policy design process leads to better policy outcomes. This strategy, which bridges the gap between SPs and SUs, models the collaboration promoted in this manual. For instance, Eschenfelder (2010) contended that collaborative working relationships have been encouraged by "nonprofit, for-profit, and government sectors to maximize administrative efficiency, avoid redundant effort, prevent costly competition for resources or clients, pursue collaborative funding opportunities, conduct joint planning and program development, and increase the impact of advocacy efforts" (p. 407; see also Alexander, 2000; Dunlop & Holosko, 2005; Eisenberg & Eschenfelder, 2009; Kohm & La Piana, 2003; Mandell, 2001; McLaughlin, 1998; Snavely & Tracy, 2000; Vogel, Ransom, Wai, & Luisi, 2007). Similarly, Bishop, Vicary, Browne, and Guard (2009) noted the importance of engaging communities "on their own terms, and not in the terms of the culture of the bureaucracies" (p. 117). Hedley, Fennel, Wall, and Cullen (2003) term this a "whole systems approach" (p. 177; also Moriarty et al., 2007), whereby people who are representative of the entire system, be they SPs or SUs, are brought together. "They can share the knowledge from their part of the system and understand how that fits into the 'whole,' thus reducing the need for a wide variety of meetings which traditionally focus only on part of the system" (Hedley et al., 2003, p. 178). Such an approach is integral to implementing meaningful change that is user focused (Moriarty et al., 2007).

Given the formative nature of this step, it is imperative that, during this group identification process, SUs and SPs select appropriate stakeholders. The history of planning in the local community should also be explored to determine if there are related groups who should be included in the scan of stakeholders at the local level. In many ways, the planning and implementation trajectory hinges on this foundation. Thus, it is essential that a comprehensive stakeholder analysis is conducted to ensure that all relevant SUs, SPs, community partners, community groups, and resources have been identified. From there, the recruitment of SUs and SPs can begin.

DESCRIPTION OF PLANNING ACTIVITIES FOR STEP 1: DEFINE STAKEHOLDER PARTICIPATION

This planning step contains three action steps. Remember that any of the three action steps might use more than one activity sheet. Upon completion of these three action steps for Planning Step 1, please use the appropriate evaluation form found at the end of the chapter to evaluate each action step. Evaluation is an important part of the overall planning process.

Action Step 1.1. Recruiting the SU Group
Action Step 1.2. Recruiting the SP Group
Action Step 1.3. Joining SU/SP Stakeholder Analyses

Action Step 1.1 (Recruiting the SU Group) describes the recruitment of the SUs who will be the core SU group involved throughout the entire planning process. Action Step 1.2 (Recruiting the SP Group) ensures that the SPs who have a stake in the planning issue are involved from the onset in the development of the ensuing SU/SP planning partnership. Action Step 1.3 (Joining SU/SP Stakeholder Analyses) brings together SUs and SPs in joint decision-making about who the stakeholders should be, for the eventual joint planning partnership. Action Step 1.3 also ensures that SUs and SPs, who have been involved in parallel planning processes to date, braid their respective data into a cohesive and negotiated understanding of stakeholder participation, and coalesce their views on stakeholder participation in the local planning initiative. Bringing stakeholders together early in the process will help to ensure that there is agreement about who needs to be involved, and at what level. Practitioners will learn how to conduct comprehensive stakeholder analyses that include both SUs and SPs. This formative planning step also educates practitioners about how to recruit and engage stakeholders in the community, and how to analyze their importance and level of involvement. This identification of SUs' and SPs' actual stake in the local issue needs to be thorough and complete to ensure recruiting of stakeholders who are missing but need to be included.

Action Step 1.1. Recruiting the SU Group

a. List of Activity Sheet(s): Recruiting the SU Group

Action Step	Activity Sheet(s)
1.1. Recruiting the SU Group	1.1.a. Building SU Knowledge of Stakeholders

b. Introduction: Recruiting the SU Group

In Action Step 1.1 we see the parallel process characteristic of this particular eight-step CDPM. While a strong commitment to SU participation is often espoused by regulatory bodies or governments, there are significant barriers to achieving this, not the least of which is the minimizing or muting of SU voice in any planning process. The approach taken in this manual is to strengthen SU voice using a long-standing social work community development approach informally called "starting where the individual is." True partnership, therefore, in this model, involves a philosophy of empowerment and respect for the real and lived experience of SUs. The practical application of this commitment to SU inclusion and voice necessitates the development of parallel planning groups at various points of time in the planning process. In this initial step therefore, it is imperative that SUs have their own identified group and share their actual experiences by identifying stakeholders and stakeholder power. Only when local SUs can exercise their decision-making power in planning will participation be meaningful and democratic (see introduction to this manual). As such, SUs in this approach need not fear the intimidation of SPs who may try to influence the choice of stakeholders and promote their choices vigorously within the planning process. Within the confines of the SU cohort, an open dialogue among members will facilitate a strong voice for eventual planning with the SP group when that step of the process is eventually implemented. Consensus reached through deliberation and dialogue in SUs' own time and in their own way strengthens initial and ongoing SU identity as partners who need to be continually recognized as necessary participants in any SU/SP planning initiative.

Action Step 1.1 describes the recruitment of the stakeholders who will be involved throughout the entire planning process. Since this is a locally driven SU/SP planning process, each community will have a unique set of stakeholder representatives that are selected by the SU/SP planning group. This involves documenting community stakeholders at the very onset of the planning process. The SU and SP planning groups initially will carry out the stakeholder analysis in separate groups, and then will combine their lists of stakeholders as a final step in the analysis. The macro practitioner will help facilitate the process of decision-making by SUs and SPs about stakeholders to be recruited. The joint SU/SP planning group can then designate stakeholders at various levels of participation; their roles may be diverse. The macro practitioner involved in the planning process will carry out a CD role to engage the identified stakeholders once these have been chosen by the SU and SP planning group. Activity Sheet 1.1.a (Building SU Knowledge of Stakeholders) is a beginning tool that can be used to support an analysis of initial stakeholder involvement in the planning process. This activity should be carried out before any decisions are made about sharing a recruitment list of stakeholders with the larger SU/SP planning group.

c. Description: Recruiting the SU Group

1. Use the sections that identify stakeholders in the following categories: (1) SUs, (2) SPs, (3) community leaders, (4) volunteers, (5) elected leaders, and (6) others.
2. Identify early on whom you would like to be involved.
3. Identify why the stakeholder is important to the overall group and its purpose.
4. Identify what the stakeholder will gain from his or her involvement.
5. Identify who knows the stakeholder and, when appropriate, how and who should contact that person or organization.

By using this structured and planned approach, SUs will participate in identifying and analyzing their choices about stakeholder involvement, and will have determined why each stakeholder is important to the planning process. Also, SUs will have reviewed how stakeholders will benefit the group, who knows the stakeholder, and who can communicate with the stakeholder about his or her interest and involvement in the planning process. This accountability of stakeholder involvement will provide data that SUs can bring to the joint SU/SP planning process. Once both SU and SP groups have carried out their separate stakeholder analyses, then decisions can be made about contacting identified stakeholders and inviting them to participate in either the parallel separate SU and SP planning groups or in the joint SU/SP planning group.

Action Step 1.2. Recruiting the SP Group

a. List of Activity Sheet(s): Recruiting the SP Group

Action Step	Activity Sheet(s)
1.2. Recruiting the SP Group	1.2.a. Building SP Knowledge of Stakeholders

b. Introduction: Recruiting the SP Group

Action Step 1.2 ensures that SPs who have a stake in the overall planning issue are involved from the onset of the ensuing SU/SP planning partnership. Action Step 1.2 has been designed to carry out the same stakeholder analysis process for SPs as in Action Step 1.1 for SUs. This second action step is a preliminary step that the SP group needs to carry out before stepping into the joint planning process with SUs—where each stakeholder list will be consolidated and subjected to joint review and decision-making about who is necessary to the planning process and who will be recruited. Macro practitioners as leaders will also help the group identify stakeholder roles and expectations. Providers will have a view of the relative importance of stakeholders necessary to achieving good planning outcomes. As a separate cohort, SPs will work together to assess what type of impact potential stakeholders will have on the planning initiative.

This action step for engaging potential planning group members uses the same categories as the SU stakeholder analysis chart, namely categories of stakeholders such as (1) SUs, (2) SPs, (3) community leaders, (4) volunteers, (5) elected leaders, and (6) others. Within these categories, SPs will undertake the formative first step for developing recruitment strategies that are necessary for successful community planning. Activity Sheet 1.2.a (Building SP Knowledge of Stakeholders) is a tool that can be used to support the analysis of stakeholder involvement in the planning process. The SP group will go through its stakeholder analysis exercise together and come to a consensus on stakeholders who should be recruited. Once the SP planning group has made decisions, it will be able to share its recruitment list of stakeholders with the larger SU/SP planning group.

c. Description: Recruiting the SP Group

1. Identify stakeholders by name in each of the following categories: (1) SUs, (2) SPs, (3) community leaders, (4) volunteers, (5) elected leaders, and (6) others.
2. Using the identified stakeholder list (#2), discuss why they are important to the group.
3. Using the identified stakeholder list (#2), discuss what each has to gain by being involved.
4. Using the identified stakeholder list (#2), discuss how a lack of participation by the stakeholder could potentially interfere with good results or success in the planning initiative.
5. Using the identified stakeholder list (#2), identify who in the group knows the specific stakeholder. This step is important for recruiting other stakeholders in the future when decisions are made in the larger planning group.
6. Create a list of primary stakeholders that the SP group believes needs to be involved in the community planning initiative. This list will be the priority list to be shared with the SU group when the two groups converge to review their individual decision-making.

Action Step 1.3. Joining SU/SP Stakeholder Analyses

a. List of Activity Sheet(s): Joining SU/SP Stakeholder Analyses

Action Step	Activity Sheet(s)
1.3. Joining SU/SP Stakeholder Analyses	1.3.a. SU/SP Joint Stakeholder Analysis: Levels of Involvement
	1.3.b. SU/SP Joint Stakeholder Analysis
	1.3.c. SU/SP Joint Stakeholder Analysis Summary
	1.3.d. Sample Recruitment Letter for SU/SP Stakeholders

b. Introduction: Joining SU/SP Stakeholder Analyses

Action Step 1.3 is about developing and documenting community stakeholders at the very beginning of the planning process. This first joint planning group process blends together the work that has been done separately by the SU and SP groups in their initial parallel planning processes. Stakeholders will be designated for various levels of participation, and their roles may be very diverse. Designations at four levels of stakeholders minimally are as follows:

1. Core members who will be involved throughout the planning process
2. Involved members who are available for consultation on the planning process
3. Supportive members who may at times be needed for forms of additional support including advocacy and resource development
4. Peripheral members who need to be kept informed but do not participate in the planning process (Public Health Ontario, 2014; see Activity Sheet 1.3.a [SU/SP Joint Stakeholder Analysis: Levels of Involvement])

The success of this step also depends on SP flexibility and respect regarding the importance and influence of SUs as stakeholders in the local project. SP decision-making regarding the importance of stakeholders rests on an ongoing dialogue shaped by process questions such as Who will be involved? Why are they important? What is their level of involvement? Who knows the stakeholder? and How will the planning initiative will be impacted either by their involvement or their disengagement? (see Activity Sheet 1.3.b [SU/SP Joint Stakeholder Analysis]). The practitioner as planning group leader will have worked with both groups to reach consensus on a stakeholder list that is the primary outcome of this joint activity. Each of these groups will present its stakeholder lists, and will continue the ongoing dialogue about the levels of involvement appropriate using Activity Sheet 1.3.a.

By working with each other to determine the specific roles and levels of involvement for each stakeholder presented, in each SU and SP list, the joint SU/SP planning group can build a collaborative working group based on inclusiveness and **shared decision-making.** One of the most important outcomes of this action step is having the necessary conversations around stakeholder involvement, required by all participants. Thus students and macro practitioners will learn how to facilitate such discussions that forthrightly table common language development to the joint SU/SP planning group. The development of a shared perception of stakeholder importance helps SUs and SPs bring a clearer expectation and understanding to the range of potential stakeholders necessary for successful planning. The planning activity itself is designed to bring SUs and SPs together in an inclusive, positive, and pragmatic exercise that will build understanding and trust for the proposed future planning steps.

c. Description: Joining SU/SP Stakeholder Analyses

1. SUs present the stakeholder list created by their SU group to the joint SU/SP planning group.
2. SPs present the stakeholder list created by their SP group to the joint SU/SP planning group.
3. SUs and SPs assess the stakeholders as to their potential interest and vested stake in the planning process.
4. SUs and SPs listen to each other regarding the levels of involvement of stakeholders, why they are important, and what the stakeholder will gain from his or her involvement.
5. SUs and SPs identify key stakeholders within the six categories of (1) SU, (2) SP, (3) community leader, (4) volunteer, (5) elected leaders, and (6) others.

Discussion between SUs and SPs will lead to a consensually agreed-on list of key stakeholders within each category.

6. The joint SU/SP planning group identifies the key stakeholders within each category and agrees that these specific stakeholders will be included on a priority list of stakeholders to be recruited. See Activity Sheet 1.3.c (SU/SP Joint Stakeholder Analysis Summary).

7. The joint SU/SP planning group assigns responsibility to identification of who should contact the stakeholders on the priority list and how this contact should take place (e.g., telephone call, mail, e-mail, personal visit). This decision about contact with the stakeholder will be based on a discussion about who has had previous contact with the stakeholder, what informal and formal relationships SUs and SPs have with the stakeholder, and whether SUs and SPs are willing to engage in stakeholder recruitment. See Activity Sheet 1.3.c.

8. The joint SU/SP planning group will jointly decide on the contents of their stakeholder recruitment letter. See Activity Sheet 1.3.d (Sample Recruitment Letter for SU/SP Stakeholders).

CASE VIGNETTE: STAKEHOLDER PARTICIPATION

In this case vignette, a local agency received funding to hire a coordinator to develop a coalition of SUs and SPs to plan for child welfare services. A small group of three to four agency representatives formed a core group, with one of the SPs taking on a chairperson role. Before a stakeholder analysis was carried out to identify members who were important to the group's purpose, the members of this core group began contacting local organizations to recruit participants. Initially the core group recruited SPs such as physicians, school principals, public health nurses, local child protection workers, and a family court judge. Since the funder had requested the involvement of SUs in the planning group, one of the members of the core group contacted a local parents group and requested representation at the first meeting. At the initial meeting of the newly formed group, the family court judge left the meeting after explaining that the parent representative at the meeting was someone who had appeared before him in a child protection case and that he could not continue with the group.

The problem of not analyzing SUs and SPs before bringing all parties together that is illustrated in this vignette could have been avoided if appropriate planning for stakeholder participation had been carried out by using the structured approach to stakeholder analysis that is proposed in this eight-step model of SU/SP partnership planning. Recruitment of SU and SP stakeholders requires a strategic planning approach that includes a detailed analysis of who has a stake in the planning issue and a democratic decision-making avenue that allows for agreement and transparency between SU/SP partners on the selection of appropriate participants.

SUMMARY AND EVALUATION OF PLANNING STEP 1: DEFINE STAKEHOLDER PARTICIPATION

Summary of Planning Step 1: Define Stakeholder Participation

This manual assists practitioners and students, in the safety of the classrooms or workshop settings, to explore the sequential EI planning steps that they will be required to use in their eventual real world planning work. The obstacles they may encounter in learning how to lead collaborative planning groups are mainly in two areas: (1) little knowledge of or experience with EI planning, and (2) little knowledge of or insights into the **politics** of community, and the complex web of stakeholder relationships that must be managed. Those with little community practice experience often misunderstand the importance of stakeholder analysis before beginning any planning process at a community level. The case vignette presented outlines clearly how easily mistakes can be made that compromise the integrity of the planning project and alienate important stakeholders in the community. Practitioners and students often appear to minimize stakeholder participation, and to provide minimal attention to the recruitment of SUs as legitimate planning participants. This lack of participation might not lead to the best results, and might lead to decisions being challenged, delayed, or overruled by community stakeholders. However, this manual is specifically designed to implement SU/SP partnerships. It provides a vehicle for leadership in planning of local community services and, more importantly, provides an opportunity for both students and macro practitioners to gain competencies in EI planning prior to stepping into the political complexity that characterizes SU/SP planning group work at local community levels.

Evaluation of Planning Step 1: Define Stakeholder Participation

Evaluation Form: Circle one number only for each question listed below.

Action Step 1.1. Recruiting the SU Group

a. How confident were you about achieving this goal?	Not confident	Somewhat confident	Very confident	Extremely confident
	1	2	3	4

b. What was the most important thing you learned about this step?

Action Step 1.2. Recruiting the SP Group

a. How confident were you about achieving this goal?	Not confident	Somewhat confident	Very confident	Extremely confident
	1	2	3	4

b. What was the most important thing you learned about this step?

Action Step 1.3. Joining SU/SP Stakeholder Analyses

a. How confident were you about achieving this goal?	Not confident	Somewhat confident	Very confident	Extremely confident
	1	2	3	4

b. What was the most important thing you learned about this step?

Your Total Score? _____

Group Discussion Notes:

(continue on back as needed)

REFERENCES

Alexander, J. (2000). Adaptive strategies of non-profit human service organizations in an era of devolution and new public management. *Non-profit Management & Leadership, 10*(3) 287–303. doi:10.1002/nml.10305

Bishop, B., Vicary, D., Browne, A., & Guard, N. (2009). Public policy, participation and the third position: The implication of engaging communities on their own terms. *American Journal of Community Psychology, 43,* 111–121. doi:10.1007/s10464-008-9214-8

Brugha, R., & Varvasovszky, Z. (2000). Stakeholder analysis: A review. *Health Policy and Planning, 15*(3), 239–246.

Bryson, J. M. (2004). *Strategic planning for public and nonprofit organizations: A guide to strengthening and sustaining organizational achievement* (3rd ed.). San Francisco: Jossey-Bass.

Chrislip, D. (2002). *Collaborative leadership field book: A guide for citizens and civic leaders.* San Francisco: Jossey-Bass.

Dowding, K., & John, P. (2011). Voice and choice in health care in England: Understanding citizen responses to dissatisfaction. *Public Administration 89*(4), 1403–1418. doi:10.1111/j.1467-9299 .2011.01960

Dunlop, J. M., & Holosko, M. J. (2005). The story behind the story of collaborative networks: Relationships do matter! *Journal of Health and Social Policy, 19*(3), 1–18. doi:10.1300/J045v19n03_01

Eisenberg, E., & Eschenfelder, B. (2009). In the public interest: Communication in non-profit organizations. In L. R. Frey & K. N. Cissna (Eds.), *Routledge handbook of applied communication research* (pp. 355–379). New York: Routledge.

Eschenfelder, B. E. (2010). Using community-based assessments to strengthen non-profit governance collaboration and service delivery. *Journal of Health and Human Services Administration, 32*(4), 405–446.

Finn, C. B. (1996). Utilizing stakeholder strategies for positive collaborative outcomes. In C. Huxham (Ed.), *Creating collaborative advantage* (pp. 152–165). Thousand Oaks, CA: Sage.

Hedley, A., Fennel, S., Wall, D., & Cullen, R. (2003). People will support what they help to create: Clinical governance large group work. *Clinical Governance, 8*(2), 174–179. doi:10.1108/ 14777270310471667

Holosko, M., Leslie, D., & Cassano, D. R. (2001). How service users become empowered in human service organizations: The empowerment model. *International Journal of Health Care Quality Assurance, 14*(3), 126–132.

Kohm, A., & La Piana, D. (2003). *Strategic restructuring for non-profit organizations: Mergers, integrations, and alliance.* Westport, CT: Praeger.

Levin, E. (2004). *Involving service users and carers in social work education* (SCIE Guide 4). London: Social Care Institute for Excellence.

Mandell, M. (2001). Collaboration through network structures for community building efforts. *National Civic Review, 90*(3), 279–288. doi:10.1002/ncr.90308

Maurer, F. A., & Smith, C. M. (2008). *Community/public health nursing practice: Health for families and populations.* Philadelphia: W. B. Saunders.

McLaughlin, T. A. (1998). *Nonprofit mergers and alliances: A strategic planning guide.* New York: John Wiley.

Moriarty, J., Rapaport, P., Beresford, P., Branfield, F., Forrest, V., Manthorpe, J., . . . Keady, J. (2007). The participation of adult service users, including older people, in developing social care. *Practice Guide for Social Care Institute for Excellence.* London: Social Care Institute for Excellence.

Ottman, G., & Laragy, C. (2010). Developing consumer-directed care for people with a disability: 10 lessons for user participation in health and community care policy and program development. *Australian Health Review, 34*(4), 390–394. doi:10.1071/AH09759

Public Health Ontario. (2014). *Planning health promotion programs: An introductory workbook.* Retrieved from https://www.publichealthontario.ca/

Snavely, K., & Tracy, M. B. (2000). Collaboration among rural non-profit organizations. *Non-profit Management & Leadership, 11*(2), 145–165.

Thomas, J. (1993). Public involvement and governmental effectiveness. *Administration and Society, 24*(4), 444–469.

Thomas, J. (1995). *Public participation in public decisions: New skills and strategies for public managers.* San Francisco: Jossey-Bass.

Vogel, A., Ransom, P., Wai, S., & Luisi, D. (2007). Integrating health and social services for older adults: A case study of interagency collaboration. *Journal of Health & Human Services Administration, 30*(2), 199–228.

INTERNET REFERENCES

University of Kansas—Community Tool Box. http://ctb.ku.edu/en/table-of-contents/participation/encouraging-involvement/identify-stakeholders/main

This site offers information and a checklist for identifying stakeholders and their interests. It suggests that stakeholders need to be identified as early as possible and offers multiple definitions of stakeholders and activities for stakeholder analysis.

Ontario Health Program Planner—Program Planning Steps. http://www.publichealthontario.ca/en/ServicesAndTools/ohpp/Pages/default.aspx

This site offers six program planning steps to help planning participants and **facilitators** make EI decisions. It provides interactive worksheets for each of the six steps in the planning model: (1) manage the planning process; (2) conduct a situational assessment; (3) set goals, targets, and outcome objectives; (4) choose strategies and activities, and assign resources; (5) develop indicators; and (6) review the plan.

Overseas Development Institute—Planning Tools: Stakeholder Analysis. http://www.odi.org/publications/5257-stakeholder-analysis

This site highlights the need for stakeholder analysis of those who have something to gain or lose in a planning process. A grid is used to organize stakeholders in different matrices according to their interest and power, and to structure discussion during the planning process.

NHS Institute for Innovation and Improvement. http://www.institute.nhs.uk/quality_and_service_improvement_tools/quality_and_service_improvement_tools/stakeholder_analysis.html

This site highlights key questions to be asked to help groups understand their key stakeholders. Stakeholders are identified in nine categories in terms of power, influence, and the extent to which they are affected by the project or change.

POWERPOINT RESOURCES

Chapter 1

Planning Step 1
Define Stakeholder Participation

Why is this planning step important?

- It defines roles and determines collaboration.
- It identifies and effectively utilizes all available resources.
- It leads to knowing and understanding involved and invested parties and their intentions, behaviors, agendas, etc.
- It generates a credible, committed, and representative group.

What does the literature say?

- User involvement has become the **policy of choice.**
- It is deemed a **whole systems approach** where people who represent the entire system are brought together for an all-encompassing **multi-lens perspective.**
- Collaborative working relationships are encouraged **in all sectors,** including nonprofit, for-profit, and government to
  - Avoid redundant efforts and deplete existing resources,
  - Maximize efficiency,
  - Pursue collaborative funding efforts and prevent costly competition, and
  - Increase impact.

Planning Step 1: Define Stakeholder Participation

Activity Sheet 1.1.a: Building SU Knowledge of Stakeholders

	STAKEHOLDER NAME	WHY STAKEHOLDER IS IMPORTANT TO THE GROUP	WHAT STAKEHOLDER WILL GAIN	WHO KNOWS THE STAKEHOLDER
Service Users				
Service Providers				
Community Leaders				
Volunteers				
Elected Leaders				
Others				

Planning Step 1: Define Stakeholder Participation

Activity Sheet 1.2.a. Building SP Knowledge of Stakeholders

	STAKEHOLDER NAME	WHY STAKEHOLDER IS IMPORTANT TO THE GROUP	WHAT STAKEHOLDER WILL GAIN	WHO KNOWS THE STAKEHOLDER
Service Users				
Service Providers				
Community Leaders				
Volunteers				
Elected Leaders				
Others				

Planning Step 1. Define Stakeholder Participation

Activity Sheet 1.3.a. SU/SP Joint Stakeholder Analysis: Levels of Involvement

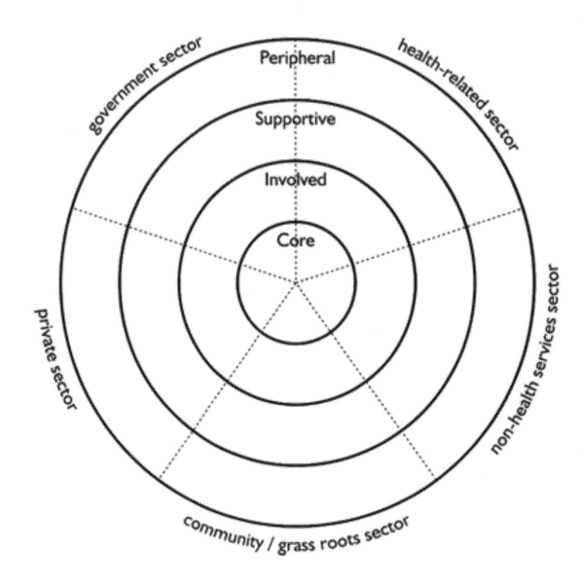

Planning Step 1. Define Stakeholder Participation

Activity Sheet 1.3.b. SU/SP Joint Stakeholder Analysis

	STAKEHOLDER NAME	WHY STAKEHOLDER IS IMPORTANT	WHAT LEVEL OF INVOLVEMENT (see Activity Sheet 1.3.a)	WHO KNOWS THE STAKEHOLDER
Service Users				
Service Providers				
Community Leaders				
Volunteers				
Elected Leaders				
Others				

Planning Step 1. Define Stakeholder Participation

Activity Sheet 1.3.c. SU/SP Joint Stakeholder Analysis Summary

STAKEHOLDER CATEGORIES	SU/SP STAKEHOLDER PRIORITY LIST	WHO WILL CONTACT STAKEHOLDER	HOW CONTACT WITH STAKEHOLDER WILL OCCUR
Service Users			
Service Providers			
Community Leaders			
Volunteers			
Elected Leaders			
Others			

Planning Step 1. Define Stakeholder Participation

Activity Sheet 1.3.d. Sample Recruitment Letter for SU/SP Stakeholders

[Insert date]

Dear [Insert stakeholder name],

Recently, funding has become available for a Joint Service User/Service Provider Community Planning Group. The purpose of this group is to bring together community members who have an interest in improving the services available to our local families. We believe the work of this new planning group is strongly connected to your interests in the area of improving services for families in [Name the community].

We believe that your knowledge and experience would add greatly to the planning process and would like to discuss with you the ways that you could be involved. This new joint Service User/Service Provider Community Planning Group has the potential to bring significant changes to the services that are delivered in our local community and we would value your participation. We believe that community groups can bring about positive changes in services through partnerships between service users and service providers and are looking forward to the opportunity of discussing this with you.

One of our planning group members will contact you [Indicate how contact will be made] within [Indicate time frame, e.g., "a week"] to speak with you and explore your interest in joining this exciting new local community planning project. We hope you will be able to join with us in working toward improving services in our local community.

Please visit our Web site at [Insert Web site address] for further information. If you have any questions, please contact me at [Insert contact information].

Sincerely,

[Insert name of planning group coordinator]

Planning Step 2

Build Mission and Purpose

OVERVIEW AND RATIONALE

The ideal long-term goal of the SU/SP joint planning group is to reform the local service delivery system. Integral to this reform is the establishment of clearly defined mission, vision, and purpose statements that will convey this intent to both the collaborative partners and the public at large. While much of the organizational literature addresses mission and vision statements for formal organizations or planning groups, it is important to note that planning groups also use mission and vision development activities to build a cohesive group and to communicate to the **external environment** (1) who they are, (2) what they hope to achieve, and (3) how they hope to achieve their objectives. Throughout this discussion of mission and purpose building, we encourage the reader to apply the knowledge and practice of mission and vision development to local planning groups as well.

Vision statements encompass an image of a desired future state. Kouzes and Posner (1996) believe vision statements all contain the following attributes: (1) idealization, (2) uniqueness, (3) future orientation, and (4) imagery. Vision statements should be short so that the imagined future state of change by the group can be communicated easily (Work Group for Community Health and Development, 2014). Mission statements are more concrete; they set out clearly what the organizations intends to do (purpose) and for whom (target population/social problem). Mission statements should be no more than one to three sentences. To develop a mission statement, ask the following questions: (1) Who are we?, (2) Who do we serve?, (3) What are our values?, and (4) What makes us unique? (Bryson, 2011).

As articulated by Yaffee, Wondolleck, Bryan, McKearnan, and Mas (2003), "Most collaborative groups develop a vision, mission or purpose statement. . . . These statements articulate a common purpose for the participants, and guide decisions about where to focus future efforts" (p. 1). Therefore, planning tasks first involve the development of a vision statement to guide their collaborative process. The strategic management (Hill & Jones, 2008), social administration (Lipton, 1996), and organizational change literature all refer to the vision statement as an enduring characteristic guiding the group or organization. In contrast to activities and objectives, a vision represents the group's commitment to a long-term, unwavering goal even "in the face of ambiguity and surprises" (Johns & Saks, 2008, p. 85). It establishes a "desired future state" toward which the entity strives to achieve (Hill & Jones, 2008, p. 15), and is a critical characteristic of a group that is both capable of and amenable to change (Johns & Saks, 2008, p. 556). Since vision statements can be used as catalysts for change, it is imperative that the planning group emphasize the need for collaboration within the service continuum, as well as for broader systemic transformation.

Establishing a joint SU/SP vision statement is instrumental in conveying to the larger community the agreed-on reason for the group's existence. Quigley (1994) proposed that a clear vision "implies an understanding of the past and present which in turn, offers a roadmap to the future" (p. 37). This clarity serves multiple purposes, two of which are (1) to inform stakeholders about the company's aspirations for the future, and (2) to motivate and inspire employees and stakeholders to act on those aspirations (Candemir & Zalluho lu, 2013; Free, 2014). Therefore, it is recommended that SUs and SPs use vision statements to describe the future state that the organization would like to aspire to, as it pertains to service development and implementation, client recruitment, the particular service context in which it is operating, and the economy (Free, 2014). By having a clear vision with a target audience, SUs and SPs have the ability to get things done, as they are more prepared to mobilize their identified resources (i.e., money, people, etc.) in ways that effectively and efficiently meet the short-term and long-term goals of the organization. Also, it is important to note that a vision statement is not a business plan, but is a living document that catalogues the history of the organization or planning group, and is later used to tell the world what the organization or planning group would like to achieve or accomplish and the steps that the organization plans to use in order to achieve those future goals (Free, 2014; Lucas, 1998).

Writing a vision statement without a clear agenda may cause organizations or planning groups to flounder. Lucas (1998) stated that having a verbose vision statement would paint too broad a picture of what people can expect from the organization or what they can relate to. Likewise, being too specific trivializes the complexity and uniqueness of the problem that the organization or planning group has set out to address (Lucas, 1998). In order to create an effective and efficient vision statement that represents an organization's uniqueness, Laslo (2013) proposed five preliminary considerations:

1. A vision statement should reflect reality and be relevant and achievable.
2. A vision statement should be compelling and motivational for all group members.
3. A vision statement should not have to be the communication piece for the public.
4. A vision statement should not go beyond the scope of the organization and speak to the whole of the greater community.
5. A vision statement should reflect a consensus by group members on the desired future state of the organization.

Within any planning group or organization, a statement of organizational purpose may mirror elements of the mission statement, and vice versa. As indicated by Holosko, Winkel, Crandall, and Briggs (2015), in both the business and nonprofit worlds "the importance of mission statements have flourished in the past 25 years, as our rapidly changing society and institutions have evolved in a variety of ways" (p. 1). These authors also noted that in the literature they examined there is a renewed interest in mission statements in both their prevalence and relevance to external organizational environments, as well as the internal functions of organizations and planning groups. "In short, mission statements are seen as the organization's lifeblood or their raison d'être [meaning reason for being], and this prominent statement ideally encapsulates the essence of what any organization strives to achieve" (Holosko et al., 2015, p. 2).

A consensual and well-noted definition of a mission statement is "a broadly defined but enduring statement of purpose that distinguishes the organization from others of its type and identifies the scope of its operations in product, or service, and market terms" (Pearce, 1983, p. 15).

Well-written mission statements typically answer these four key questions: (1) Who are we? (2) What do we do? (3) What makes us unique? and (4) What are our core values? (Angier, 2005; Bart & Tabone, 2000; Bryson, 2011; Candemir & Zalluho lu, 2013; Ehmke, Dobbins, Gray, Boehlje, & Miller, 2004; Holosko et al., 2015; Smith, 2014; Tofttoy & Chatterjee, 2004). In both business and nonprofit organizations, mission statements are typically nested in a model normally hierarchically presented as vision→mission→values→purpose→goals→objectives→activities→outcomes (Holosko et al., 2015). This linear configuration depicts how alignment, performance, and outcomes can be readily assessed using any organization's mission statement.

To create an effective, updated, and relevant mission statement that distinguishes one organization from the other, it is important to write a parallel strategic plan (Salisbury & Griffis, 2014; Worth, 2014). According to Worth (2014), "a *strategic plan* is more than a strategy; it is a *process* that produces *a product*" (p. 160; emphasis in original). This helps the organization to focus its efforts as well as differentiate itself from other organizations (Gow, 2009). The strategic planning process starts where the organization is, identifies where it wants to go, and then creates a roadmap for the organization to reach its goal (Worth, 2014). However, ultimately it is the mission statement that guides the creation of events and activities that a group or organization undertakes (Gow, 2009). Worth (2014) outlined nine steps to aid with effectively writing a mission and purpose statement (p. 162):

1. Plan to plan by determining the process, the players, and their roles
2. Clarify the organization's mission, vision, and values
3. Assess the situation by scanning the external environment and the organization's internal realities
4. Identify the key strategic questions that need to be addressed
5. Develop clearly defined goals, strategies, and objectives
6. Write and communicate the plan
7. Develop operational and implementation plans
8. Execute the plan
9. Evaluate results

Like the vision statement, the mission statement plays an important role in outlining how the agency will meet the needs of its constituents (Bolon, 2005; Morphew & Hartley, 2006; Smith, 2014). For example, Lipton (1996) stated that "a mission must appeal to the broadest stakeholder constituency as possible and rise above the interests of any single stakeholder group. It must engage people and require little or no explanation" (p. 86). A mission statement sets the parameters for the working group and is the primary directive from which the group or organization operates (Hardina, Middleton, Montana, & Simpson, 2007, p. 132). According to Hummel (1996, as cited in Hardina et al., 2007), a mission statement should include a definition of the problem, a statement of the social problem to be addressed, one or more pertinent goals, identification of core values, and a description of the target population. Without a clear mission and purpose, the organization will fail to address issues or concerns under which it was formed, and will fail to carry the potential to reach designated audiences (Bolon, 2005). Figure 2.1 shows selected examples of mission statements highlighted by Smith (2014) and Worth (2014). These statements vary in content because they target different audiences, create particular experiences, and state what a company does. Similarly, the mission statements vary in length based on the type of services that the organization provides.

Figure 2.1. Selected Organizations and Their Mission Statements

Name of Organization	Sample Mission Statement
Coca-Cola	To refresh the world in mind, body, and spirit; to inspire moments of optimism through our brands and actions; to create value and make a difference everywhere we engage. http://www.coca-colacompany.com/our-company/mission-vision-values
Special Olympics	The mission of Special Olympics is to provide year round sports training and athletic competition in a variety of Olympic type sports for children and adults with intellectual disabilities, giving them continuing opportunities to develop physical fitness, demonstrate courage, experience joy and participate in sharing of gifts, skills and friendship with their families, other Special Olympics athletes and the community http://resources.specialolympics.org/Topics/General_Rules/Article_01.aspx
Starbucks	To inspire and nurture the human spirit—one person, one cup and one neighborhood at a time. http://www.starbucks.com/about-us/company-information/mission-statement
Nike	Bring inspiration and innovation to every athlete* in the world. (*If you have a body, you are an athlete.) http://about.nike.com/
Domestic Violence Shelter	To ensure a safe environment for women and children who have been victims of physical and emotional violence, while strengthening their abilities to function independently in a positive lifestyle free of violence.
Family Services Agency	To promote family strength and stability in a manner that allows each individual to achieve his or her potential while at the same time supporting strong and productive interrelationships among family members.
Drug and Alcohol Counseling	To promote and support the achievement of a positive and productive lifestyle, including steady employment and stable relationships, for those formerly addicted to chemical substances.

While every organization has a reason to exist, each should be able to clearly articulate what it would like to accomplish, both for short- and long-term processes. With this understanding, Morphew and Hartley suggest that mission and purpose statements operate as instructional tools for building any organization (2006) In this regard, we suggest that planning groups operate in much the same way as corporate and nonprofit organizations by developing their vision and mission statements to communicate to the external environment who they are, what is unique about them, and what they hope to achieve. In other words, a mission statement is used to "help organizational members distinguish between activities that conform to institutional imperatives and those that do not; provide a shared sense of purpose that has the capacity to inspire and motivate those within an institution; and communicate its characteristics, values, and history to key external constituents" (Morphew & Hartley, 2006, p. 457). Bolon (2005) further extended this notion a bit by underscoring the idea that a clear mission statement will help to distinguish between organizations that provide similar services. This sharper clarity helps to inspire and motivate individuals within an institution about (1) how to clearly communicate its characteristics, values, and history to key external constituents (Cochran, David, & Gibson, 2008); (2) how to help to propel the organization forward and to visualize its ideal future (Castro & Lohmann, 2014); and (3) how to help with strategic planning and the implementation of activities (Salisbury & Griffis, 2014).

While there are specific steps that must be taken when writing a mission statement, it is important to also be cognizant of some barriers that may arise during this process. Lee, Barker, and Mouasher (2013) suggested that, when writing mission and purpose statements, it is important to also write parallel goals and objectives that are achievable, measurable, and realistic; failing to do so could result in a lack of awareness, interest, and involvement from investors, community partners, and clients. Similarly, without a clear mission the organization may not be able to gain momentum for eventual change (Lee et al., 2013). Reasons for this lack of clarity could be based on unrealistic expectations that are actually highlighted in the mission (Candemir & Zalluho lu, 2013). Finally, it is important to note that organizations and planning groups have to commit themselves to taking the necessary steps to define their own mission, clarify their vision, and lay the foundation needed if they hope to get the support or community buy-in: this process takes time, commitment, and tenacity in order to fully execute this essential organizational activity.

DESCRIPTION OF PLANNING ACTIVITIES FOR STEP 2: BUILD MISSION AND PURPOSE

This planning step contains three action steps. Remember that any of the three action steps might use more than one activity sheet. Upon completion of these three action steps for Planning Step 2, please use the appropriate evaluation form found at the end of the chapter to evaluate each action step. Evaluation is an important completion part of the overall planning process.

Action Step 2.1. Creating a Joint SU/SP Vision Statement
Action Step 2.2. Building a Joint SU/SP Mission and Purpose Statement
Action Step 2.3. Redefining the SU/SP Mission Statement

Action Step 2.1 (Creating a Joint SU/SP Vision Statement) involves a commitment by both SUs and SPs to work together to develop a clear vision statement that signifies their ongoing commitment to the planning partnership, and what they hope to achieve by working together. Action Step 2.2 (Building a Joint SU/SP Mission and Purpose Statement) involves putting this commitment into words by preparing a mission statement that represents a consensual understanding of why the group is coming together, what the group hopes to achieve, and the value base for facilitation of the planning process. Finally, Action Step 2.3 (Redefining the SU/SP Mission Statement) incorporates the agreements between SUs and SPs into a negotiated redefined mission statement that will provide a pathway for working together throughout the planning process, and for communicating with external stakeholders about the work of the group. Action Step 2.3 is foundational to the success of the SU/SP group initiative as it demonstrates the important principle of trust and commitment between SUs and SPs. Without a solid commitment to the vision and mission created by this unique group, there is some risk that individuals or groups may stray away from their original purpose. The mission statement then, because of its necessity to the planning process offers both SUs and SPs their quasi marching orders in the accomplishment of their eventual planning goals. The mission statement articulated and agreed-on supports the joint venture of the SU/SP partnership in its early stages, and solidifies the group's commitment to its stated purpose.

Finally, our collective experiences in writing mission statements in a variety of health and human service programs, organizations, and planning groups revealed that almost all stakeholders wish to be involved in defining their mission. The enthusiasm to do this task and be part of building the mission is high. It has been noted in many consulting experiences that nothing galvanizes a group like building the mission statement.

Action Step 2.1. Creating a Joint SU/SP Vision Statement

a. List of Activity Sheet(s): Creating a Joint SU/SP Vision Statement

Action Step	Activity Sheet(s)
2.1. Creating a Joint SU/SP Vision Statement	2.1.a. Building a Joint SU/SP Vision Statement

b. Introduction: Creating a Joint SU/SP Vision Statement

This initial important step provides a negotiated pathway for SUs and SPs as they come together to establish the purpose of their group and describe their ideal vision of what outcomes they hope to see as a result of the SU/SP parallel planning process. The vision is a broad outcome statement that does not describe how the group members will work together or what they will do, but rather gives a focus to creating and projecting on what would be an ideal scenario as a result of planning for the local community. Visioning exercises typically ask participants to envision a future where resources are not limited, and planning does not have to incorporate economic constraints. In this way, visioning is a futuristic endeavor that eventually moves toward the development of a shared mission statement.

Given existing or perceived power differentials between SUs and SPs, **consensual decision-making** is critical in this action step. Practitioners will learn how to lead a group through a set of proscribed visioning exercises, and encourage consensual decision-making. Practitioners leading this group will help participants to envision the future perceived outcome of the planning process, articulate an ideal scenario they would strive for, and examine their shared values. Importantly in this step, the development of a shared vision gives some opportunity for SUs and SPs to negotiate their differences early on, and come to some agreement about their commitment to working together. Without a shared vision, the risk of going off track with the unfolding planning process is likely.

Activity Sheet 2.1.a (Building a Joint SU/SP Vision Statement) is a beginning tool that seeks to develop a group identity for the SU/SP partnership. This activity sheet asks the following questions to structure the SU/SP planning group responses: (1) What can the local SU/SP planning group offer the local community? (2) What are we capable of doing as an SU/SP planning group? (3) What will success look like for the community in one year? and (4) What will success look like for the SU/SP planning group in one year? The most important part of the vision statement activity for SUs and SPs is to put the vision statement at the forefront of the SU/SP planning group process to remind members that they are involved in a joint planning process to democratize decision-making among SUs and SPs, and also to work together to improve services for their local community. The vision statement provides the purpose and direction for SUs and SPs and encourages them to work together for the good of the local community and to work on overcoming their differences and to work toward a common goal of improving services in the local community. The development of the joint vision statement is the first step to working more specifically on the mission statement and purpose statement. This step is critical to the establishment of SU/SP consensual decision-making; the joint vision statement must precede the development of a mission statement that will eventually be communicated to the larger community.

c. Description: Creating a Joint SU/SP Vision Statement

1. Differentiate with the SU/SP joint planning group the differences among vision statements, purpose statements, and mission statements.
2. Develop a common language for the planning group that defines the vision statement as an ideal future that the SU/SP joint planning group would like to achieve.
3. Facilitate the development of the vision statement by asking what would be ideal for both SU and SP groups.
4. Facilitate the negotiations around the vision statement to bring the group to a consensual decision that represents their resolution of differences of opinion around the desired outcome of the joint planning group.

Action Step 2.2. Building a Joint SU/SP Mission and Purpose Statement

a. List of Activity Sheet(s): Building a Joint SU/SP Mission and Purpose Statement

Action Step	Activity Sheet(s)
2.2. Building a Joint SU/SP Mission and Purpose Statement	2.2.a. Building a Joint SU/SP Mission and Purpose Statement

b. Introduction: Building a Joint SU/SP Mission and Purpose Statement

Action Step 2.2 brings SUs and SPs in a mission-driven and purpose-building exercise in a collaborative planning process. Practitioners will learn how to lead the SU/SP group through a mission development exercise that is based on four critical questions: (1) Who are we? (2) Whom do we serve? (3) What are our values? and (4) What makes us unique?

This activity rests on the importance of a coherently developed mission statement that clearly defines what the planning initiative is, whom it proposes to serve, what community need it will meet, and how it proposes to meet that need. In order for the community to understand the mission and purpose of the planning group, the group needs to define the nature of the planning process in the local community, and must reach a consensus on their mission and purpose. Bringing SUs and SPs together early in the process will help ensure that all participants understand the general direction of the planning initiative.

Once again, as with the previous vision statement, the joint planning group must strive to overcome any power disparities to reinforce a fair, open, and equitable planning process. It is important to use consensus development models of priority setting, to allow the group to move forward. Using a well-developed series of questions for this process will assist practitioners keep diverse SU and SP groups on track, to reach a statement of mission and purpose that can be easily understood by the larger community. The questions in Activity Sheet 2.2.a simplify the process of mission development by representing a holistic approach to developing group identity for SUs and SPs together. Blending these two groups together into positive interactions requires the use of structured formats and approaches, that allow data from each group to be reciprocally and openly presented for consideration and negotiation within the joint planning session. The incorporation of a mission and purpose statement in the joint SU/SP planning process solidifies the planning group's commitment to working together collaboratively, to meet the needs of the local community. Practitioners will also learn how to create a mission and purpose statement that can be used to help the community understand the joint planning group's work in the short and the long term.

c. Description: Building a Joint SU/SP Mission and Purpose Statement

1. Revisit the discussion of the respective meaning of mission statements, vision statements, and purpose statements with the joint planning group.
2. Develop a common language for the planning group that defines mission as a declaration of organizational purpose agreed upon by the SU/SP planning group.
3. Highlight the importance of SU/SP collaboration as the critical factor in the implementation of the EI planning process.
4. Develop a mission statement based on the four essential questions in Activity Sheet 2.2.a: (1) Who are we? (2) Whom do we serve? (3) What are our values? (4) What makes us unique? (Bryson, 2011).
5. Facilitate the development of a statement that is based on joint planning group consensus, and resolve any differences of opinion, between SU and SP participants.

6. Create a brief, concise mission statement that reflects group consensus about the identity and purpose of the group, and allows SUs and SPs to further develop a shared understanding of how to work together.

7. Expand upon the development of the mission statement by developing a short and concise purpose statement.

Action Step 2.3. Redefining the SU/SP Mission Statement

a. List of Activity Sheet(s): Redefining the SU/SP Mission Statement

Action Step	Activity Sheet(s)
2.3. Redefining the SU/SP Mission Statement	2.3.a. SU/SP Mission Matrix
	2.3.b. SU/SP Consolidated Mission Statement

b. Introduction: Redefining the SU/SP Mission Statement

Finally, Action Step 2.3 is designed to help practitioners learn how to implement a process to develop and test the utility of the mission and purpose statement agreed upon in Action Step 2.2. By reviewing and refining the mission and purpose statement from the previous step, further consensual decision-making between SUs and SPs is reinforced. The importance of this "learning laboratory" of joint planning for mission and purpose development cannot be understated. By successfully cooperating on the mission and purpose of the joint planning group, a process has been established that highlights collaboration and respect for each other's similarities and differences. Achieving success in collaborating on a joint mission and purpose statement in the early stages of planning, forecasts potentially successful outcomes, when the more contentious issues of identifying needs and prioritizing services are eventually brought to the joint planning table. Implementing the process to review and refine the mission statement in the early stages of planning not only gives a sense of direction to the entire group, it also conveys a cohesive message regarding shared values and purpose that can be communicated to the larger community. The SU/SP joint planning group will need to discuss important questions such as, (1) What is the purpose of the joint planning group? (2) What is unique about this joint planning group? (3) Is our existence important to the local community? and (4) Can we successfully negotiate required decisions on priority needs, intervention planning, and grant applications?

While Action Step 2.3 may appear superfluous given the work previously accomplished in Steps 1 and 2, it is designed to further enhance the SU/SP planning group's function. Importantly, this step of redefining the mission will not be implemented until a joint mission statement is developed in Step 2. Activity Sheet 2.3.a requires SUs and SPs to identify the mission statement components they have developed in three areas: (1) purpose, (2) target population, and (3) activities. This summary mission matrix activity sheet allows SUs and SPs to compare their responses in all three areas and to work on consolidating their joint mission statement. Once there is joint planning group consensus however, on the mission and purpose of the planning group, it is important to once again return to the parallel process planning model and separate meetings and undertake a review of the accomplishments by exploring with individuals their separate understanding of the decisions that they have negotiated. Activity Sheet 2.3.b requires that all SU/SP participants sign the final joint mission statement as testimony to their negotiated agreement. Endorsing this mission statement helps to counteract mission drift in the future planning process where there may be a change of direction or interest. Participants can be brought back to their signed agreements with the statement of mission and purpose as a way of ensuring that mission drift is minimal and of holding participants accountable to their original signed agreement. The practitioner has the responsibility to co-ordinate the responses from each group to ascertain whether there has been a de facto commitment by both groups to the mission, or whether there have been accommodations that may become limiting factors to the success of future planning steps.

c. Description: Redefining the SU/SP Mission Statement

1. Facilitate responses from SUs and SPs by asking them to identify individually in separate groups what is the purpose, target population, and activities of the planning initiative in separate SU/SP groups (Activity Sheet 2.3.a).
2. Coordinate responses of both SU and SP groups, and facilitate SUs and SPs in a joint planning group to work together, to develop a shared understanding of the purpose of their work using Activity Sheet 2.3.a.
3. Develop a mission statement that has been uniquely crafted from individual responses, separate SU and SP groups, and finally a collaborative response from a joint SU/SP planning group that has reached consensus on a unique mission statement for this task.
4. Create a concise mission statement that reflects the purpose, target population, and activities that compose the joint SU/SP planning group using Activity Sheet 2.3.b.

CASE VIGNETTE: BARRIERS AND FACILITATORS TO BUILDING A MISSION STATEMENT

This case vignette illustrates the perils of jumping too quickly into planning steps of mission and purpose building, and reminds us that all communities are unique and there really is no cookie-cutter approach to planning. While there was a specific barrier to the development of a mission statement in this case, the context of a top-down government mandate for planning was also part of the larger problem. This actual problem of planning was based on a project funded by government to organize prevention coalitions in three separate cities. The story cannot be told without identifying that only one agency in one community received funding, and was responsible for the administration of the budget and supervision of staff. A coordinator was hired by the agency that received this funding. The funding was to be used to develop prevention coalitions addressing youth alcohol and drug addiction in each of the selected communities. However, when the coordinator began meeting with local SUs and SPs in each community, it became apparent that the communities who did not receive funding had their own ideas about how they would use the coordinator's time.

In one community there was an influential SP who did not agree with the funder's decision to target youth alcohol and drug addiction as being the community's social problem. Instead, this SP wanted to use the resources allocated to bring more children's mental health services to the local community. In meeting with this SP, the coordinator clearly outlined the mandate for the project and stated that funding was not available for children's mental health services because the project was originally funded for targeted youth alcohol- and drug-addicted populations. At the initial meeting of the newly formed coalition, the influential SP took over the vision- and mission-planning activities from the chairperson to lead the coalition, and she or he tried to reshape the project's mission and purpose to include his or her preferred children's mental health agenda.

The problem presented in this vignette is two-pronged. First, government funding was given to only one of the communities with no allocated budget for either of the other locations. Second, the coordinator was employed by the one agency that had received funding. Geographically, these communities were distant from each other, and each had its own unique problems and important stakeholders who held power in their respective local communities. The lack of dedicated resources for each community weakened the commitment of nonfunded locales to the mandate and mission prescribed by government agendas. Proceeding with a joint mission and purpose-building activity without a signed agreement that signaled dedication to the mandate of the project proved to be problematic. This case vignette highlights the importance of recognizing the uniqueness of local communities and their individual power dynamics. Building a joint mission and purpose in community planning requires a shared vision—not only between SPs and SUs but also between central government and local communities. The good news is that with much diplomacy and tact the recalcitrant SP was encouraged to work with the mandate and "get in the game" for the good of their community.

SUMMARY AND EVALUATION OF PLANNING STEP 2: BUILD MISSION AND PURPOSE

Summary of Planning Step 2: Build Mission and Purpose

This chapter discussed Planning Step 2 on mission and purpose building. In it, practitioners learn how to lead a group through a visioning exercise and how to encourage consensus decision-making about establishing a meaningful mission statement. It is only when there's a legitimate shared understanding of how the SU/SP partnership will work together that success will be attainable. This beginning step then brings together the responses of both groups, and encourages SUs and SPs to create a scenario where open and shared understanding can lead to shared commitment and attachment to the overall planning group. The trust developed thus leads to a fused and collaborative mission and purpose statement that not only guides the SU/SP partnership, but also leads to a more comprehensive and cohesive message to stakeholders in the larger community.

Evaluation of Planning Step 2: Build Mission and Purpose

Evaluation Form: Circle one number only for each question listed below.

Action Step 2.1. Creating a Joint SU/SP Vision Statement

a. How confident were you about achieving this goal?	Not confident	Somewhat confident	Very confident	Extremely confident
	1	2	3	4

b. What was the most important thing you learned about this step?

Action Step 2.2. Building a Joint SU/SP Mission and Purpose Statement

a. How confident were you about achieving this goal?	Not confident	Somewhat confident	Very confident	Extremely confident
	1	2	3	4

b. What was the most important thing you learned about this step?

Action Step 2.3. Redefining the SU/SP Mission Statement

a. How confident were you about achieving this goal?	Not confident	Somewhat confident	Very confident	Extremely confident
	1	2	3	4

b. What was the most important thing you learned about this step?

Your Total Score? _____

Group Discussion Notes:

(continue on back as needed)

REFERENCES

Angier, D. (2005). *How to write a mission statement*. South Burlington, VT: Success Network International, Inc.

Bart, C. K., & Tabone, J. C. (2000). Mission statements in Canadian not-for-profit hospitals: Does process matter? *Health Care Management Review, 25*(2), 45–63.

Bolon, D. S. (2005). Comparing mission statement content in for-profit and not-for-profit hospitals: Does mission really matter? *Hospital Topics, 83*(4), 2–9.

Bryson, J. (2011). *Strategic planning for public and nonprofit organizations. A guide to strengthening and sustaining organizational achievement*. Hoboken, NJ: John Wiley & Sons.

Candemir, A., & Zalluho lu, A. E. (2013). Exploring the innovativeness and market orientation through mission and vision statements: The case of Istanbul Stock Exchange companies. In *Proceedings of 9th International Strategic Management Conference, Procedia: Social and Behavioral Sciences, 99*, 619–628. doi:10.1016/j.sbspro.2013.10.532

Castro, R., & Lohmann, G. (2014). Airport branding: Content analysis of vision statements. *Research in Transportation Business & Management, 10*, 4–14. doi:10.1016/j.rtbm.2014.01.001

Cochran, D. S., David, F. R., & Gibson, C. K. (2008). A framework for developing an effective mission statement. *Journal of Business Strategies, 25*(2), 27–39.

Ehmke, C., Dobbins, C., Gray, A., Boehlje, M., & Miller, A. (2004). *Developing vision and mission statements*. Purdue University Cooperative Extension Service, EC-720.

Free, M. (2014). Vision, mission . . . purpose? *Production Machining, 14*(11), 17–19.

Gow, P. (2009). Missions, mantras, and meaning: What should mission statements do? *Independent School, 69*(1), 24–30.

Hardina, D., Middleton, J., Montana, S., & Simpson, R. (2007). *An empowering approach to managing social service organizations*. New York: Springer.

Hill, C., & Jones, G. (2008). *Strategic management: An integrated approach*. Mason, OH: South-Western Cengage Learning.

Holosko, M. J., Winkel, M., Crandall, C. A., & Briggs, H. (2015). A content analysis of mission statements of our top 50 schools of social work. *Journal of Social Work Education, 51*(2), 222–236. doi:10.1080/10437797.2015.1012922

Johns, G., & Saks, A. (2008). *Organizational behavior: Understanding and managing life at work* (7th ed.). Toronto, ON: Pearson Education Canada.

Kouzes J. M., & Posner, B. Z. (1996). Envisioning your future: Imagining ideal scenarios. *The Futurist, 30*(3), 14–19.

Laslo, R. (2013). Strategic planning: Making it real! *Municipal World, 123*(12), 27–28.

Lee, K., Barker, M., & Mouasher, A. (2013). Is it even espoused? An exploratory study of commitment to sustainability as evidenced in vision, mission, and graduate attribute statements in Australian universities. *Journal of Cleaner Production, 48*, 20–28. doi:10.1016/j.jclepro.2013.01.007

Lipton, M. (1996). Demystifying the development of an organizational vision. *Sloan Management Review, 37*(4), 83–92.

Lucas, J. R. (1998). Anatomy of a vision statement. *Management Review, 87*(2), 22–26.

Morphew, C. C., & Hartley, M. (2006). Mission statements: A thematic analysis of rhetoric across institutional type. *Journal of Higher Education, 77*(3), 456–471.

Pearce, J. A. (1983). The company mission as a strategic tool. *Sloan Management Review, 23*(3), 15–24.

Quigley, J. V. (1994). Vision: How leaders develop it, share it, and sustain it. *Business Horizons, 37*(5), 37–41. doi:10.1016/0007-6813(94)90017-5

Salisbury, P., & Griffis, M. R. (2014). Academic library mission statements, Web sites, and communicating purpose. *Journal of Academic Librarianship, 40*(6), 592–596.

Smith, D. J. (2014). Have you formed a personal mission statement? *Grand Rapids Business Journal,* GRBJ.com.

Tofttoy, C. N., & Chatterjee, J. (2004). Mission statements and the small business. *Business Strategy Review, 15*(3), 41–44. doi:10.0000/j.0955-6419.2004.00326.x

Work Group for Community Health and Development at the University of Kansas. (2014). *Community Tool Box, Chapter 8, Developing a strategic plan, Section 2: Proclaiming your dream: Developing vision and mission statements.* University of Kansas.

Worth, M. J. (2014). *Nonprofit management: Principles and practices* (3rd ed.). Los Angeles: Sage.

Yaffee, S., Wondolleck, J., Bryan, T., McKearnan, S., & Mas, A. (2003). *Collaborative resource management: Sample vision, mission, and purpose statements.* Ecosystem Management Initiative, School of Natural Resources and Environment, University of Michigan, Ann Arbor.

INTERNET REFERENCES

Free Management Library—Copyright Carter McNamara MBA, Ph.D. http://managementhelp.org/strategicplanning/mission-vision-values.htm

"The Basics of Developing Mission, Vision and Values Statements" found at this Web site defines the differences among mission, vision, and values statements. These online resources set out clearly the steps needed to develop mission, vision, and values statements. These guidelines have been adapted from the *Field Guide to Nonprofit Strategic Planning and Facilitation* published by the Authenticity Consulting LLC.

University of Kansas—Community Tool box. http://ctb.ku.edu/en/table-of-contents/structure/strategic-planning/vmosa/main

This sites offers an overview of strategic planning that addresses the development of vision, mission, objectives, strategies, and action plans (VMOSA). A step-by-step process outlining how community groups can use VMOSA is presented, along with an explanation of each of the sections that make up VMOSA.

Three Sigma, Inc.—Making Your Mission Operational. http://www.threesigma.com/mission_operational.htm

This site contains a printable version of the document entitled "Making Your Mission Operational." An operational mission is defined as a process model for transforming your mission into work. This model offers a series of questions on mission and purpose to assist organizations to define the fundamental reason for their existence.

Top NonProfits.com—50 Example Mission Statements. https://topnonprofits.com/examples/nonprofit-mission-statements/

This site suggests a one-sentence mission statement can be used to help guide decisions about priorities, actions, and responsibilities. It provides a link to a site that addresses vision statements and provides examples of fifty mission statements from diverse organizations.

POWERPOINT RESOURCES

Chapter 2

Planning Step 2

Build Mission and Purpose

Why is this planning step important?

- It clearly sets out what the organization intends to do, and for whom.
- It guides decisions for focusing current and future efforts in a collaborative manner.
- It conveys to participants, service users, and service providers the reason for the group's existence.

What does the literature say?

- A vision statement is a **living document,** and not a business plan (Free, 2014).
- A verbose vision or mission statement will paint too broad a picture, and cannot be evaluated.
- The simpler the language, the better.

Planning Step 2. Build Mission and Purpose

Activity Sheet 2.1.a. Building a Joint SU/SP Vision Statement

WHAT CAN THE LOCAL SU/SP PLANNING GROUP OFFER THE LOCAL COMMUNITY?	WHAT ARE WE CAPABLE OF DOING AS AN SU/SP PLANNING GROUP?	WHAT WILL SUCCESS LOOK LIKE FOR THE COMMUNITY IN ONE YEAR?	WHAT WILL SUCCESS LOOK LIKE FOR THE SU/SP PLANNING GROUP IN ONE YEAR?

Planning Step 2. Build Mission and Purpose

Activity Sheet 2.2.a. Building a Joint SU/SP Mission and Purpose Statement

WHO ARE WE?	WHOM DO WE SERVE?	WHAT ARE OUR VALUES?	WHAT MAKES US UNIQUE?

Planning Step 2. Build Mission and Purpose

Activity Sheet 2.3.a. SU/SP Mission Matrix

MISSION COMPONENT	SERVICE USERS	SERVICE PROVIDERS
Purpose		
Target Population		
Activities		

Source: Bryson (2011).

Planning Step 2. Build Mission and Purpose

Activity Sheet 2.3.b. SU/SP Consolidated Mission Statement

DATE	SU/SP FINAL JOINT MISSION STATEMENT
	SIGNED BY:

Planning Step 3
Identify Community Strengths

OVERVIEW AND RATIONALE

Broadly defined, asset mapping is an evaluation process that assesses the need for human services by exploring the existence of a problem within a specific client population (Grinnell, Gabor, & Unrau, 2012). It is often used as a tool to collect input from a cross-section of community members with knowledge of, and involvement in, particular social problems of interest. Asset mapping has several purposes, some of which include (1) determining the extent of a social problem and the nature of the target population's needs (Rossi, Lipsey, & Freeman, 2003), (2) identifying gaps in service delivery and future programming needs (Gupta, 1999), and (3) preventing or eliminating duplication of services (Beaulieu, 2002).

The mapping process gathers pertinent data that are used to "match clients' needs with potential programs" (Grinnell et al., 2012, p. 118). This process extends beyond simply expressing that a particular problem exists: it is designed to "find out more about the nature, scope and locale of the social problem" (Grinnell et al., 2012, p. 125). In simpler terms, asset mapping is used to fill a gap within a community and answers the questions (1) What is? and (2) What should be? based on the current state of a particular social problem and its desired outcome (see figure 3.1) (Beaulieu, 2002).

Asset mapping is highly congruent with the EI approach which we have proposed in this manual. In fact, some authors view it as an essential component of a larger conceptual framework for EIP (Rugs, Hills, Moore, & Peters, 2010; Simpson, 2002, 2004; Simpson & Flynn, 2007). As stated by DeVillaer (1990), "Asset mappings encompass a variety of methodologies including social indicator analyses, examination of treatment utilization data, key informant interviews, and community opinion surveys"

Figure 3.1. Purpose of Needs Assessment

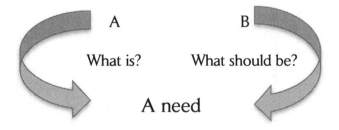

A   B

What is?   What should be?

A need

Gap between A and B

(as cited in Rugs et al., 2010, p. 30). Results from a well-constructed asset map can "create a sense of urgency and severity of a problem, thus motivating an investment of resources from interested parties" (Rugs et al., 2010, p. 30). Similarly, in turn it can "stimulate community ownership of a solution" (Amodeo & Gal, 1997, p. 230). When implemented correctly, asset mapping promotes the evolution of a willing community coalition into working groups with tangible goals and outcomes (Rugs et al., 2010, p. 35).

Central to asset mapping is the engagement of key stakeholders and partners toward the creation of community coalitions that are inclusive of "SPs, researchers, policy-makers, and clients" (Rugs et al., 2010, p. 30). When consumers are active participants in any coalition, there is a legitimate forum for their voices to be heard. As greater emphasis is placed on the adoption of EIPs, community-based multipartner collaborations will increase in use. Asset mapping provides a field-tested mechanism to develop an eventual consensus about future community research, training, and service planning.

One of the more straightforward and simpler types of asset mapping is the well-regarded strengths, weaknesses, opportunities, and threats (SWOT) analysis (Hill & Westbrook, 1997). SWOT, as the acronym suggests, is a listing of all strengths, weaknesses, opportunities, and threats that are currently present within an environment (Everett, 2014). SWOT analyses identify both the internal (strengths and weaknesses), and external (opportunities and threats) impacts on communities, overall (Dyson, 2004; Pickton & Wright, 1998). When focused internally, SWOT analyses explore what resources or lack thereof, are present (Worth, 2014). Externally, SWOT scans the "political, economic, social, technological and competitive environment with a view to identifying opportunities or threats" (Dyson, 2004, p. 632) that are relevant to the survival of the organization, and/or the improvement of the community. An example of a SWOT matrix as outlined by Worth (2014) is shown in figure 3.2.

Figure 3.2. An Example of a SWOT Matrix

SWOT ANALYSIS

Helpfulness and Origin	Helpful to achieving the objective	Harmful to achieving the objective
Internal Origin	STRENGTHS	WEAKNESS
Attributes of the organization	Characteristics of the organization that place it at an advantage over others	Characteristics of the organization that place it at a disadvantage relative to others
External Origin	OPPORTUNITIES	THREATS
Attributes of the organization	Elements within the environment that enhance its chances of success	Elements within the environment that prevent success

One main benefit of a SWOT analysis is its identification of current in-depth insights regarding the consensual strengths and weaknesses of the community or organization. However, Everett (2014) and Houben, Lenie, and Vanhoof (1999) provided a comparative list of advantages and disadvantages using SWOT analysis. Advantages of using SWOT included identifying possibilities for change not previously considered and the optimization of time used for the research were identified. However, some of the disadvantages of using SWOT were that it reduced creativity and encouraged superficial scanning of the strengths and weaknesses of the community or organization. The list of advantages and disadvantages using SWOT analysis are shown in figure 3.3.

Figure 3.3. Advantages and Disadvantages of Using SWOT Analyses

Advantages

1. It gathers the historical knowledge of many people concerning the topic and is very complete.
2. The checklist forces the manager to look at every aspect of the company independently of any knowledge of the subject and awareness of the problem.
3. It optimizes the time used for the research.
4. It explores possibilities for new efforts of solutions to problems.
5. It helps make decisions about the best path for the initiative. It identifies opportunities for success in context of threats to success. It can clarify directions and choices.
6. It helps to determine where change is possible. It helps to create an inventory of strengths and weaknesses that can reveal priorities as well as possibilities.
7. It standardizes the methodology and makes it possible to compare different companies and sectors.

Disadvantages

1. It does not measure the subjectivity of the given information.
2. The manager has to follow a procedure and cannot change according to the company situation, and so loses some flexibility.
3. The checklists do not stimulate the creativity.
4. It yields banal or misleading results.
5. It has a weaker theoretical basis.
6. It implies that organizational factors can be neatly categorized as positive or negative.
7. It encourages superficial scanning and impromptu categorization.
8. It promotes list building as opposed to thoughtful consideration.
9. It promotes muddled conceptualizations.
10. It does not look at trade-offs among factors.

Another form of asset mapping uses the **participatory action research** (PAR) approach. Minkler (2000) defined PAR as "a systematic investigation, with the collaboration of those affected by the issue being studied, for the purposes of education and taking action or effecting social change" (p. 192). PAR explicitly engages individuals who are directly affected by the issue(s) under investigation (Alvarez & Gutierrez, 2001; Cassano & Dunlop, 2005). However, "PAR is not necessarily a set of proscribed procedures to follow when gathering information, but a philosophy and empirical approach to gathering and using available information" (Incite! Women of Color Against Violence (hereafter Incite!), 2015, p. 79). According to Minkler (2000, p. 192), PAR approaches are:

1. Participatory
2. Co-operative, engaging community members and researchers in a joint process in which both contribute equally
3. A co-learning process for researchers and community members

4. A method for systems development and local community capacity-building
5. An empowering process by which participants can increase control over their lives by nurturing community strengths and problem-solving abilities
6. A way to balance research and action

Some basic principles of PAR are outlined by Incite!

1. Participants are experts who can describe their own experiences, and have many different ways of knowing and getting information about their conditions.
2. Participants control the process and gathering, coupled with the use of information about their communities. They decide what information they need to make the necessary changes they want, and how to get it. They decide what questions they need to answer and how. They lead and are integrally involved in all aspects of the design & implementation of the research, and of the analysis and distribution of the information gathered.
3. Participants gather information to inform and direct their actions for change.
4. Participants reflect on the information they have gathered, and the ways in which they are gathering it throughout the process. They also reflect on the actions they have taken and decide if they need more information before taking further action.
5. The people we gather information with and from are active, not passive participants in the process. Participants use information gathering to build community and movement, to develop leadership, and to empower themselves to make change.
6. Participants are not trying to "prove" an assumption or hypothesis; they want to learn more about themselves and their communities as a way to make change.
7. Participants agree on principles and values that will guide their information gathering and stay accountable to them throughout the process. (Incite! 2015, p. 79)

The PAR approach represents a participatory empowerment model of working with communities that is compatible with the eight-step planning process designed for the SU/SP planning process. The nonprescriptive, **bottom-up planning approach** that is the foundation of PAR is the same participatory approach that is used in the SU/SP planning group where the collection of EID and the joint decision-making requires both SUs and SPs to be involved from the very beginning of the planning initiative.

Ultimately, when assessing any community, it is important to understand the lens that is being used. For instance, it is important to understand the difference(s) between needs and assets. Some researchers have underscored that when conducting needs assessments, they often operate through what is termed a *deficit lens* as a way of forcing community leaders to highlight their communities' worst sides, in order to attract maximum resources from external, and sometimes internal, support. This deficit lens creates one-dimensional images of communities and the individuals within them, based on a disease risk profile or social problem category, such as low income, welfare moms, the handicapped, or high-crime neighborhood (Kretzmann & McKnight,

1993; Mathie & Cunningham, 2002; Sharpe, Greaney, Lee, & Royce, 2000). Contrarily, asset-based evaluations "mean identifying, supporting, and mobilizing existing community resources and capacities for the purpose of creating and achieving a shared vision" (Sharpe et al., 2000, p. 206. A contrast between a needs approach and an asset approach to community assessment is illustrated in figure 3.4.

Figure 3.4. Needs vs. Assets Approaches to Community Assessment

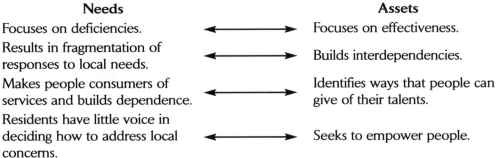

Needs		Assets
Focuses on deficiencies.	←——→	Focuses on effectiveness.
Results in fragmentation of responses to local needs.	←——→	Builds interdependencies.
Makes people consumers of services and builds dependence.	←——→	Identifies ways that people can give of their talents.
Residents have little voice in deciding how to address local concerns.	←——→	Seeks to empower people.

Finally, it is the "thoughtful planning and direct engagement of invested parties that are necessary steps to achieve successful outcomes benefiting all" (Rugs et al., 2010, p. 36). As stated by Kretzmann and McKnight (1996), when researchers, policy-makers, and direct-care providers holistically understand the relationship between an individual and his or her environment, then programs will be created that adequately, effectively, and efficiently address the needs of the actual individuals who are seeking services.

DESCRIPTION OF PLANNING ACTIVITIES FOR PLANNING STEP 3: IDENTIFY COMMUNITY STRENGTHS

This planning step contains three action steps. Remember that any of the three action steps might use more than one activity sheet. Upon completion of these three action steps for Planning Step 3, please use the appropriate evaluation form found at the end of the chapter to evaluate each action step. Evaluation is an important part of the overall planning process.

Action Step 3.1. SUs Lead in Mapping Community Assets
Action Step 3.2. SPs Review Community Asset Maps of SUs
Action Step 3.3. SPs Collaborate with SUs to Develop a Joint Asset Map

Action Step 3.1 (SUs Lead in Mapping Community Assets) describes the role that SUs will play as they use the EID sheets designed for this planning step; SUs will initiate this action step as a bottom-up planning process. Working in the collaborative planning group, they will set goals and identify activities that need to be carried out, assess the resources and skills that already exist in the local community, and identify how these resources and skills can be utilized within the planning initiative to improve services in the local community.

Action Step 3.2 (SPs Review Community Asset Maps of SUs) addresses how a well-constructed asset map can be created through a variety of methods that include interviews, surveys, **focus groups,** and **secondary data sources.** In addition, since the planning initiative depends on Web-based reporting, SUs can upload data from organizations and community residents into a Web-based source that could also include pictures and graphic representations to further explain the asset map.

Action Step 3.3 (SPs Collaborate with SUs to Develop a Joint Asset Map) utilizes a number of activity sheets that assist SUs in creating six mapping categories: (1) assets of individuals, (2) assets of associations, (3) assets of organizations, (4) physical assets of the community, (5) economic assets of the community, and (6) cultural assets (Brighter Futures Together, 2015). Realistically, having SUs take the lead in this asset mapping stage of the planning process is designed to increase the participation of SUs and create a more holistic appraisal of existing community resources.

Action Step 3.1. SUs Lead in Mapping Community Assets

a. List of Activity Sheet(s): SUs Lead in Mapping Community Assets

Action Step	Activity Sheet(s)
3.1. SUs Lead in Mapping Community Assets	3.1.a. SUs Identify Individual, Association, and Organizational Assets 3.1.b. SUs Identify Physical, Economic, and Cultural Assets 3.1.c. SUs Create GIS Asset Map Profile

b. Introduction: SUs Lead in Mapping Community Assets

While **community asset mapping** attempts to replace the deficit-based approaches of needs assessment with a more participatory, strengths-based data collection method, it does not in and of itself create a level playing field between SUs and SPs. To this end, this planning model is based on a community asset mapping exercise that recommends, initially at least, SU asset maps. Action Step 3.1 then gives legitimacy to the view that creating an asset map is more than just gathering strengths-based data; instead, the asset map is perceived here as a vehicle of empowerment. The parallel planning process for SUs and SPs has been developed to offset the likelihood that SPs will take it upon themselves to decide what levels of decision-making and influence SUs will have within the planning initiative.

c. Description: SUs Lead in Mapping Community Assets

SUs complete the asset mapping activity by identifying the resources that are available in the local community. There are six categories of assets that will be mapped by SUs as they complete Action Step 3.1. By having SUs take the lead in this asset mapping process, it is hoped that not only the formal individuals, associations, organizations, physical, economic, and cultural assets of the community will be highlighted, but also that SUs will also bring knowledge of the informal assets of the local community to build a more enhanced community asset map made up of formal and informal assets.

A number of activity sheets have been created for this action step to support the development of the SU asset mapping process. Activity Sheet 3.1.a (SUs Identify Individual, Association, and Organizational Assets) and Activity Sheet 3.1.b (SUs Identify Physical, Economic, and Cultural Assets) are structured to allow the data collected by SUs to be placed into three asset categories: (1) individuals, (2) associations, and (3) organizations. Within each of these categories, subcategories of types of assets will be constructed to allow SUs to collect similar data in each respective category. For example, the activity sheet for assets of individuals will identify factors such as knowledge, skills, and interest (Activity Sheet 3.1.a). Similarly, physical assets may include green space, community gardens and markets, or unused buildings that could be converted to neighborhood youth centers (Activity Sheet 3.1.b). These categories of assets allow for a more comprehensive submission of the data to the Web-based model of reporting and provide the framework for the asset map profile. Offering a visual representation of the community profile through mapping of demographic and social indicator data and/or graphic representations of the community through an asset map profile will increase the participatory nature of the asset mapping exercise by SUs when they use Activity Sheet 3.1.c (SUs Create GIS Asset Map Profile). That being said, of course SUs only will decide what asset information they wish to explore and through what data collection methods. Diverse data collection methods such as focus groups, interviews, surveys, and secondary data can all be organized into the categories of asset mapping: individuals, associations, organizations, physical assets, economic assets, and cultural assets. The final action step of counting these assets in each category allows for input to a GIS mapping program that can plot the assets graphically on an asset map profile for the local community.

Action Step 3.2. SPs Review Community Asset Maps of SUs

a. List of Activity Sheet(s): SPs Review Community Asset Maps of SUs

Action Step	Activity Sheet(s)
3.2. SPs Review Community Asset Maps of SUs	3.2.a. SPs Review Matrix for SU Asset Map 3.2.b. SPs Develop Information Sheet for Joint Asset Mapping Activity

b. Introduction: SPs Review Community Asset Maps of SUs

Action Step 3.2 (SPs Review Community Asset Maps of SUs) signifies the first step that SPs need to undertake before they bring their review to the joint planning group in Action Step 3.3 (SPs Collaborate with SUs to Develop Joint Asset Map). SPs will review the asset map prepared by SUs who will have uploaded their assets that make up each category, to use their own knowledge of the system, and to reanalyze how and where the asset map could be further enhanced. SPs will examine the community assets compiled by SUs and designate additions, enhancements, changes, or questions according to the categories of (1) assets of individuals, (2) assets of associations, (3) assets of organizations, (4) physical assets of the community, (5) economic assets of the community, and (6) cultural assets. Thus, the information gathered by SUs will be filtered through an SP lens using a **summary** review matrix that can potentially identify duplications or missing information (Activity Sheet 3.2.a [SPs Review Matrix for SU Asset Map]). In addition, further information can be identified by SPs who may have information on previous asset mapping initiatives, or on future grant funding that may increase community assets in any of the categories of interest. The documentation of supplementary information that will be presented to the joint planning group provides important and valuable knowledge in this planning step (Planning Step 3: Identify Community Strengths).

c. Description: SPs Review Community Asset Maps of SUs

A number of activity sheets for this action step facilitate the development of the review by SPs of the SU-led community asset map. The first two sheets are used to allow SPs to review the Web-based report posted by the SU group. Activity Sheet 3.2.a uses the established categories of the asset map described previously. In reviewing the prescribed categories of asset mapping, SPs may identify duplications or add emerging programs or consolidate data that have been corrected. The SP review matrix for asset mapping leads subsequently to a document that establishes SP information that will be shared. Thus, Activity Sheet 3.2.b (SPs Develop Information Sheet for Joint Asset Mapping Activity) becomes an important factor in facilitating the joint planning process in Action Step 3.3. When the information from Activity Sheet 3.2.b is uploaded to the Web-based reporting system, SUs will be able to see the review and information that has been added to promote the collaborative effort among the partners. In this way, both the SU asset map posted online and the SP information sheet posted online give partners an opportunity to discover the community resources that already exist and to learn what other community members are interested in pursuing through the SU/SP planning initiative.

Action Step 3.3. SPs Collaborate with SUs to Develop Joint Asset Map

a. List of Activity Sheet(s): SPs Collaborate with SUs to Develop Joint Asset Map

Action Step	Activity Sheet(s)
3.3. SPs Collaborate with SUs to Develop Joint Asset Map	3.3.a. SU/SP Asset Map Comparison Sheet for Joint Asset Mapping Activity 3.3.b. SU/SP Joint Asset Map Profile for Web-based Reporting

b. Introduction: SPs Collaborate with SUs to Develop Joint Asset Map

Finally, in Action Step 3.3 the coming together of SUs and SPs is a collaborative effort that recognizes the value of the perceptions of both partners. This joint asset-mapping action step encourages SPs to add their knowledge and experience about community strengths to the planning process. SUs in this instance have taken the lead in the development of the community asset map and have presented their **findings** (online) to the SPs to increase transparency and trust between planning members. SPs have utilized the Web-based reporting mechanism to analyze and review the findings of SUs regarding the categories of asset mapping: (1) individuals, (2) associations, (3) organizations, (4) physical assets, (5) economic assets, and (6) cultural assets. A compilation of the categories of the SU asset map has been provided to the SP group early on in the process, by using the Web-based reporting method. The ability of the SPs to utilize data collected by SUs has enhanced their ability to prepare responses that will inevitably strengthen the overall community asset map. Their preparation for the joint asset-mapping meeting between SUs and SPs includes the completion of Activity Sheet 3.3.a (SU/SP Asset Map Comparison Sheet for Joint Asset Mapping Activity).

c. Description: SPs Collaborate with SUs to Develop Joint Asset Map

While the SUs and SPs have been working independently in parallel groups to create their asset maps, this final action step requires that they now collaborate to produce a joint SU/SP asset map. Since transparency has been the hallmark of both SUs and SPs, they have been able to review and discuss their respective findings through the Web-based reporting system. Indeed, there will be no surprises when both SUs and SPs have had an opportunity to gain information about what each other is thinking. The premeeting information provided by the Web-based reporting system allows both SUs and SPs to understand their community assets in ways that can promote unique responses. Creating a joint SU/SP asset map using Activity Sheet 3.3.b (SU/SP Joint Asset Map Profile for Web-based Reporting) affords the local partnership an opportunity to strengthen their involvement as partners who seek to reshape their community services and their potential to expand existing resources and services for the local community. The knowledge and experience of both SUs and SPs will join together to coconstruct an asset map that represents the overall identified strengths and resources available in the local community. Here, practitioners will learn the importance of increasing SU participation by amplifying SU voice and encouraging a meaningful role for SUs in EI planning. By providing leadership in this asset-mapping action step, SUs will be establishing their bona fide legitimacy as meaningful representative partners in the planning initiative.

CASE VIGNETTE: COLLABORATING ON COMMUNITY ASSET MAPS

Community asset mapping is not without its own challenges in local communities. Building consensus among SUs and SPs about what is needed in any community is indeed a worthy goal that needs to be undertaken. The story in this case reflects the diverse opinions of SUs and SPs about what actually constitutes a "service delivery system of care."

A children's service coordinating committee in one community began a community asset mapping activity by using different committees for SUs and SPs. Administrators assumed that both of their respective community asset maps would be similar, and that when meeting together as a joint group, there would be no major issues between the two groups, but this was not the case. When the SUs and SPs eventually reviewed together the two separately constructed asset maps, their obvious discrepancies concerned both groups. SUs reported some community services identified as duplicative and redundant. SPs were shocked at the levels of informal support services reported as community assets by SUs. The gap between the two groups' perceptions of community assets was so great that SPs began to question whether they should go back to deficit approaches in order to identify needs, rather than stay with the preferred asset-based approach. This lack of acceptance of SUs' asset maps as valuable did little to promote the principle of inclusion that had been espoused in their earlier mission statement. Fixed ideas about professional services kept SPs from actually listening to SUs, whose lived experiences showed them that informal supports do indeed matter in communities of care.

This case vignette highlights the importance of principles such as inclusion, participation, and respect for providing the foundation and rationale for collaborative relationships between SUs and SPs. The negativity of SPs toward the work carried out by SUs undermined the very assumptions that underlie asset mapping approaches to service improvement. In this case, the two separate committees reworked their asset maps and got together again in one large joint planning group. However, once more the resistance of SPs to acknowledge the importance of informal supports services as community assets put an end to this joint planning initiative. SUs again lost their voice and retreated from the planning process, vowing never to engage with that particular group of SPs again. The type of tokenism noted herein mirrors the literature on SU participation, which reveals that when SUs speak, SPs often placate them and turn a deaf ear. This community asset mapping initiative thus provided the participants with yet another learning laboratory on how SUs often remain disempowered in their various community interactions with SPs.

SUMMARY AND EVALUATION OF PLANNING STEP 3: IDENTIFY COMMUNITY STRENGTHS

Summary of Planning Step 3: Identify Community Strengths

Planning Step 3 of the SU/SP planning process assumes that SUs are the primary producers of knowledge about what services are needed in the local community. The construction of the asset map by SUs will be uploaded to the Web-based reporting system, where SPs can access it, and prepare for their SP group review, prior to the final action step that brings SUs and SPs together to create the comprehensive asset map to be eventually used throughout this planning process. The purpose of having SUs take the lead in this planning step is to showcase the experiential knowledge of community that users bring to the planning table. Highlighting the participatory planning process to be undertaken with SUs in the lead is congruent with asset mapping, which focuses on the strengths of community. In this planning step the strengths of SUs are recognized: only the SUs will decide which data collection methods to use and what asset information to explore.

Evaluation of Planning Step 3: Identify Community Strengths

Evaluation Form: Circle one number only for each question listed below.

Action Step 3.1. SUs Lead in Mapping Community Assets

a. How confident were you about achieving this goal?	Not confident	Somewhat confident	Very confident	Extremely confident
	1	2	3	4

b. What was the most important thing you learned about this step?

Action Step 3.2. SPs Review Community Asset Maps of SUs

a. How confident were you about achieving this goal?	Not confident	Somewhat confident	Very confident	Extremely confident
	1	2	3	4

b. What was the most important thing you learned about this step?

Action Step 3.3. SPs Collaborate with SUs to Develop a Joint Asset Map

a. How confident were you about achieving this goal?	Not confident	Somewhat confident	Very confident	Extremely confident
	1	2	3	4

b. What was the most important thing you learned about this step?

Your Total Score? _____

Group Discussion Notes:

(continue on back as needed)

REFERENCES

Alvarez, A., & Gutierrez, L. (2001). Choosing to do participatory research: An example and issues of fit to consider. *Journal of Community Practice, 9*(1), 1–20.

Amodeo, M., & Gal, C. (1997). Strategies for ensuring use of asset mapping findings: Experiences of a community substance abuse prevention program. *Journal of Primary Prevention, 18*(2), 227–242.

Beaulieu, L. J. (2002). *Mapping the assets of your community: A key component for building local capacity* (SRDC 227). Southern Rural Development Center.

Brighter Futures Together (2015). *Brighter Futures Together Toolkit.* Sustainable Communities North East Initiative (SCNEI), UK.

Cassano, D. R., & Dunlop, J. M. (2005). Participatory action research with South Asian immigrant women: A Canadian example. *Critical Social Work, 6*(1), 1–15.

DeVillaer, M. (1990). Client-centered community needs assessment. *Evaluation and Program Planning, 13*(3), 211–219.

Dyson, R. G. (2004). Strategic development and SWOT analysis at the University of Warwick. *European Journal of Operational Research, 152*(3), 631–640.

Everett, R. F. (2014). A crack in the foundation: Why SWOT might be less than effective in market sensing analysis. *Journal of Marketing & Management Special Issue, 1*(1), 58–78.

Grinnell, R., Gabor, P., & Unrau, Y. (2012). *Program evaluation for social workers. Foundations of evidence-based programs.* New York: Oxford University Press.

Gupta, K. (1999). *A practical guide to asset mapping.* San Francisco: Jossey-Bass Pfeiffer.

Hill, T., & Westbrook, R. (1997). SWOT analysis: It's time for a product recall. *Long Range Planning, 30*(1), 46–52.

Houben, G., Lenie, K., & Vanhoof, K. (1999). A knowledge-based SWOT-analysis system as an instrument for strategic planning in small and medium sized enterprises. *Decision Support Systems, 26*(2), 125–135.

Incite! Women of Color Against Violence. (2015). Stop *law enforcement violence toolkit.* Incite!

Kretzmann, J. P., & McKnight, J. L. (1993). *Building communities from the inside out: A path toward finding and mobilizing a community's assets.* Chicago: ACTA.

Kretzmann, J. P., & McKnight, J. L. (1996). Asset-based community development. *National Civic Review, 85*(4), 23–29.

Mathie, A., & Cunningham, G. (2003). From clients to citizens: Asset-based community development as a strategy for community-driven development. *Development in Practice, 13*(5), 474–486.

Minkler, M. (2000). Using participatory action research to build healthy communities. *Public Health Reports, 115*(2–3), 191–197.

Pickton, D. W., & Wright, S. (1998). What's SWOT in strategic analysis? *Strategic Change, 7*(2), 101–109.

Rossi, P. H., Lipsey, M., & Freeman, H. E. (2003). *Evaluation: A systemic approach* (7th ed.). Thousand Oaks, CA: Sage.

Rugs, D., Hills, H. A., Moore, K. A., & Peters, R. H. (2010). A community planning process for the implementation of evidence-based practice. *Evaluation and Program Planning, 34*(2011), 29–36.

Sharpe, P. A., Greaney, M. L., Lee, P. R., & Royce, S. W. (2000). Assets-oriented community assessment. *Public Health Reports, 115*(2–3), 205–211.

Simpson, D. D. (2002). A conceptual framework for transferring research to practice. *Journal of Substance Abuse Treatment, 22*(4), 207–211.

Simpson, D. D. (2004). A conceptual framework for drug treatment process and outcomes. *Journal of Substance Abuse Treatment, 27*(2), 99–121.

Simpson, D. D., & Flynn, P. M. (2007). Moving innovations into treatment: A stage-based approach to program change. *Journal of Substance Abuse Treatment, 33*(2), 111–120.

Worth, M. J. (2014). *Nonprofit management: Principles and practices* (3rd ed.). Los Angeles: Sage.

INTERNET REFERENCES

The Asset-Based Community Development (ABCD) Institute. http://www.abcdinstitute.org/publications/downloadable/

This site identifies the ABCD Institute as an organization that considers local assets as the primary building blocks of sustainable CD. There are a large number of downloadable publications available online in categories such as (1) general, (2) community, (3) education, (4) health, (5) inclusion, and (6) global development. The ABCD Institute is located at Northwestern University, Evanston, Illinois.

The Asset-Based Community Development (ABCD) Institute—ABCD Toolkit. http://www.abcd institute.org/toolkit/index.html

This toolkit offers a variety of Web-based resources arranged into three categories: (1) talking point tools, (2) asset mapping tools, and (3) facilitating tools. Within all three categories, there is a wide range of downloadable information and activity sheets designed to support community asset mapping initiatives.

Strengthening Nonprofits: A Capacity Builders Resource Library. http://www.strengtheningnon profits.org/

This site offers a six-step model for conducting a community assessment with an e-learning component that contains an audio file and a guidebook. The six steps are outlined as follows: (1) define the scope, (2) go solo or collaborate, (3) collect data, (4) determine key findings, (5) set priorities and create an action plan, and (6) share your findings.

University of Kansas, Community Tool Box: Section 8. Identifying Community Assets and Resources. http://ctb.ku.edu/en/table-of-contents/assessment/assessing-community-needs-and-resources/identify-community-assets/main

This site defines community assets and/or community resources as anything that can be used to improve the quality of life in a community. Sections of the document outline definitions of community assets, how to identify them, and how to map community assets to meet needs and strengthen the community as a whole.

POWERPOINT RESOURCES

Chapter 3
Planning Step 3

Identify Community Strengths

Why is this planning step important?

- It sets the stage for what the community does well and determines assets, weaknesses, resources, and limitations.
- It guides asset mapping, an evaluation process that assesses the need for human services by exploring existing problems.
- By assessing strengths it can promote growth or generation of a willing community group with tangible goals and outcomes.

What does the literature say?

- An asset map can **create a sense of urgency and severity of a problem** to motivate an investment of resources from interested parties.
- SWOT analysis (**s**trengths, **w**eaknesses, **o**pportunities, and **t**hreats) scans the environment for trends, and for internal and external components to consider for creating and sustaining community coalitions.
- Asset maps and their components fill a gap within a community based on current state of a particular social problem and its desired outcome.

Planning Step 3. Identify Community Strengths

Activity Sheet 3.1.a. SUs Identify Individual, Association, and Organizational Assets

ASSET MAP CATEGORY	SUs' IDENTIFICATION OF ASSETS
1. Individuals	
2. Associations	
3. Organizations	

Planning Step 3. Identify Community Strengths

Activity Sheet 3.1.b. SUs Identify Physical, Economic, and Cultural Assets

ASSET MAP CATEGORY	SUs' IDENTIFICATION OF ASSETS
1. Physical	
2. Economic	
3. Cultural	

Planning Step 3. Identify Community Strengths

Activity Sheet 3.1.c. SUs Create GIS Asset Map Profile

ASSET MAP CATEGORY	SU TOTAL NUMBER OF ASSETS BY CATEGORY	GIS INPUT NUMBER OF ASSETS BY CATEGORY
Individuals		
Associations		
Organizations		
Physical Assets		
Economic Assets		
Cultural Assets		

Planning Step 3. Identify Community Strengths

Activity Sheet 3.2.a. SPs Review Matrix for SU Asset Map

ASSET MAP CATEGORY	ASSETS	DUPLICATIONS	EMERGING SERVICES	QUESTIONS
Individuals				
Associations				
Organizations				
Physical Assets				
Economic Assets				
Cultural Assets				

Planning Step 3. Identify Community Strengths

Activity Sheet 3.2.b. SPs Develop Information Sheet for Joint Asset Mapping Activity

ASSET MAP CATEGORY	CATEGORY CHANGES
Individuals	
Associations	
Organizations	
Physical Assets	
Economic Assets	
Cultural Assets	

Planning Step 3. Identify Community Strengths

Activity Sheet 3.3.a. SU/SP Asset Map Comparison Sheet for
Joint Asset Mapping Activity

ASSET MAP CATEGORY	SERVICE USERS ASSET MAPPING	SERVICE PROVIDER ASSET MAPPING
Individuals		
Associations		
Organizations		
Physical Assets		
Economic Assets		
Cultural Assets		

Planning Step 3. Identify Community Strengths

Activity Sheet 3.3.b. SU/SP Joint Asset Map Profile for Web-based Reporting

ASSET MAP CATEGORY	JOINT TOTAL NUMBER OF ASSETS BY CATEGORY	GIS INPUT NUMBERS BY CATEGORY OF ASSETS
Individuals		
Associations		
Organizations		
Physical Assets		
Economic Assets		
Cultural Assets		

Planning Step 4

Identify Community Needs Using EID

OVERVIEW AND RATIONALE

Long and established beliefs about the necessity of collecting data on local community needs are today being linked with Web-based technology in order to better facilitate such data collection and dissemination. This technology has helped providers understand how clients view services, has created a bidirectional approach to understanding treatment approaches, and has provided insights into the processes that patients access when utilizing health care and/or treatment services (Kvarnström, Hedberg, & Cedersund, 2013; Williamson, German, Weiss, Skinner, & Bowes, 1989). Some of these information technology approaches to treatment include explanations of how and why SUs access treatment, how they communicate with their SPs, and/or how SPs can improve their service quality. This knowledge becomes important when SUs and SPs in a community planning process are carrying out parallel processes associated with data collection and routine sharing. The development, implementation, evaluation, and execution of a Web-based logging application for these groups simplify data collection and provide a mechanism for SUs and SPs to learn from each other about their gathering of EID on community needs.

While traditional community needs assessments utilize a variety of qualitative and quantitative methods such as focus groups, interviews, surveys, or preexisting large data sets that may include social indicator data, these methods are not always effective in influencing behavior change (Carpenter, Nieva, Albaghal, & Sorra, 2005). However, using Web-based technology data collection fields can be tailored more precisely to suit local needs (Turner, Yorkston, Hart, Drew, & McClure, 2006). Needs assessments, whether Web based or paper based, are critical to SU/SP planning because they provide EID on the current local problem/need and are a mechanism for collaboration on what needs to be done to solve the problem and/or meet the identified need.

This chapter's planning activity sheets for Action Step 4.1, Action Step 4.2, and Action Step 4.3 demonstrate how information transmission between the SU planning group and SP planning group can be coordinated, thus increasing the overall transparency of each of the eight planning steps. In Planning Step 4 of the CDPM described in this manual there is a work plan (Activity Sheet 4.1.a. SU/SP Data Collection Work Plan). This work plan outlines a set of planning activities that must be carried out in a stepwise manner for SU/SP collection of EID for the needs assessment component of the planning process. While the work plan provides a pathway for EID collection, it is in no way prescriptive. Both SUs and SPs must agree on the questions to be answered by the needs assessment process. The collection of EID is critical to the SU/SP planning process. It is within Planning Step 4 that SUs and SPs utilize EID to accurately identify local problems and needs and begin the recognition of what priority needs should be included in the scope of their collaborative planning process. In this way, needs assessments carried out using EID provide the foundation for how SUs and SPs will decide on priority needs and interventions. Without EID collected and analyzed in the local context and within the current time frame for planning, the probability of reaching a joint conclusion by SUs and SPs on recommended intervention models could be compromised by politics and power struggles. EID is critical in the SU/SP planning process for a successful outcome for all planning members and for the local community.

The utilization of SUP in identifying community needs cannot be understated. Research conducted by Kvarnström, Willumsen, Andersson-Gare, and Hedberg (2012) found that information transmission, conditions for SUP, and interaction for increased understanding were important variations that contributed to SUP. A study by Holosko, Leslie, and Cassano (2001) found that the involvement of SUs not only provided clients with a voice in creating the service that best suited their needs, but also empowered them to create an identity that best represented and gave voice to their most immediate and/or pressing needs. Other researchers have also found that while SUs were willing to cooperate with SPs, they were hesitant to do so, resulting in service utilization gaps that have included the underutilization of services and/or improper diagnosis of clients and their symptoms (Forest, Risk, Masters, & Brown, 2000; Fudge, Wolfe, & McKevitt, 2008; Holosko, 1996; McLaughlin, 2009; Oxman, Thomson, Davis, & Haynes 1995; Williamson et al., 1989). This bidirectional process is important because often practitioners, researchers, and SPs ignore and dismiss suggestions of SUs that appear to be based on the notion that the SU is unaware of medical practices or proper protocols for dealing with the need (Abraham, 1993; Fudge et al., 2008).

The use of Web-based reporting to share EID has a positive impact on the interaction between SUs and SPs during the community needs assessment phase of the planning process. An example is unique collaborative communication styles that have created a shared power dynamic between SPs and SUs based on Web-based communication (Kvarnström et al., 2012). Likewise, Web-based reporting has narrowed the communication gap between SPs and SUs. However, it is important to explore and describe the differences between traditional data dissemination and Web-based dissemination. Researchers suggest that information dissemination is not a linear process, but instead is increasingly a dynamic and fluid process (Carpenter et al., 2005; Kvarnström et al., 2013; Zhang, Huang, Su, Zhao, & Zhang, 2014). In other words, the funneling of information does not always travel from person A, to person B, to person C, and so on, but rather from person A, to person D, to person X, to person M, and so on.

Traditional information dissemination includes the utilization of manuscripts, publications, and/or conferences as mechanisms for sharing pertinent research findings (Oxman et al., 1995). Although this process has been instrumental in informing SPs about **promising practices** regarding treatment and service utilization, it now appears that having this singular mode to inform change has some technical limitations. For instance, some research (Oxman et al., 1995; Williamson et al., 1989) found that physicians were not always updated on treatment and/or medication information as a result of delayed processing or limited opportunities associated with traditional information-sharing methods. Since traditional information-sharing methods may include manuscript publication, which is often a process that includes peer review, manuscript approval, and distribution in printed form, updated information is not always readily available and accessible. However, when such information becomes accessible it becomes normally accessible only to those individuals associated with colleges and universities (Williamson et al., 1989), as individuals who frequently attend academic conferences may obtain or attend presentations regarding a particular topic of interest. This venue, which has a limited audience (primarily practitioners, academics, and/or graduate students), may attract only those participants who directly provide a specific intervention or work with a specific population, thus limiting how such information is shared and knowledge is gained (Oxman et al., 1995).

Contrarily, Web-based dissemination is seen as the process of disseminating various forms of information to a wide array of individuals in a short time frame (Zhang, et al., 2014). This dissemination also allows for information to be updated and presented in a timely manner, and to reach diverse and nontraditional populations. Much of the research on Web-based dissemination underscores the concept of gossip dissemination, or the process of sending information to one network of people, that in turn sends the information to another network, and so on (Eugster, Guerraoui, Kermarrec, Massoulié, 2004; Even & Monien, 1989). This process ultimately ends in what is known as the broadcast, at which point the information has been fully shared and almost all participants are fully aware of the depth and breadth of the problem (Even & Monien, 1989).

The practicality of Web-based reporting has many advantages. The ability to draw from multiple sources in order to make an informed decision is the most obvious and supported notion. Kvarnström et al. (2013) found that when an SU presents a problem, the SP has both various networks that she or he may draw on for promising practices and updated information that may help to best meet the needs of the SU. This information further empowers the SUs to make decisions based on choices that best meet their needs (Kvarnström et al., 2013). Finally, the process of Web-based information dissemination allows an SU to find information on his or her own and ask questions about that information, hence further empowering SUs to take control of their own health and well-being.

Ultimately, it is argued that the dissemination of information is a process; it is important that SPs explore the mechanisms necessary to distribute their pertinent information. Carpenter et al. (2005) posit that there are no past formulae regarding how and when to disseminate information. Rather, they suggest that researchers craft dissemination plans into their research agenda so that they incorporate the unique needs of SUs. As such, they have created a six-step rubric to assist with this process:

1. Research findings and products: What is going to be disseminated?
2. End users: Who will apply it to practice?
3. Dissemination partners: Who are the individuals, organizations, or networks through whom you can reach end users?
4. Communication: How will you convey the research outcomes?
5. Evaluation: How have you determined what worked and what did not?
6. Dissemination work plan: Where do you start? (Carpenter et al., 2005).

Thus, the development of a dissemination plan helps to place into perspective the various components of any project, and in turn, the **long-term objectives** of that project. Since every project is different, having unique plans in place that are tailored to specific events helps to improve the ways and manner in which information ultimately gets shared.

DESCRIPTION OF PLANNING ACTIVITIES FOR PLANNING STEP 4: IDENTIFY COMMUNITY NEEDS USING EID

This planning step contains three action steps. Remember that any of the three action steps might use more than one activity sheet. Upon completion of these three actions steps for Planning Step 4, please use the appropriate form found at the end of the chapter to evaluate each action step. Evaluation is an important completion part of the overall planning process.

Action Step 4.1. SU/SP Establish Data Collection Work Plan for Community Needs Assessment

Action Step 4.2. SU/SP Complete Data Collection Work Plan

Action Step 4.3. SU/SP Report Findings on Dedicated Web Site

Action Step 4.1 (SU/SP Establish Data Collection Work Plan for Community Needs Assessment) involves a commitment by SUs and SPs to develop a plan for establishing what data are required for their eventual community needs assessment, to identify who has responsibility for data collection, and to set time lines for completion (Activity Sheet 4.1.a).

Action Step 4.2 (SU/SP Complete Data Collection Work Plan) requires the completion of the data collection work plan that designates specific data collection responsibilities that may include secondary data sources (i.e., social indicator data, census data, previous needs assessment studies, research literature), as well as **primary data** sources (i.e., focus groups and **key informant** interviews). Action Step 4.2 contains a variety of activity sheets created to facilitate transparency between SUs and SPs as they monitor their progress in collecting the community needs assessment data. An example of GIS mapping of community needs assessment data is also included in Action Step 4.2 (specifically Activity Sheet 4.2.c) to illustrate how spatial analysis of local community data can enhance the SU/SP assessment of community needs (Dunlop, 2010).

In Action Step 4.3 (SU/SP Report Findings on Dedicated Web Site), SUs and SPs systematically report on their data collection activities and prepare a joint analysis of the findings. Once the preliminary community needs/assets report is uploaded to the dedicated Web site (Activity Sheet 4.3.a [Preliminary Community Needs Assessment Report: TOC]), SUs and SPs will review it and assess whether they have the information they need to proceed with the next step in the needs assessment planning process (Step 5: Identify Services and Set Priorities Using EID).

Action Step 4.1. SU/SP Establish Data Collection Work Plan for Community Needs Assessment

a. List of Activity Sheet(s): SU/SP Establish Data Collection Work Plan for Community Needs Assessment

Action Step	Activity Sheet(s)
4.1. SU/SP establish data collection work plan for community needs assessment	4.1.a. SU/SP Data Collection Work Plan

b. Introduction: SU/SP Establish Data Collection Work Plan for Community Needs Assessment

This step begins the process of reviewing and examining the issues that are of concern to the SUs and SPs who have joined together in the planning initiative. All planning initiatives focus on defining clearly how the problem is defined within the local community. Possible questions include (1) Who is affected by the problem? (2) What stakeholders are willing to be involved in the solution? (3) Is there a general agreement about what is causing the problem? and (4) What are the consequences of maintaining the status quo?

c. Description: SU/SP Establish Data Collection Work Plan for Community Needs Assessment

Activity Sheet 4.1.a identifies a broad range of data that may be available. There is, however, no cookie cutter approach to developing and implementing a community needs assessment. Macro practitioners will need to consider carefully factors such as accessibility and accuracy of available data and resources when deciding which methods to undertake. Most importantly, data collection methods must be meaningful to both SUs and SPs. Activity Sheet 4.1.a contains a number of steps to assist SUs and SPs in completing this planning activity. Choosing what data to collect is a primary collaborative task for SUs and SPs: **data sources** can be tailored to each individual community planning initiative. Since this manual is interdisciplinary in focus, the indicator data chosen will reflect the specific data collection needs of the SU/SP planning group. Therefore, quantitative secondary data sources may include not only demographic information, but also crime statistics; health indicator data; social and economic data; social service statistics; previous needs assessment reports; literature reviews in the relevant discipline; and federal, regional, and municipal data. Primary quantitative data can be collected using a variety of methods such as client satisfaction surveys or community surveys. Complementary qualitative data can be collected using methods such as (1) focus group interviews, (2) key informant interviews, (3) SU interviews, (4) SP interviews, and (5) community forums.

Action Step 4.2. SU/SP Complete Data Collection Work Plan

a. List of Activity Sheet(s): SU/SP Complete Data Collection Work Plan

Action Step	Activity Sheet(s)
4.2. SU/SP Complete Data Collection Work Plan	4.2.a. SU/SP Summary of Data Collection, Completed
	4.2.b. SU/SP Summary of Data Collection, Not Completed
	4.2.c. Sample GIS Map: Data Analysis Tool for Needs Assessment

b. Introduction: SU/SP Complete Data Collection Work Plan

In order to collect EID for a community needs assessment, it is important for SUs and SPs to define what they need to know and what evidence (e.g., information) they eventually will need to make ethical decisions about potential community solutions. While there are a number of quantitative and qualitative methods that may be used, it is not necessary to include all potential data sources in a community needs assessment. In Action Step 4.2 SUs and SPs revisit their jointly created mission and purpose statements to solidify their commitment to conducting a needs assessment based on their agreed-on target population or social problem. Next, they will need to identify what resources are available within the planning group to implement the data collection work plan. It is unlikely that all the expertise required will exist within the planning group, so SUs/SPs will jointly identify the resources external to the planning group that they will need to hire on a consulting basis. These consultants can complete specific components of the data collection work plan that require technical or research expertise not found in the SU/SP planning group's expertise.

c. Description: SU/SP Complete Data Collection Work Plan

1. Revisit the mission and purpose statement to solidify commitment to the agreed-on problem and population.

2. Identify resources available within the planning group to complete the data collection work plan.

3. Identify resources external to the planning group who will be needed for the SU/SP group to complete the data collection work plan (e.g., GIS mapping, Web-based reporting system).

4. Identify secondary data sources that will meet the objectives of the needs assessment, such as census data; social indicator data; literature reviews; other needs assessment studies conducted in the community; health status indicators; crime statistics; and federal, regional, and municipal statistics in the identified problem area.

5. Review data collection methods and decide what methods you will use to collect data in the local community. Use the checklist contained in Activity Sheet 4.1.a to identify data sources that are relevant to the objectives of the planning group.

6. Explore the feasibility of collecting the identified data given the identified resources within the SU/SP planning group.

7. Explore the use of consultants for specific needs assessment data analysis such as GIS mapping and Web-based, reporting and identify the cost of these services and potential funding sources.

8. Decide who will collect data through a negotiated process that involves SUs and SPs having equal responsibility for data collection.

9. Identify what training SUs and SPs need to be able to carry out their responsibilities within the community needs assessment data collection work plan.

10. Develop the data collection tools for both quantitative and qualitative data collection methods (e.g., focus group interview guides, key informant interview guides, community forum participant feedback sheets).

11. Identify the timelines for completion of data collection and select and hire the consultant who will train SUs and SPs on the use of Web-based reporting systems.

12. Discuss the data analysis tasks to ascertain who has the required knowledge and skill to analyze statistical data and thematic content analysis of the qualitative responses.

13. Identify how data analysis will be carried out, the deadline for completion, and who has the requisite skills. If consultants will be hired to analyze the data, the planning group should set a timeline for completion of that analysis (Activity Sheets 4.2.a [SU/SP Summary of Data Collection, Completed] and 4.2.b [SU/SP Summary of Data Collection, Not Completed]).

14. Before the preliminary needs assessment report is constructed, SUs and SPs will decide on how the asset mapping data they collected in an earlier planning step will be incorporated into the final needs assessment preliminary research report.

15. After data have been collected and analyzed, preliminary findings should be jointly evaluated by the SU/SP planning group to assess whether the SU/SP preliminary community needs assessment report (Activity Sheet 4.3.a) meets the objectives set by the group, or whether more information and analysis are necessary.

Action Step 4.3. SU/SP Report Findings on Dedicated Web Site

a. List of Activity Sheet(s): SU/SP Report Findings on Dedicated Web Site

Action Step	Activity Sheet(s)
4.3. SU and SP Report Findings on Dedicated Web Site	4.3.a. SU/SP Preliminary Community Needs Assessment Report: TOC

b. Introduction: SU/SP Report Findings on Dedicated Web Site

Finally, Action Step 4.3 is the last step in the sequence here that started with the development of a data collection work plan. The use of a dedicated Web site to share information between SUs and SPs and their consultants has facilitated the free exchange of ideas and opinions as the needs assessment process unfolds. The challenge in this step is how to present these findings as clearly as possible, and how to engage people in reviewing and deciding on whether they have been successful in meeting their objectives. If the SU/SP planning group made a decision to employ consultants to analyze the data, are planning group members satisfied with the consultant's report or do they still have questions that need to be answered regarding the analysis? Are there comments on how the training they received before beginning the data collection either facilitated or constrained their data collection experience? Finally, after reviewing the preliminary report, are the SU/SP planning group members satisfied that they will be able to use the data to inform priority setting and **gap analysis** in future planning steps?

c. Description: SU/SP Report Findings on Dedicated Web Site

Prepare the preliminary needs assessment report using Activity Sheet 4.3.a (SU/SP Preliminary Community Needs Assessment Report: TOC).

1. Introduction to the preliminary needs assessment. Describe the objective of the needs assessment process and the social problem and population the SU/SP planning initiative is addressing in the local community.

2. Stakeholder identification. Present the stakeholder analysis chart and identify perceived level of stakeholder involvement.

3. Method. Describe the steps of the needs assessment data collection work plan and identify the instruments used for recording data. Report on methods used to analyze data collected.

4. Identification of community assets and needs. Bring the asset map into this section and summarize the preliminary results of the needs assessment.

5. Definition of local geographical community. Use GIS mapping to create a community profile using census data.

6. Quantitative data. Report on the statistical analysis from census data, social indicator data, and other secondary data sources relevant to the social problem and population.

7. Qualitative data. Report on the thematic analysis of primary data collection through focus groups, key informant interviews, etc.

8. Summary and recommendations. Prepare a summary of the preliminary needs assessment report and identify recommendations for further data collection; proceed to the next step of the needs assessment process in Planning Step 5: Identify Services and Set Priorities Using EID.

CASE VIGNETTE: USING EID AND WEB-BASED REPORTING TO IDENTIFY COMMUNITY NEEDS

It is said that a picture is a worth a thousand words, and in this case vignette the picture was a geographical representation of data that identified specific service needs in a local community. The backstory of this case illustrates the importance of using emerging technology such as GIS in conducting community needs assessments as part of community planning.

Planning in rural areas is often difficult because of the large geographical distances between SUs and SPs. Consequently, the planning process can be rather laborious and slow. Bringing Web-based reporting into the planning process facilitated shared decision-making and allowed SUs and SPs to establish priority needs without the burden of having to meet in a specific physical location.

With the emergence of technology such as GIS that facilitates data sharing between SUs and SPs, community needs assessments are readily available online. While GIS mapping using technology such as MapInfo Pro is not easy to use, university students in a geography department created the GIS maps in this case as part of their coursework. The graphic display of data on community needs that is possible with GIS provides an immediate visual story for SUs/SPs across time and space. In this case, in a rural planning initiative, data were collected using the traditional means such as focus groups, surveys, and interviews. Additionally, larger interfacing data sets such as census information and social indicator data were uploaded into a mapping program to produce a geographically based unique community profile for each of the local rural communities.

This use of technology and particularly the dramatic visual impact of GIS mapping created a shared world of planning for all participants in real time. Not only did this online sharing of data facilitate decision-making about identified priority needs for each community, but it also increased the transparency of the overall planning process. As such, virtual community needs assessments afforded both SU and SP groups a powerful empirical tool for better understanding their local communities overall.

SUMMARY AND EVALUATION OF PLANNING STEP 4: IDENTIFY COMMUNITY NEEDS USING EID

Summary of Planning Step 4: Identify Community Needs Using EID

Effective EIP requires that macro practitioners learn how to work collaboratively with SUs and SPs using data to identify priority needs in the community. The needs assessment data collection work plan (Activity Sheet 4.1.a) requires SUs and SPs to bond together in a joint planning process that builds transparent ongoing consensus. Thus, as they each identify what data are required to complete the needs assessment and designate responsibility for its collection, they acknowledge the contributions of each other as full **joint partners** in this overall process. The practical needs assessment process described in this planning step can be implemented to identify populations or problems across the interdisciplinary spectrum and can legitimize **funding proposals** that seek to create, enhance, or expand programs and services in their respective local communities.

Evaluation of Planning Step 4: Identify Community Needs Using EID

Evaluation Form: Circle one number only for each question listed below.

Action Step 4.1. SU/SP Establish Data Collection Work Plan for Community Needs Assessment

a. How confident were you about achieving this goal?	Not confident	Somewhat confident	Very confident	Extremely confident
	1	2	3	4

b. What was the most important thing you learned about this step?

Action Step 4.2. SU/SP Complete Data Collection Work Plan

a. How confident were you about achieving this goal?	Not confident	Somewhat confident	Very confident	Extremely confident
	1	2	3	4

b. What was the most important thing you learned about this step?

Action Step 4.3. SU/SP Report Findings on Dedicated Web Site

a. How confident were you about achieving this goal?	Not confident	Somewhat confident	Very confident	Extremely confident
	1	2	3	4

b. What was the most important thing you learned about this step?

Your Total Score? _____

Group Discussion Notes:

(continue on back as needed)

REFERENCES

Abraham, L. K. (1993). *Mama might be better off dead: The failure of healthcare in America.* Chicago: University of Chicago Press.

Carpenter, D., Nieva, V., Albaghal, T., & Sorra, J. (2005). Development of a planning tool to guide research dissemination. In K. Henriksen, J. B. Battles, E. S. Marks, & D. I. Lewin (Eds.), *Advances in patient safety: From research to implementation* (Vol. 4, *Programs, tools, and products*). Rockville, MD: Agency for Healthcare Research and Quality.

Dunlop, J. M. (2010). *Hate crime activity in the City of London.* Unpublished manuscript. School of Social Work, Kings University College at the University of Western Ontario, London, ON, Canada.

Eugster, P. T., Guerraoui, R., Kermarrec, A. M., & Massoulié, L. (2004). Epidemic information dissemination in distributed systems. *Computer, 37*(5), 60–67. doi:10.1109/MC.2004.1297243

Even, S., & Monien, B. (1989, March). On the number of rounds necessary to disseminate information. In *Proceedings of the first annual ACM symposium on parallel algorithms and architectures* (pp. 318–327). New York: Association for Computing Machinery.

Forest, S., Risk, I., Masters, H., & Brown, N. (2000). Mental health service user involvement in nurse education: Exploring the issues. *Journal of Psychiatric and Mental Health Nursing, 7*(1), 51–57. doi:10.1046/j.1365-2850.2000.00262.x

Fudge, N., Wolfe, C. D. A., & McKevitt, C. (2008). Assessing the promise of user involvement in health service development: Ethnographic study. *British Medical Journal, 336*(7639), 313–317. doi:10.1136/bmj.39456.552257.BE

Holosko, M. (1996). Service user input: Fact or fiction? The evaluation of the trauma program, Department of Rehabilitation, Sault Ste. Marie, ON, Canada. *Canadian Journal of Program Evaluation, 11*(2), 111–126.

Holosko, M., Leslie, D., & Cassano, D. R. (2001). How service users become empowered in human service organizations: The empowerment model. *International Journal of Health Care Quality Assurance, 14*(3), 126–132.

Kvarnström, S., Hedberg, B., & Cedersund, E. (2013). The dual faces of SU participation: Implications for empowerment processes in interprofessional practice. *Journal of Social Work, 13*(3), 287–307. doi:10.1177/1468017311433234

Kvarnström, S., Willumsen, E., Andersson-Gare, B., & Hedberg, B. (2012). How service users perceive the concept of participation, specifically in interprofessional practice. *British Journal of Social Work, 42*(1), 129–146. doi:10:1093/bjsw/bcr049

McLaughlin, H. (2009). What's in a name: "Client," "patient," "customer," "consumer," "expert by experience," "service user"—What's next? *British Journal of Social Work, 39*(6), 1101–1117. doi:10.1093/bjsw/bcm155

Oxman, A. D., Thomson, M. A., Davis, D. A., & Haynes, R. B. (1995). No magic bullets: A systematic review of 102 trials of interventions to improve professional practice. *Canadian Medical Association Journal, 153*(10), 1423–1431.

Turner, C., Yorkston, E., Hart, K., Drew, L., & McClure, R. (2006). Simplifying data collection for process evaluation of community coalition activities: An electronic Web-based application. *Health Promotion Journal of Australia, 17*(1), 48–53. doi:10.1071/HE06048

Williamson, J. W., German, P. S., Weiss, R., Skinner, E. A., & Bowes, F. (1989). Health science information management and continuing education of physicians: A survey of U.S. primary care practitioners and their opinion leaders. *Annals of Internal Medicine, 110*(2), 151–160. doi:10.7326/0003-4819-110-2-151

Zhang, N., Huang, H., Su, B., Zhao, J., & Zhang, B. (2014). Information dissemination analysis of different media towards the application for disaster pre-warning. *PLOS ONE, 9*, 1–12. doi:10.1371/journal.pone.0098649

INTERNET REFERENCES

City of Calgary, Community Assessment Handbook. http://www.calgary.ca/CSPS/CNS/Pages/Publications-guides-and-directories/Community-Assessment-Handbook/Community-Assessment-Handbook.aspx

The manual provides a framework and tools for learning about a community's needs and strengths and then how to set priorities. A table of contents is provided that identifies the sections of a community assessment such as what a community assessment is and why to conduct one. Also included is a section on information collection and analysis and establishing community priorities.

University of Kansas—Community Tool Box—Developing a Plan for Assessing Local Needs and Resources. http://ctb.ku.edu/en/table-of-contents/assessment/assessing-community-needs-and-resources/develop-a-plan/main

This site provides an overview of how to develop a plan for understanding the community's needs and how to utilize its resources. One of the most important steps in developing the plan is to determine what data are already available and decide who will collect the data and who will analyze the data.

Ontario Centre of Excellence for Children and Youth Mental Health: Bringing People and Knowledge Together to Strengthen Care—Learning Module—Needs Assessment. http://www.excellencefor childandyouth.ca/node/1166

This e-learning site provides a learning module online that addresses needs assessment using EIP. The learning module on needs assessment sets out the objectives of the module and leads the learner through a three-step process of identifying the need for a change, conducting critical appraisals of need, and selecting the right EI intervention to meet the need.

Centre for Parent Information and Resources—Tips and Tools for Disseminators. http://www.parent centerhub.org/repository/dissem-tools

This Web site provides a variety of tip sheets and tools to support the development of a dissemination plan for projects that use Web site based reporting. It offers a series of Webpages that outline six tips for writing for the Web including understanding how people read on the Web and how to "chunk" your information.

POWERPOINT RESOURCES

Chapter 4

Planning Step 4

Identify Community Needs Using
EID

Why is this planning step important?

- It facilitates transparency between SUs and SPs as they implement their data collection work plan.
- It facilitates a base template, method, or approach to collaboration of SUs and SPs.
- It facilitates agreement on what EID needs to be collected based on SU/SP agreement about target or social problem.

What does the literature say?

- Information dissemination is a not a linear process. Rather, it is dynamic and fluid.
- Web-based dissemination is seen as the process of sharing varied forms of information with a wide array of people in a condensed time frame, often in different ways.
- With Web-based technology EID collection can be tailored more precisely to suit local needs.

Planning Step 4. Identify Community Needs Using EID

Activity Sheet 4.1.a. SU/SP Data Collection Work Plan

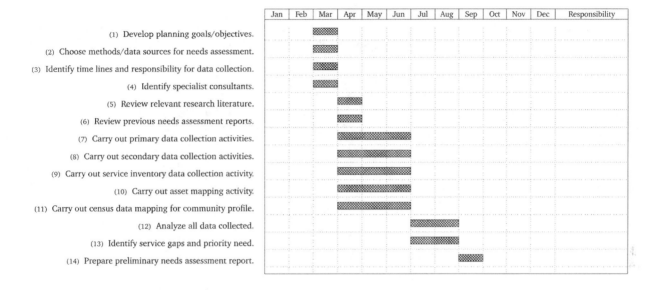

	Jan	Feb	Mar	Apr	May	Jun	Jul	Aug	Sep	Oct	Nov	Dec	Responsibility
(1) Develop planning goals/objectives.			▓										
(2) Choose methods/data sources for needs assessment.			▓										
(3) Identify time lines and responsibility for data collection.			▓										
(4) Identify specialist consultants.			▓										
(5) Review relevant research literature.				▓									
(6) Review previous needs assessment reports.				▓									
(7) Carry out primary data collection activities.				▓▓▓▓									
(8) Carry out secondary data collection activities.				▓▓▓▓									
(9) Carry out service inventory data collection activity.				▓▓▓▓									
(10) Carry out asset mapping activity.				▓▓▓▓									
(11) Carry out census data mapping for community profile.				▓▓▓▓									
(12) Analyze all data collected.							▓▓						
(13) Identify service gaps and priority need.							▓▓						
(14) Prepare preliminary needs assessment report.								▓					

Planning Step 4. Identify Community Needs Using EID

Activity Sheet 4.2.a. SU/SP Summary of Data Collection, Completed

WHAT HAS NOT BEEN COMPLETED?	WHO IS RESPONSIBLE?	WHAT IS THE DATE FOR COMPLETION?

Planning Step 4. Identify Community Needs Using EID

Activity Sheet 4.2.b. SU/SP Summary of Data Collection, Not Completed

WHAT HAS NOT BEEN COMPLETED?	WHO IS RESPONSIBLE?	WHAT IS THE DATE FOR COMPLETION?

Planning Step 4. Identify Community Needs Using EID

Activity Sheet 4.2.c. Sample GIS Map: Data Analysis Tool for Needs Assessment

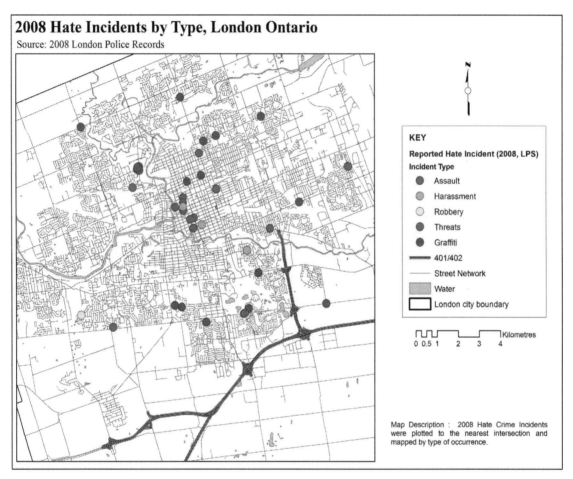

2008 Hate Incidents by Type, London Ontario
Source: 2008 London Police Records

KEY

Reported Hate Incident (2008, LPS)
Incident Type
- Assault
- Harassment
- Robbery
- Threats
- Graffiti
- 401/402
- Street Network
- Water
- London city boundary

Kilometres
0 0.5 1 2 3 4

Map Description : 2008 Hate Crime Incidents were plotted to the nearest intersection and mapped by type of occurrence.

Source: Dunlop (2010).

Planning Step 4. Identify Community Needs Using EID

Activity Sheet 4.3.a. SU/SP Preliminary Community Needs Assessment Report: TOC

Table of Contents

List of appendices

1. Introduction to the preliminary needs assessment report
2. Stakeholder identification
3. Data collection methods
4. Identification of community assets and needs
5. Definition of local geographical community: GIS maps
6. Quantitative data: census data and social indicator data
7. Qualitative data: focus groups and key informant interviews
8. Summary and recommendations: preliminary community needs assessment report

Reference list

Planning Step 5
Identify Services and Set Priorities Using EID

OVERVIEW AND RATIONALE

The planning approach to determining priorities and allocating resources has traditionally emphasized consultations and priority-setting exercises that attempt to balance available budgets with stated priorities of various interest groups, organizations, and government stakeholders (Pirkis, Harris, Buckingham, Whiteford, & Townsend-White, 2007). The planning process developed for this SU/SP planning process places value on EI decisions about priorities for service development at local levels. The term *EI decisions* echoes the need for planning processes to use reliable data that include empirical social indicators and health data to describe community problems, along with levels of services needed, and the kinds of services that are currently available in the local community. Campbell (2010) highlighted four additional methodological steps to this priority setting process:

1. The issue must be relevant to the local community as determined by an accepted criteria set forth by the local planning group.
2. The eventual decisions—and the reasons behind them—must be publicized to the community-at-large.
3. The outcomes must include a process to challenge, revise, and/or reverse decisions.
4. Community leaders must be able to enforce the above three conditions.

Using information from the designated SU/SP planning model in the priority setting process, the next step is to develop a service inventory approach that is based on standardized procedures that will be used to address identified community problems. The EID collection activities in this step of the SU/SP planning process incorporate not only a listing of services, but also an extended inventory that contains, for example, information on geographical area, target population, and staffing complement. This planning step brings SUs and SPs together to address community concerns, identify accessible community resources, and find cost-effective ways to address and report back on the identified issues (Pollock, St. George, Fenton, Crowe, & Firkins, 2014). Thus, it is important to create a shared space wherein SUs and SPs are able to have a voice in identifying varying viewpoints on issues that the community feels are important (Grimm, 2013; Holosko, Leslie, & Cassano, 2001; Pollock et al., 2014). Various researchers (Chenane, Brennan, Steiner, & Ellison, 2015; Rose, Gómez, & Valencia-Garcia, 2003) have pointed out that having such a shared space helps to

1. Better understand the actual needs of the community/communities;
2. Ensure that identified problem areas are accurately documented;
3. Empower different parts of the community;
4. Foster accountability with community members, funders, and researchers;
5. Safeguard procedures that prioritize areas based on severity;
6. Create feasible outcomes based on identified needs;
7. Produce rationales to prioritize need importance for service delivery;
8. Strengthen weaker parts of a community and enhance already strong parts; and
9. Create service cascades that outline local service provision.

As previously mentioned, the term *service inventory* for the purposes of this manual is defined as the procedural steps used to identify and define service information surrounding the issue(s) under investigation. It is important to note that while the service inventory attempts to capture larger amounts of data regarding the community and the identified priority needs that it currently faces, this inventory will need to be updated in a predetermined time frame in order to capture additional timely and topical trend changes within the overall community over time (MacDonald, Moen, & St. Louis, 2013). We should also note here that different problems might require slight amendments or modifications to the data collection plan.

Having an **inventory of existing services** is an important component of any responsible planning process. Service inventories capture data on local community services and provide an easily accessible listing for review. These service inventories use various categories to describe local service components that are important for review and analysis in the planning process. Although the development of a service inventory is unique to each planning process, there are general categories that can be used such as (1) name of institution, (2) program name, (3) ages served, (4) services offered, (5) hours of service, (6) requirements to be eligible for service, and (7) information on institutional Web sites and contact information. The service inventory for homeless youth in Vancouver is a good example of a service inventory designed to (1) capture data on youth services and (2) present information in a concise but comprehensive manner (Basi, Clelland, Khind, Morris, & Severinson 2012). Figure 5.1 serves as an example of a community-based service inventory in a public health setting.

Once data from the inventory are completed, they should be added to the Web-based reporting mechanism that allows for a preliminary analysis of the services provided. This analysis may lead to the publication of joint compilations of data from SU and SP planning groups. It also identifies factors associated with changes that are most likely to occur if a particular outcome is desired, therefore identifying the gap between what is and what should be (Sukeri, Alonso-Betancourt, & Emsley, 2015). The use of the Web-based application for this inventory of services and gap analysis allows for simplification of data reporting and SU/SP accountability. More importantly, it supports SU/SP ease of accessibility to the data needed for subsequent gap analyses and priority setting. The electronic reporting also allows for SU/SP group members to independently make immediate comparisons between the inventory of services created by SUs and SPs. Any community planning process also requires research summaries in order to help overcome the ever-looming political issues and make the EID

Figure 5.1. An Example of a Service Inventory of Programs in Vancouver for Homeless Youth

Institution	Program	Ages Served	Services Offered	Hours	Requirements	More Information
Covenant House (I)	Crisis Shelter	16–22	3 meals, 54 bed crisis shelter	24 hours	12 hours clean	http://www.covenanthouse bc.org Crisis shelter
Covenant House (II)	Community Support Services	16–24	Street outreach (food, counseling, minor medical attention), daily drop-in, and housing support workers	24/7	Difficulty accessing social services	http://www.covenanthouse bc.org/what/css
Covenant House (III)	Rights of Passage (ROP)	Up to 24	Transitional living program that provides 6–24 months of supported living; 24 hour youth workers	Youth Workers Available 24/7	Application process and strict guidelines	http://www.covenanthouse bc.org/what/rights_of_passage
Directions Youth Services	Day Resource Centre	18 & Under	Access to housing support workers, life skills support and programming, counseling, needs assessment and service referrals, and assistance in accessing community services such as health and mental health assessment and support, drug and alcohol intervention, shelter services	M–F 8:00 a.m to 4:00 p.m.		http://www.fsgv.ca/program pages/youthservices/resource centre-directionsyouthservice centre.html
Directions Youth Services	"Dawn to Dusk" Night Resource Centre & Peer Support	21 & under	Drop-in program for homeless and at-risk youth. Access to laundry, showers, clothing, toiletries, peer counseling, health services (including a doctor & street nurse clinic), and service referrals, 1 hot meal	M–Sun 4:00 p.m. to 12:00 a.m.		Same as above

Source: Basi, S., Clelland, T, Khind, N., Morris, A. & Severinson, P. (2012). *Housing Homeless Youth in Vancouver: Key Barriers and Strategic Responses.* School of Public Policy, Simon Fraser University, Vancouver, B.C.

readily available to both SUs and SPs simultaneously (Krizek, Forysth, & Schivley-Slotterback, 2009).

As with all such strategies, there are both strengths and weakness. Pealer, Weiler, Pigg, Miller, & Dorman (2001) provide strengths-based perspectives for using Web-based reporting systems, three of which are (1) time effectiveness: participants are able to complete surveys at their convenience; (2) cost efficiency; less money spent on travel times and paying for administering survey; and (3) accessibility: individuals are able to easily find the survey online and provide their feedback. Conversely, Smyth, Dillman, Christian, and O'Neill (2010) presented some weaknesses to Web-based reporting, three of which are (1) selection bias: only reaching a selected group of people; (2) incomplete information: missing data based on skipped or ignored questions; and (3) lower response rates: individuals choosing not to respond based on personal decisions.

Overall, the strategies outlined herein create a skeleton framework for identifying services and setting priorities. Following these presented guidelines (1) allows for honest feedback from SUs and SPs, (2) creates conversations between SUs and SPs, and (3) allows for different types of analyses. Furthermore, this approach is a process of cooperative action, whereby planning group members can categorize community resources into a service inventory that identifies what supports are already in the community, what duplications in services exist, and what gaps exist. An analysis using a comprehensive service inventory provides an opportunity for SUs and SPs to work not only toward meeting the identified priority need, but also toward avoiding competition in a resource-scarce local environment.

DESCRIPTION OF PLANNING ACTIVITIES FOR PLANNING STEP 5: IDENTIFY SERVICES AND PRIORITIES USING EID

This planning step contains three action steps. Remember that any of the three action steps might use more than one activity sheet. Upon completion of these three action steps for Planning Step 5, please use the appropriate evaluation forms found at the end of the chapter to evaluate each action step. Evaluation is an important completion part of the overall planning process.

Action Step 5.1. SUs and SPs Create an Inventory of Existing Services
Action Step 5.2. SUs and SPs Conduct a Gap Analysis
Action Step 5.3. SUs and SPs Decide on Priorities

The action steps in Planning Step 5 are designed to promote collaboration and negotiation between SUs and SPs as they work through priority setting in the planning process. There are a large number of planning activity sheets in this planning step. These planning activities can be seen as sequential steps toward good decision-making; more than that, though, they are skill-building exercises where SUs and SPs learn to value, respect, and listen to each other's opinions. Arriving at a consensus on priority needs and interventions is a complicated process between SUs and SPs, or between and among the members of any planning group, for that matter. The structured activities in this planning step will provide a mechanism for dialogue and discussion and help SUs and SPs learn to work together toward their common goal of improving their local communities.

Action Step 5.1 (SUs and SPs Create an Inventory of Existing Services) describes the planning process that ensures that a list of programs and services is prepared so it encompasses a broad spectrum of potential agencies across multidisciplinary domains. Establishing who provides the service, where it is provided, to whom it is provided, what exactly is provided, and what geographical area is deemed to be the catchment area prepares the way for a more specific analysis of duplications, gaps, and possible changes to services in the community. In Action Step 5.1 the SU/SP planning group conducts a scan of the whole service system to identify local relevant services applicable to the identified need. This whole service scan can be applied to any target population: for example, if the identified need is youth programming, then the whole service system scan will identify all the agencies that are providing services to youths in the local community. This is a first step scan that will be followed by more-specific drilling down of examination of local services. Using service categories such as community-based, community resources, health, and recreation, the joint SU/SP planning group will make decisions about which local services are most relevant to their identified priority need. From that planning activity, the SU/SP planning group will negotiate further targeting of specific local services that they jointly agree should be examined more closely for suitability as an SP in the problem area or to the target population.

Action Step 5.2 (SUs and SPs Conduct a Gap Analysis) expands on the simple collection and description of local services by assessing current duplications in services and changes to services, such as expansions or terminations. Finally, and most importantly in Action Step 5.2, the Web-based inventory of services supports the use of reliable data as it enables SUs and SPs to compare their data independently to make corrections, add new data about impending services, or amend their interpretations of specific services.

Action Step 5.3 (SUs and SPs Decide on Priorities) requires SUs and SPs to determine priorities, which is a rather difficult undertaking, since there are always more needs in a community than resources to meet them (see introduction, part II, to this manual). To complete this specific action step, a number of activity sheets provide a road map to assist SUs and SPs to assess what problem areas are most feasible to address given the scarce resource environment that characterizes planning in local communities. In Action Step 5.3 the use of rating criteria to facilitate decision-making regarding service gaps is supported by EID collection. While there may be differences of opinion between SUs and SPs about what services are a community priority, the use of EID is an effective field-tested tool to determine service priorities in local community planning.

Action Step 5.1. SUs and SPs Create an Inventory of Existing Services

a. List of Activity Sheet(s): SUs and SPs Create an Inventory of Existing Services

Action Step	Activity Sheet(s)
5.1. SUs and SPs Create an Inventory of Existing Services	5.1.a. SU/SP Service Description Chart
	5.1.b. SU/SP Identification of Community-based Services
	5.1.c. SU/SP Identification of Community Resources
	5.1.d. SU/SP Identification of Health Services
	5.1.e. SU/SP Identification of Recreation Services
	5.1.f. SU/SP Identification of Local Services
	5.1.g. SU/SP Examine Specific Local Services

b. Introduction: SUs and SPs Create an Inventory of Existing Services

Action Step 5.1 essentially begins the process of identifying and tabling forthrightly what services are currently provided in the local community. The EID collection activities in this action step include not only a listing of services, but also a more comprehensive inventory identifying who provides the service, what services are provided, the geographical area served, and the target group and staff complement. Since SUs and SPs will be sharing their service inventories, the data collection instruments for each group must be the same. While a number of different approaches are possible, the service inventory data collection in this planning step contains a service description chart, a categorical examination of service sectors, and a beginning exploration of general and specific services.

c. Description: SUs and SPs Create an Inventory of Existing Services

Activity Sheet 5.1.a (SU/SP Service Description Chart) identifies the data to be collected in the following categories: (1) agency name, (2) address and phone, (3) e-mail address, (4) contact person, and (5) a description of the programs and services offered. Data collection on existing community resources is carried out by SUs and SPs using a broad-based categorical listing of services. These instruments collect data on agency name, type of service, target group, and geographical area services in four broad categorical areas: (1) community-based services (Activity Sheet 5.1.b [SU/SP Identification of Community-based Services]), (2) community resources (Activity Sheet 5.1.c [SU/SP Identification of Community Resources]), (3) health services (Activity Sheet 5.1.d [SU/SP Identification of Health Services]), and (4) recreation services (Activity Sheet 5.1.e [SU/SP Identification of Recreation Services]). At this point, all data previously collected are compiled and summarized in three thematic categories: (1) who provides the service, (2) where the service is provided, and (3) what service is provided (Activity Sheet 5.1.f [SU/SP Identification of Local Services]). Following this action step that builds knowledge of general local services, data are compiled and summarized in more detail to describe specific services that need to be included in the service inventory in Activity Sheet 5.1.g (SU/SP Examine Specific Local Services). This activity sheet is used to gather information from SUs and SPs about their knowledge and experiences with specific agencies and their programs, services, target population, and geographical and staffing complement. When completed, a reconstructed inventory of services using Activity Sheet 5.1.g is uploaded to the planning group Web site for review by SUs and SPs in preparation for its use in subsequent planning steps.

Action Step 5.2. SUs and SPs Conduct a Gap Analysis

a. List of Activity Sheet(s): SUs and SPs Conduct a Gap Analysis

Action Step	Activity Sheet(s)
5.2. SUs and SPs Conduct a Gap Analysis	5.2.a. SU/SP Service Planning Review
	5.2.b. SU/SP Use EID in Service Planning
	5.2.c. SU/SP Review Local Service Gaps and Needs

b. Introduction: SUs and SPs Conduct a Gap Analysis

A data collection instrument for identifying services ensures that all data collected follow the same format and are easily retrievable, and that documentation is sufficiently expansive to bring real meaning to the SU/SP planning group as members complete their analysis services in the local community. Identifying gaps in the service system utilizes all of the EID collected in the needs assessment phase of planning and matches those identified needs with the resources or services that are currently available. The importance of collecting accurate and reliable EID steps to the forefront: while various planning activities are carried out in order to identify gaps in the community service system, the credibility and legitimacy of the SU/SP planning group rests on the quality of the data and quality of the analysis of data in the summarized needs assessment report. While the needs assessment itself is a form of priority setting because it produces specific identifiable needs in the community, it is only one component of this gap analysis. What is best for the community requires yet another look at the community and its services.

c. Description: SUs and SPs Conduct a Gap Analysis

In this Action Step 5.2 the comparison between needs and resources produces a gap analysis that can be used for priority setting. While no gap analysis is perfect because each depends on reliable up-to-date data from many community partners, it is possible to structure the analysis to make it readily available for timely deliberation and decision-making. Action Step 5.2 uses the service inventory that was uploaded to the planning group Web site. The purpose of this further review of service information is to capture emerging service changes that may not have been previously identified during the service inventory data collection phase. Activity Sheet 5.2.a (SU/SP Service Planning Review) provides an opportunity to further assess program or service changes that SUs or SPs have become aware of since the initial service inventory was completed. This service planning review is filtered through a framework that includes (1) service name, (2) service duplication, (3) proposed or planned service enhancement, (4) proposed or planned service expansion, and (5) proposed or planned service termination. This review is carried out jointly by SUs and SPs to consolidate information on program changes within the local community. It is possible that service changes are being made or planned in the local community; if so, it is necessary for the SU/SP planning group to review and discuss these changes. While it is assumed that SPs may have more of a conduit to this information, this may not necessarily be the case if active SUs have experienced changes in their local service provision. Documenting changes or planned changes in services through the use of Activity Sheet 5.2.a allows the SU/SP planning group to conduct its review of local services in a knowledgeable, comprehensive, and informed manner.

After the initial assessment of services, duplication(s), and gaps, a more detailed review is carried out to build EID decision-making skills. Data from the service inventory are reviewed using the following criteria: (1) name of service, (2) acceptance of the service by SUs, (3) whether services are evaluated, (4) whether the service reports EID results, and (5) if so, whether there is consultation with SUs about changes (Activity Sheet 5.2.b [SU/SP Use EID in Service Planning]). The EID planning process results in a gap analysis conducted by the SU/SP planning group. The gap analysis is completed by comparing the needs assessment data collected and analyzed in a previous planning step with the service inventory completed in Action Step 5.1. The need to always make decisions about priorities for funding of services requires that the gap analysis be valued at a local community level. Specifically, to engage support from community stakeholders and funders, planning groups are required to prove that the identified gap is real and that resources are truly needed to alleviate the identified community problem.

The final planning activity in this step is to consolidate the review, assessment, and decision-making previously carried out (Activity Sheet 5.2.c [SU/SP Review Local Service Gaps and Needs]). This planning activity provides an opportunity for SUs/SPs to consolidate their work and complete the gap analysis required for the final needs assessment report, which has seven components: (1) services offered, (2) gaps in services, (3) duplications of services, (4) importance of service to identified need, (5) priority services, (6) planned service expansion, and (7) planned service termination. A service gap analysis will be uploaded to the Web-based reporting system. The identified service gaps will then be transparent to all SUs/SPs who will need these data as they begin the decision-making and priority-setting planning activities. This planning model places value on EID decisions; the structured planning activities carried out in Action Step 5.2 are necessary tools to ensure that SUs and SPs are on the same page.

Action Step 5.3. SUs and SPs Decide on Priorities

a. List of Activity Sheet(s): SUs and SPs Decide on Priorities

Action Step	Activity Sheet(s)
5.3. SUs and SPs Decide on Priorities	5.3.a. SU/SP Service Planning: Priority Setting Skill Development 5.3.b. SU/SP Service Planning: Decision-Making on Priority Needs 5.3.c. SU/SP Three-Round Voting Template

b. Introduction: SUs and SPs Decide on Priorities

Making decisions about priorities is difficult because often there are many needs and few resources. The EID in this action step attempts to determine priorities based on accurate needs assessment data, the EID service inventory, and a set of structured activity sheets developed to guide participatory decision-making. Priority setting, then, is a relatively democratic process, whereby placing a higher priority on something means a choice has been made between alternatives. Pragmatically, needs assessment data and priority setting go hand in hand, but this pairing needs to be offset by choice of the criteria that meet the requirements of the SU/SP planning group to respond to stakeholder concerns about what needs are of most importance to the local community. Priority setting is just one more step in the planning process to access needed resources that focus on alleviating local social problems. The ability of the SU/SP planning group to respond to these local community concerns is enhanced through the selection of choice criteria for each of the planning activities carried out in this step.

c. Description: SUs and SPs Decide on Priorities

Activity Sheet 5.3.a (SU/SP Service Planning: Priority Setting Skill Development) matches service inventory data with needs assessment data and asks SUs and SPs to drill down to specific service characteristics by identifying five specific components: (1) name of the agency, (2) service offered, (3) does the service meet a priority need? (4) does the service report evidence-based results? and (5) does the service include a mechanism for SU feedback? The uniqueness of this planning activity is its identification of service components that address (1) EI results and (2) a mechanism for SU feedback. In order to complete this Action Step 5.3, SUs and SPs must discuss and decide on whether the service offered meets the priority need. If the service offered passes this level of assessment, the next level of examination questions the orientation to EID of the agency and the service in question. If evidence-based results are reported by the agency, these data pass the second approval level and move toward the next assessment, which is its commitment to SU involvement. If the agency and service have made the commitment to create a mechanism for SU feedback, then all three levels of assessment have been completed and the agency and service can move to a position where they may be considered as a viable option for decision-making in the next step of the planning. This summary sheet (Activity Sheet 5.3.a) is then uploaded to the Web-based reporting system as a first step in preparing the SU/SP group for the shared planning meeting to decide on priorities for further development in the local community.

Since a list of identified priorities is of little value, it is necessary to drill down to more-specific questions and choices regarding needs that require further action and advocacy. Activity Sheet 5.3.b (SU/SP Service Planning: Decision-Making on Priority Needs) contains the identified choice categories for decision-making activity on priority needs as follows: (1) cost of service, (2) benefits of service to the target population, (3) impact on other services, (4) community acceptance, (5) service previously offered, and (6) future adaptability of the service. It is important to remember here that in the previous planning activity (Activity Sheet 5.3.a) SUs and SPs used the EID needs assessment to define priority needs. Using the list of identified gaps in service, a priority need is established by the SU/SP group through the use of the nominal group technique approach. This approach is used widely in health and social services to narrow down lists of gaps to a single priority. SUs and SPs can decide on an open or secret ballot voting mechanism before beginning the priority-setting exercise. If a secret ballot is chosen by the SU/SP group, then SUs and SPs use the list of identified gaps/needs in the first round and anonymously write their first priority on a ballot collected by the facilitator (Activity Sheet 5.3.c [SU/SP Three-Round Voting Template]). These priorities are posted on a white board or flip chart. In the second round, participants anonymously vote for their priority based on the reduced list of gaps/needs. The third round requires participants to again anonymously vote for their priority based on the condensed list of gaps/needs from Round 2. Activity Sheet 5.3.c is then used to identify the top-ranked priority identified by the group and is uploaded to the Web-based reporting system to inform all participants of the decision-making process. This combination of EID needs assessment and structured priority setting, which takes community concerns as a critical choice factor, can move the planning group forward to the next step of determining appropriate intervention models to meet these identified gaps/needs.

CASE VIGNETTE: EXAMINING SERVICES AND SETTING PRIORITIES USING EI DECISION-MAKING

This case vignette illustrates how collecting EID can significantly influence community planning—but it is not a guarantee that decisions will reflect the views of all stakeholders. A local advisory group consisting of SUs, SPs, and community leaders was appointed by a regional government to decide what services should be offered through a new community-based senior center. The first step of the planning process went easily; members were required to collect information on what local seniors' services currently existed in the community using an EID collection instrument. This step was completed quickly, and members gathered service data, uploaded their data to a Web site, reviewed and agreed on the descriptions of services, and compiled their data into a service inventory to be used for future gap analysis. The planning group leader was relieved that the data collection process had been so easily completed and looked forward to the next step of conducting a gap analysis and determining an agreed-on priority need for senior services. The leader's relief was short lived, however.

While the purely descriptive data seemed innocuous when reported, when analytical questions were necessary, conflict became the reigning norm for the group. A more in-depth analysis of each agency service was carried by the planning group using questions such as these: (1) Is the service a duplication? (2) Is the service acceptable to SUs? (3) Does the SP use evaluation to consult with SUs about change? (4) Are there changes in the service being planned? and (5) Does the agency report evidence-based results? Indeed, differences of opinion in community planning are to be expected, and it is a given that there will never be enough resources to meet the needs for all services. Thus, EI priority setting in community planning attempts to facilitate decision-making through acknowledgment that the professional knowledge of SPs is not enough. The question here is this: Why did the group get stuck at this place in their planning process, and why were they unable to move ahead with a gap analysis and priority need decision? The main reason was once again SP resistance to the knowledge and lived experience of SUs. Fortunately, the planning group facilitator was able to bring SUs and SPs to a new understanding that their need to set priorities in service planning was not about labeling services as good or bad, but about deciding on the urgency or need for the target population to receive the service. SPs recognized the importance of community participation and democratic decision-making and worked with SUs even though there were disagreements. Subscribing to principles of inclusiveness and transparency, this planning group agreed on a priority need for senior services after three rounds of voting, demonstrating that although they were not all in agreement, they could eventually reach consensus on the need for an assessment clinic for Early Stage Alzheimer's at the new Seniors' Community Centre.

SUMMARY AND EVALUATION OF PLANNING STEP 5: IDENTIFY SERVICES AND SET PRIORITIES USING EID

Summary of Planning Step 5: Identify Services and Set Priorities Using EID

Planning Step 5 is an important part of the planning process because it culminates in a critical decision-making process between SUs and SPs. This step comprises three sequential action steps: (1) development of a joint service inventory, (2) a gap analysis using EID, and (3) a decision regarding the priority need to be addressed. The collection of data regarding local services and the development of a comprehensive service inventory is the platform for informed democratic decision-making. Once the data collection for the service inventory is completed by SUs and SPs, they are uploaded to the Web-based application where it can be reviewed, analyzed, and merged into a joint compilation for use in a gap analysis where priority needs and current services are compared. The culmination of this planning step is a consensus decision made by SUs and SPs about the most important priority need for service that leads to the logical progression to Planning Step 6: Plan Service Using EID.

Evaluation of Planning Step 5: Identify Services and Set Priorities Using EID

Evaluation Form: Circle one number only for each question listed below.

Action Step 5.1. SUs and SPs Create an Inventory of Existing Services

a. How confident were you about achieving this goal?	Not confident	Somewhat confident	Very confident	Extremely confident
	1	2	3	4

b. What was the most important thing you learned about this step?

Action Step 5.2. SUs and SPs Conduct a Gap Analysis

a. How confident were you about achieving this goal?	Not confident	Somewhat confident	Very confident	Extremely confident
	1	2	3	4

b. What was the most important thing you learned about this step?

Action Step 5.3. SUs and SPs Decide on Priorities

a. How confident were you about achieving this goal?	Not confident	Somewhat confident	Very confident	Extremely confident
	1	2	3	4

b. What was the most important thing you learned about this step?

Your Total Score? _____

Group Discussion Notes:

(continue on back as needed)

REFERENCES

Basi, S., Clelland, T., Khind, N., Morris, A., & Severinson, P. (2012). *Housing homeless youth in Vancouver: Key barriers and strategic responses.* School of Public Policy, Simon Fraser University, Vancouver, B.C., Canada.

Campbell, S. (2010). *Deliberative priority setting—a CIHR KT module.* Canadian Institute of Health Research.

Chenane, J. L., Brennan, P. K., Steiner, B., & Ellison, J. M. (2015). Racial and ethnic differences in the predictive validity of the level of service inventory-revised among prison inmates. *Criminal Justice and Behavior, 42*, 286–303.

Grimm, D. (2013). Whole community planning: Building resiliency at the local level. *Journal of Business Continuity & Emergency Planning, 7*, 253–259.

Holosko, M., Leslie, D., & Cassano, D. R. (2001). How service users become empowered in human service organizations: The empowerment model. *International Journal of Health Care Quality Assurance, 14*(3), 126–132.

Krizek, K., Forsyth, A., & Schivley-Slotterback, C. (2009). Is there a role for evidence-based practice in urban planning and policy? *Planning Theory & Practice, 10*(4), 450–478.

MacDonald, G., Moen, A. C., & St. Louis, M. (2013). The national inventory of core capabilities for pandemic influenza preparedness and response: An instrument for planning and evaluation. *Influenza and Other Respiratory Viruses, 8*, 189–193.

National Association of County and City Health Officials. (2010). *First things first: Prioritizing health problems.* National Association of County and City Health Officials.

Pealer, L. N., Weiler, R. M., Pigg, Jr., R. M., Miller, D., & Dorman, D. (2001). The feasibility of a Web-based surveillance system to collect health risk behavior data from college students. *Health Education & Behavior, 28*, 547–559.

Pirkis J., Harris, M., Buckingham, W., Whiteford, H., & Townsend-White, C. (2007). International planning directions for provision of mental health services. *Administration and Policy in Mental Health and Mental Health Services Research, 34*, 377–387.

Pollock, A., St. George, B., Fenton, M., Crowe, S., & Firkins, L. (2014). Development of a new model to engage patients and clinicians in setting research priorities. *Journal of Health Research & Policy, 19*, 12–18.

Rose, V. J., Gómez, C. A., & Valencia-Garcia, D. (2003). Do community planning groups (CPGs) influence HIV prevention policy? An analysis of California CPGs. *AIDS Education and Prevention, 15*, 172–183.

Smyth, J. D., Dillman, D. A., Christian, L. M., & O'Neill, A. C. (2010). Using the Internet to survey small towns and communities: Limitations and possibilities in the early 21st century. *American Behavioral Scientist, 53*(9), 1423–1448.

Sukeri, K., Alonso-Betancourt, O., & Emsley, R. (2015). Needs-based gap analysis for service transformation in the Eastern Cape. *South African Journal of Psychiatry, 21*, 3–7.

INTERNET REFERENCES

The James Lind Alliance: Overview of Priority Setting Partnerships (PSPs). http://www.jlaguidebook.org/jla-guidebook.asp?val=15

This site sets out objectives for the PSPs between patients and clinicians who work through the priority-setting process together. One of the objectives of the PSP is to reach an agreement by consensus on a prioritized top-ten list of uncertainties about the effects of treatments.

National Collaborating Centre for Methods and Tools: A Planning Tool for Priority Setting.
http://www.nccmt.ca/registry/view/eng/106.html

This site presents four priority-setting methods (sticker dot voting, or dotmocracy, paired comparisons, decision boxes, and grid analysis). Resources provided include a conceptual framework of elements necessary for successful priority setting such as stakeholder engagement and information management.

National Association of County and City Health Officials: The Community Guide Toolkit.
http://www.ebprevention.org/cg/review-and-select-strategies.html

This site offers a toolkit with downloadable resources on reviewing and selecting appropriate evidence-based strategies to improve community health. The Web site also provides links to other helpful tools and links to evidence-based intervention sources such as the U.S. SAMHSA's National Registry of Evidence-based Programs and Practices.

U.S. Agency for Healthcare Quality and Research: Assess Data and Set Priorities for Improvement.
http://www.ahrq.gov/professionals/systems/primary-care/businessstrategies/busstrat2.html

This Web site provides a chart that helps clinicians assess their outcomes and provides a number of tools that focus on **efficiency** as a way to improve care. Guidelines are given for promoting the transparency of data through the use of information technology that can harvest already existing data and make them user friendly.

POWERPOINT RESOURCES

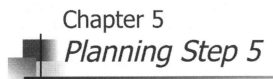

Chapter 5
Planning Step 5

Identify Services and Set Priorities Using EID

Why is this planning step important?

- It identifies the gap between what *is* and *what should be.*
- It creates a shared space wherein SUs and SPs have a voice to address community concerns, identify accessible community resources, and find cost-effective ways to address identified issues.
- It sets priorities that are relevant to the community; leads to eventual decisions with structured and validated reasoning; and provides a template for processing to challenge, revise, and reverse decisions and to enable SUs and SPs to improve local conditions.

What does the literature say?

- Web-based reporting has some weaknesses: selection bias, incomplete information, lower response rates. It also has some strengths: time effectiveness, cost efficiency, accessibility, accountability.
- Inventory needs to be updated in a predetermined time frame to capture additional timely and topical trend changes within the overall community over time.
- Having a shared space can
  - Safeguard procedures, produce rationales, empower different parts of community, create feasible outcomes, strengthen weaker parts of a community, and enhance effective ones, etc.

Planning Step 5. Identify Services and Set Priorities Using EID

Activity Sheet 5.1.a. SU/SP Service Description Chart

AGENCY NAME	ADDRESS AND PHONE NUMBER	E-MAIL ADDRESS	CONTACT PERSON	DESCRIPTION OF THE PROGRAM AND SERVICES OFFERED

Printed Name _____

Signature _____   Date:_____

Please check only one of the boxes below:

I CONSENT TO SHARING THIS INFORMATION IN THE SERVICE INVENTORY   ☐

I DO NOT CONSENT TO SHARING THIS INFORMATION IN THE SERVICE INVENTORY   ☐

Planning Step 5. Identify Services and Set Priorities Using EID

Activity Sheet 5.1.b. SU/SP Identification of Community-based Services

SERVICE TYPE	AGENCY NAME	TARGET POPULATION	GEOGRAPHICAL AREA SERVED
Neighborhood Youth Centers			
Outpatient Substance Abuse			
Youth Substance Abuse			
Child Protection Services			
Group Homes/Halfway Houses			
Residential Treatment Centers/ Addictions			
Family Violence Program/Shelters			
Homeless Shelters			
Mental Health Crisis Services			
Community Resource Centers			
Non-Profit Counseling			
Seniors Centers/Day Programs			
Private Counseling			
Specialized Day Care			
Case Management Services			
Employment Services			
Parenting Programs			
Family Resource Centers			
Suicide Crisis Line			
Suicide Prevention Services			
Other:			
Other:			

Planning Step 5. Identify Services and Set Priorities Using EID

Activity Sheet 5.1.c. SU/SP Identification of Community Resources

SERVICE TYPE	AGENCY NAME	TARGET POPULATION	GEOGRAPHICAL AREA SERVED
Service clubs			
Multicultural centers			
Community coordinating groups			
Churches/religious institutions			
Alcoholics Anonymous			
Habitat for Humanity			
Housing Cooperatives			
Block parents			
Al-Anon			
Alateen			
Narcotics Anonymous			
Gamblers Anonymous			
Neighborhood residents' associations			
MADD			
Cultural groups			
Volunteer associations			
Labor unions			
Economic development projects			
Community development projects			
Gay-straight alliances			
Other:			
Other:			

Planning Step 5. Identify Services and Set Priorities Using EID

Activity Sheet 5.1.d. SU/SP Identification of Health Services

SERVICE TYPE	AGENCY NAME	TARGET POPULATION	GEOGRAPHICAL AREA SERVED
General hospitals			
Children's hospitals			
Chronic care hospitals			
Long-term care homes			
Respite homes			
Family physicians			
Family health teams			
Community health centers			
AIDS organizations			
Public health: Environmental			
Public health: Maternal and child			
Public health: Health screening			
Public health: Health promotion			
Addictions: Assessment and referral			
Addictions: Detox centers			
Addictions: Residential treatment centers			
Immunization clinics			
Walk-in medical clinics			
Other:			
Other:			

Planning Step 5. Identify Services and Set Priorities Using EID

Activity Sheet 5.1.e. SU/SP Identification of Recreation Services

SERVICE TYPE	AGENCY NAME	TARGET POPULATION	GEOGRAPHICAL AREA SERVED
Municipal recreation department			
YWCA			
YMCA			
Bowling leagues			
Baseball leagues			
Hockey leagues			
Public swimming pools			
Public skating rinks			
Girl Guides/Girl Scouts			
Boy Scouts			
Public parks/nature trails			
Dance programs			
Horse riding facilities, camps			
Skate parks			
Yoga programs			
Walking programs			
Bike trails/bike lanes			
Martial arts training			
Other:			
Other:			

Planning Step 5. Identify Services and Set Priorities Using EID

Activity Sheet 5.1.f. SU/SP Identification of Local Services

WHO PROVIDES SERVICE?	WHERE IS SERVICE PROVIDED?	WHAT SERVICE IS PROVIDED?

Planning Step 5. Identify Services and Set Priorities Using EID

Activity Sheet 5.1.g. SU/SP Examine Specific Local Services

AGENCY	SERVICE	TARGET GROUP	GEOGRAPHICAL AREA	STAFF ROLES

Planning Step 5. Identify Services and Set Priorities Using EID

Activity Sheet 5.2.a. SU/SP Service Planning Review

SERVICE NAME	SERVICE DUPLICATION	PROPOSED OR PLANNED SERVICE ENHANCEMENT	PROPOSED OR PLANNED SERVICE EXPANSION	PROPOSED OR PLANNED SERVICE TERMINATION

Planning Step 5. Identify Services and Set Priorities Using EID

Activity Sheet 5.2.b. SU/SP Use EID in Service Planning

NAME OF SERVICE	ACCEPTANCE OF THE SERVICE BY SUs	WHETHER SERVICES ARE EVALUATED	WHETHER THE SERVICE REPORTS EID RESULTS	IF SO, WHETHER THERE IS CONSULTATION WITH SUs ABOUT CHANGES

Planning Step 5. Identify Services and Set Priorities Using EID

Activity Sheet 5.2.c. SU/SP Review Local Service Gaps and Needs

SERVICES OFFERED	GAPS IN SERVICES	DUPLICATIONS OF SERVICE	IMPORTANCE OF SERVICE TO IDENTIFIED NEED	PRIORITY SERVICES	PLANNED SERVICE EXPANSION	PLANNED SERVICE TERMINATION

Planning Step 5. Identify Services and Set Priorities Using EID

Activity Sheet 5.3.a. SU/SP Service Planning: Priority Setting Skill Development

NAME OF THE AGENCY	SERVICE OFFERED	DOES THE SERVICE MEET A PRIORITY NEED?	DOES THE SERVICE REPORT EVIDENCE-BASED RESULTS?	DOES THE SERVICE INCLUDE A MECHANISM FOR SU FEEDBACK?

Planning Step 5. Identify Services and Set Priorities Using EID

Activity Sheet 5.3.b. SU/SP Service Planning: Decision-Making on Priority Needs

COST OF SERVICE	BENEFITS OF SERVICE TO THE TARGET POPULATION	IMPACT ON OTHER SERVICES	COMMUNITY ACCEPTANCE	SERVICE PREVIOUSLY OFFERED	FUTURE ADAPTABILITY OF THE SERVICE

Planning Step 5. Identify Services and Set Priorities Using EID

Activity Sheet 5.3.c. SU/SP Three-Round Voting Template

IDENTIFIED GAP/NEED	ROUND 1 VOTE	ROUND 2 VOTE	ROUND 3 VOTE

Source: Adapted from National Association of County and City Health Officials (2010).

Planning Step 6
Plan Service Using EID

OVERVIEW AND RATIONALE

In the past decade or so, the notion of EIP has helped us to understand how we use evidence to direct our practice, the organizational and cultural contexts where we work, and most importantly our clients' perspectives (Chaffin & Freidrich, 2004; Dill & Shera, 2009). This shift has not only led to more practitioners serving as evidence providers and experts to academic research, but it also has increased the awareness and need for incorporating SUs into the scenario from the onset. SU involvement in the processes of planning and providing services, particularly in mental health services, has been expanding over the past two decades (Beresford, 2007). Furthermore, Sackett, Strauss, Richardson, Rosenberg, and Haynes (2000) pointed out the importance of integrating and relying on SUs in any evidence-based approach by highlighting the need for integration of the best possible research evidence combined with clinical expertise, along with patient values. These latter three are considered the cornerstones of EIP.

Chamberlin (2005) contended that SU involvement must be applied to all aspects of service delivery—from professional training, research, service design, delivery, and evaluation for an effective intervention and long-term sustainability, to the application to real-world service delivery. Furthermore, he cautioned that unless multiple opportunities for open and ongoing dialogue between SUs and those applying intervention (i.e., offering services) is sustained, authentic SU involvement will never truly occur (Chamberlin, 2005).

SHARED DECISION-MAKING

Traditionally, interventions were created, generated, and implemented by researchers, stakeholders, and organizations each with a vested interest at hand, which were intended to be delivered to SUs, clients, patients, and so on. In the past decade, however, there has been a shift in recognition advocating for SUs to become more involved in the planning process for services at each step of the way. In other fields, ideas such as public health's community-based participatory research, and the more patient-centered medical model have helped cement the notion that effective interventions must include the **consumer voices,** wants, and needs of the SUs, or those actually participating and utilizing said intervention.

Da Silva (2012) referred to decision-making as both a process and a philosophy; he said that decision-making requires a collaboration and reciprocal communication process between professionals and clients/patients. While current literature on the topic notes that shared decision-making between SUs and SPs is often recommended for local planning groups it is less common in day-to-day practice. Furthermore, while there is recognition that SU input is necessary and can help to create an effective, practical, and sustainable intervention or program, SPs today might still want to limit the extent to which SUs have decision-making stakes or power (Carey, 2009; Daykin, Sanidas, Tritter, Rimmer, & Evans, 2004; McDaid, 2009). More research and investigation needs to take place to ascertain both the importance of shared and perceived equal decision-making, as well as programs or interventions that have seen success or opposition to such a notion.

ELEMENTS OF SUCCESSFUL SUP

One easy way to visualize an example of elements of SUP is by using "The Ladder of Participation—Example of a Model of Service User Involvement" that was utilized in the Service User Involvement Framework developed in Wales (Welsh Assembly Government, 2004a). This resource helps to facilitate understanding of the levels of involvement that characterize SUP. The seven rungs of the ladder offer SUs an opportunity to choose the level at which they want to be involved based on their individual choices, current situation, or specific interest in the organization offering SUP. The rungs of the ladder are shown in descending order of importance:

1. Initiating: SUs generate ideas for actions and make all major decisions. Staff are available for consultation but refrain from taking charge.
2. Implementing: SUs are offered responsibilities to implement a project and monitor its outcomes.
3. Decision sharing: SUs share responsibilities to implement a project and monitor its outcomes.
4. Representation: SUs actually represent their views and opinions of peers on specific items whether through message boards, forums, focus groups, and so on.
5. Consultation: Staff generate main ideas and make key decisions but consult SUs in the process, taking into account their views and providing timely feedback on actions and decisions.
6. Positive contributions: SUs are asked about their opinions but cannot control the questions asked or how their answers will be used for research. For example, an SU satisfaction survey could be developed by staff with no input from SUs.
7. Information: Staff has control of information dissemination deciding when, what, and how it will be shared with SUs.

New roles for SUs in community planning include deciding on needed services and being central to their ultimate design. While it is generally accepted that the priorities of SUs and SPs are not the same, decisions on service delivery at the local level does need to include the opinions of both SUs and potential SUs (McLaughlin, 2009). Dowding and John (2011) stated that anything that reduces SU voice in planning for health and human services is not likely to improve care. In an earlier study by Minkler, Thompson, Bell, and Rose (2001), community participation by SUs and community members demonstrated that SUs can play a genuine role in establishing community needs, deciding on priority interventions, and being involved in funding proposals (the entire purpose for writing this manual!). SPs must challenge the social construction of SUs as outsiders and develop new understandings of the meaning of an authentic SU voice.

The devaluing of SUs in interprofessional groups inhibits full participation in partnerships and in decision-making. SPs who cannot listen or do not "hear" the actual voices of experience and knowledge that SUs bring to the group will inevitably impede SU participation and negate any real involvement in meaningful intervention planning. One of the most challenging issues is the devaluing of SU knowledge, which appears to hold little influence on SP decision-making (Cotterell et al., 2011). The policy rhetoric surrounding SU/SP focuses on increasing democratic participation and social inclusion. SU engagement, on the other hand, requires more than policy documents. This recognition of the importance of SUP in planning calls for a different route to working in more-inclusive ways. A commitment to SUP in principle is not enough; what is needed is evidence that collaboration between SUs and SPs is happening at local community levels.

Figure 6.1 sets out a process whereby organizations can measure SU involvement and assess their progress in SUP implementation (Welsh Assembly Government, 2004b). The checklist in figure 6.1 measures the means of participation within three dimensions: (1) commissioning and planning structures, (2) meetings, and (3) service providers. The checklist provides a comprehensive list of questions within each dimension where organizations can check on their current status regarding SUP.

Figure 6.1. Checklist for Service User Involvement

MEANS OF PARTICIPATION IN DIFFERENT AREAS

Commissioning and Planning Structures	Check
Does your partnership actively seek to involve service users in its work?	☐
Has your partnership or group considered user involvement when developing its terms of reference and structures?	☐
Is user involvement meetings-based or are other mechanisms employed?	☐
Is information on the structure and aims of the partnership or group readily available to service users?	☐
Do commissioners and planners have a clear understanding of the importance of user involvement?	☐
Are service users involved in the needs assessment process?	☐
Are service users involved in the development of service specifications to meet identified need?	☐
Are there opportunities for service users to be involved in the commissioning or procurement process?	☐
Are service users involved in the monitoring and evaluation of services?	☐
Is performance and activity information fed back to service users?	☐
Are changes and developments reported to service users?	☐
Would commissioners accept the finding of user-led research?	☐
Are there regular opportunities for service users to provide feedback on services either as an individual or as a group?	☐
Do commissioners allocate resources to support service user involvement?	☐
Are service users asked how they would like to be involved in commissioning?	☐
Do you regularly review your approach to service user involvement?	☐

Meetings

Are meetings held at times and in locations that are accessible to and appropriate for service users?   ☐

Are your meetings promoted in areas where service users will be?   ☐

Are minutes of your meetings readily available to service users?   ☐

Are you able to provide training and support to service users wishing to participate in meetings?   ☐

Are you able to give enough time for service users to prepare for meetings?   ☐

Do you support service users by meeting their out of pocket expenses incurred through attending meetings?   ☐

Do you use jargon and technical terms in your meetings?   ☐

Do those present have a clear understanding of the importance of user involvement?   ☐

Do you use means of communication other than e-mail?   ☐

Is the structure and culture of your meeting such that service users will feel able to contribute?   ☐

Service Providers

Do you have a service user charter?   ☐

Is information on how to make complaints or pay compliments made available to service users?   ☐

Are staff trained in delivering client-centered support and involving service users in their care plans?   ☐

Are clients able to access advocacy support?   ☐

Are service users involved in the staff recruitment process?   ☐

Are there regular opportunities for service users to provide feedback on services either as an individual or as a group?   ☐

Is there regular interaction between service users and senior management?   ☐

Are service users aware of who the commissioners of the service are?   ☐

Are service users involved in the development and review of their care plans?   ☐

Are service users involved when changes are made to the service base e.g. redecoration or renovation?   ☐

Are service users involved when changes are made to the structure of the service e.g. opening times, staff structures, out of hours support?   ☐

Are service users or ex-service users involved on your board of management?   ☐

Do service users have the opportunity to use their skills to support the delivery of the service e.g. peer support, befriending at drop-in?   ☐

Are service users involved in budget setting or management?   ☐

Are there opportunities for service users to represent the organization?   ☐

Do you operate any peer education or user led assertive outreach schemes?   ☐

Do you involve service users in the delivery of harm reduction messages?   ☐

Is the advice of service users sought when seeking to work with specific groups e.g. black and minority ethnic groups, stimulant users, etc.?   ☐

Are service users asked how they would like to be involved in services?   ☐

Are service users involved in the induction and general training of staff?   ☐

Are service users involved in the induction of new service users?   ☐

Do you advertise and promote service user forums?   ☐

Are service users informed of the range of treatment options available
to them?   ☐

Are service users encouraged to take a proactive lead in the development
and review of their own care plan?   ☐

Do you regularly review your approach to service user involvement?   ☐

Source: Welsh Assembly Government (2004b, pp. 13–15).

While decisions on intervention are intended to be collaborative, it is true that SU participation in decision-making regarding interventions and funding ranges widely across communities and nations. More specifically, the term *involvement* in planning contains many variations about who is involved, what they are involved in, how they are involved, and the type of impact their involvement might have on community planning (Morrow, Ross, Grocott, & Bennett, 2010).

DESCRIPTION OF PLANNING ACTIVITIES FOR PLANNING STEP 6: PLAN SERVICE USING EID

This planning step contains three action steps. Remember that any of the three action steps might use more than one activity sheet. Upon completion of each of these three action steps for Planning Step 6, please complete the appropriate evaluation form found at the end of the chapter. Evaluation is an important completion part of the overall planning process.

Action Step 6.1. SU/SP Examine and Propose Intervention Models

Action Step 6.2. SU/SP Rate Intervention Models

Action Step 6.3. SU/SP Develop Web-based Summary and Joint Recommendations
            for Priority Intervention Model

Action Step 6.1 (SU/SP Examine and Propose Intervention Models) brings SUs and SPs together to examine intervention models that have been identified by the consultant as EI programmatic responses, that have been used and found effective in other locations. Working together collaboratively, they will examine each intervention model and propose specific EI interventions that need further review and discussion. They will also develop rating criteria with the assistance of the consultant to ensure equitable analysis of the intervention model. Action Step 6.2 (SU/SP Rate Intervention Models) uses a priority-setting exercise similar to that used to identify the priority gap to explore the SUs' and SPs' jointly chosen intervention models. Previously, SUs and SPs worked together to identify their priority need, and now they work together using their rating criteria to identify the specific intervention that they believe will best meet that priority gap or need. Action Step 6.3 (SU/SP Develop Web-based Summary and Joint Recommendations for Priority Intervention Model) demonstrates the results of the priority setting exercise by SUs and SPs by providing joint recommendations for the priority intervention to be addressed in the local planning process.

All three action steps move the planning process from the general to the specific by using the priority needs collaboratively established by SUs and SPs. The major tasks of planning are contained within the three action steps: (1) SUs and SPs work with a research consultant to examine intervention models and develop intervention model rating criteria, (2) SUs and SPs rate intervention models using a jointly agreed-on rating criteria, and (3) SUs and SPs develop a Web-based summary and joint recommendations for the priority intervention model.

Action Step 6.1. SU/SP Examine and Propose Intervention Models

a. List of Activity Sheet(s): SU/SP Examine and Propose Intervention Models

Action Step	Activity Sheet(s)
6.1. SU and SP Examine Intervention Models	6.1.a. SU/SP Brief Summary of Intervention Models 6.1.b. SU/SP Intervention Model Rating Criteria

b. Introduction: SU/SP Examine and Propose Intervention Models

Action Step 6.1 builds on SUs' and SPs' previous experiences with priority setting, where they worked together to identify the priority need/gap in Planning Step 5. This joint planning process of reviewing intervention models has given them another opportunity to improve their collaboration, communication, negotiation, and decision-making skills. Their previous successes with joint decision-making regarding priority needs will inevitably influence the planning process when they now examine various intervention models. Action Step 6.1 also results in the development of intervention model rating criteria. SU/SP planning group members examine various rating criteria presented by the consultant and decide on what criteria they will use to rate the intervention models in Action Step 6.2. At the end of Action Step 6.1, SU/SP planning group members will have examined three specific intervention models and reviewed a specific set of rating criteria for deciding on a priority intervention.

c. Description: SU/SP Examine and Propose Intervention Models

The consultant working with the SUs and SPs will prepare intervention model descriptions using Activity Sheet 6.1.a (SU/SP Brief Summary of Intervention Models) to provide summaries that contain the following categories: (1) name of intervention, (2) brief description, (3) objectives, (4) activities, and (5) EI results. Before reviewing the intervention models, the consultant will facilitate a discussion of rating criteria for the intervention model using research-based decision criteria for health and human services, such as (1) appropriateness: fit with mandate, fit with desires of funder, and fit with desire of stakeholders; (2) impact: number reached and expected degree of change; and (3) capacity: skills available and financial cost (Activity Sheet 6.1.b [SU/SP Intervention Model Rating Criteria]) (Public Health Ontario, 2011). Decision-making on selection criteria is a joint SU/SP planning process facilitated by the macro practitioner/consultant that results in agreed-on rating criteria for intervention model review in Action Step 6.2. The SU/SP planning group in Action Step 6.1 examines the EI results of various intervention models researched and presented by the macro practitioner/consultant and chooses three specific intervention models for further review. Within Action Step 6.1, the SU/SP planning group also develops rating criteria for intervention model review as shown in Activity Sheet 6.1.b.

Action Step 6.2. SU/SP Rate Intervention Models

a. List of Activity Sheet(s): SU/SP Rate Intervention Models

Action Step	Activity Sheet(s)
6.2. SU/SP Rate Intervention Models	6.2.a. Building SU/SP Analysis Skills
	6.2.b. Building SU/SP Planning Skills

b. Introduction: SU/SP Rate Intervention Models

Action Step 6.2 puts the previous development of rating criteria and choice of intervention model into practice. Action Step 6.2 incorporates specific rating criteria chosen by the SU/SP planning group and requires analysis and decision-making by SUs and SPs voting on their priority intervention to meet the identified need. When reviewing the optional intervention models, SUs and SPs may decide on one that can be adapted, amended, or implemented as designed. As well, they will review interventions for community suitability for implementation in the local context, and critique the theoretical framework and EID that grounds various intervention models. In this action step, both SUs and SPs will have opportunities to systematically explore how using EID for program development and evaluation can improve service delivery to clients in their local community.

c. Description: SU/SP Rate Intervention Models

This step begins the process of analyzing and rating intervention models to see what priorities for service development are best suited to the local priority need or gap in service. Using the rating criteria established for decision-making on interventions, SUs and SPs begin an analysis of current services to ascertain whether the identified gap is being met. Activity Sheet 6.2.a (Building SU/SP Analysis Skills) collects data on the state of the local service system so that SUs and SPs can analyze whether a new service is required, or whether there are existing programs and services that could be expanded or enhanced, to meet the priority need. These data reflect the name of the agency, the service provided, the identified need, whether the agency is partially meeting the identified need, whether the agency is completely meeting the priority need, and finally whether the agency is meeting the identified service need. Once these data are collected, it is possible to analyze whether the specific intervention model fills the identified need/gap, whether it offers a priority service that could be expanded or enhanced, and where on the rating scale an enhancement or expansion of the existing intervention model would rank (Activity Sheet 6.2.a). At this point, it still unknown whether a new intervention model needs to be introduced or whether the existing service system, with recommended changes, has the possibility of responding appropriately to the identified need/gap in the local community. This review of current local services and how they do or do not meet the identified need is an important step in conducting a gap analysis. By gathering information on local services and programs and using the needs assessment data collected in the planning process, a determination can be made if there is a legitimate gap in service provision in the local community that requires a new intervention model.

Activity Sheet 6.2.b (Building SU/SP Planning Skills) transitions more specifically into decisions about services using EID. Activity Sheet 6.2.b is used by the SU/SP joint planning group to review the existing local service system in more depth by examining (1) gaps in service, (2) duplications of service, (3) services to be augmented, (4) services to be expanded, and (5) services to be replaced. Importantly here is the SUs' and SPs' ability to gather recently emerging changes in the service system. While the needs assessment data have been collected and analyzed, there may have been recent changes in current services that can affect the gap analysis carried out by the SU/SP planning group. Expanding a service planning analysis beyond the time-framed service inventory gives the SU/SP planning process an added dimension. By incorporating program changes that may be happening in the local community but that have not been formally announced, a more realistic portrayal of the service system is possible. The SU/SP planning group needs to ensure that they have an up-to-date snapshot of the local service system before recommending a new intervention model be developed to meet the identified priority need in the local community.

Action Step 6.3. SU/SP Develop Web-based Summary and Joint Recommendations for Priority Intervention Model

a. List of Activity Sheet(s): SU/SP Develop Web-based Summary and Joint Recommendations for Priority Intervention Model

Action Step	Activity Sheet(s)
6.3. SU/SP Develop Web-based Summary and Joint Recommendations for Priority Intervention Model	6.3.a. SU/SP Three-Round Voting Template 6.3.b. SU/SP Summary of Recommended Intervention Model

b. Introduction: SU/SP Develop Web-based Summary and Joint Recommendations for Priority Intervention Model

This Action Step 6.3 places importance on EID about intervention model priorities. The EID collected on intervention models and reviewed jointly by SUs and SPs allowed for participatory decision-making, using well-established rating criteria agreed on before SUs and SPs commenced the intervention rating process. The use of a consultant or a macro practitioner to analyze EI intervention models specifically targeted to the priority need/gap established by SUs/SPs was a valuable addition to the planning process. Similarly, the use of a facilitator/consultant to help the group establish fair and equitable rating criteria for model review was important to the promotion of determining intervention priorities and democratic decision-making.

c. Description: SU/SP Develop Web-based Summary and Joint Recommendations for Priority Intervention Model

Using the identified intervention models reviewed in Activity Sheet 6.1.b, the recommended intervention model is established through a nominal group technique. SUs and SPs will decide on whether to use an open or secret ballot voting mechanism before beginning the priority intervention model exercise. Using the list of reviewed intervention models, SUs and SPs in the first round may anonymously write their first priority model on a ballot collected by the facilitator (Activity Sheet 6.3.a [SU/SP Three-Round Voting Template). These identified priority interventions are posted on a white board or flip chart. In Round 2, participants may anonymously vote for their priority intervention based on the reduced list of intervention models from Round 1. Round 3 requires another vote for the intervention priority based on the condensed list of intervention models from Round 1. Activity Sheet 6.3.a is then used to identify the top priority intervention model that the group will be recommending.

Activity Sheet 6.3.b (SU/SP Summary of Recommended Intervention Model) incorporates all of the EID utilized by SUs/SPs to reach an agreement about the highest-priority intervention model to recommend for implementation and, in turn, to recommend for funding. While there may be differences of opinion about what intervention model would best meet the identified gap/need, the use of rating criteria to facilitate decision-making is supported by the aforementioned EID. Examining the research evidence on the effectiveness of the proposed intervention model is only one way of using EI planning, but it is a critical step in ensuring that decisions are grounded in available research. The SU/SP group will provide a summary of its recommendations using Activity Sheet 6.3.b as the template and uploading the document to the Web-based reporting system. The identified priority intervention model will then be transparent to all who will need these data as they begin the next step of identifying funding sources and **sponsors,** and preparing a proposal for funding. Once SUs and SPs are "on the same page" regarding the recommenced priority intervention, they can begin the real work of planning for implementation by researching funding sources and preparing to work with their consultants on program proposal development and budget preparation. While making decisions about priority intervention models is time-consuming and difficult, the desire for SUs and SPs to meet unmet needs in their community through securing resources is the driving force behind the joint collaborative model of this entire text.

CASE VIGNETTE: FACILITATION OF RATING OF PRIORITY INTERVENTION BY SUs/SPs

This vignette describes what happens when SUs and SPs take the rather harrowing step of choosing a priority intervention to be eventually implemented. Practitioners responsible for facilitating planning groups must honestly ask themselves: (1) Is it really possible to please everyone? and (2) If not, how will the so-called winners and losers work together? In this vignette, there was a "happy ending," and consensus between SUs and SPs. This is not to say that the journey to consensus was not fraught with intermittent conflict and controversy, however.

A joint decision was made by the SU/SP group to hire an external consultant to facilitate the group's joint planning process. The consultant, an employee of a local university, was given the EID collected in the previous planning steps, including the main priority need established by the SU/SP groups and was asked to present three potential intervention models for review. To put it mildly, SUs and SPs were shocked when presented with the proposed intervention models at their first meeting with the consultant. There were two initial pressing issues tabled: (1) There was no connection between the identified priority need and the proposed intervention model. (2) The consultant had not developed objective rating criteria for reviewing planned interventions. Since the SPs had recommended the consultant, there was suspicion by some SUs that their views were being discounted behind the scenes. This led to accusations that SPs had stage-managed the planning process to achieve their own agenda.

Despite objections to the contrary by SPs, the planning process ultimately ground to a halt. Then the consultant apologized to the planning group and stated that he had no experience at all with planning, conducting literature searches, and developing rating criteria. In fact, he simply did not know how to do the tasks. SPs were embarrassed by their choice of consultant, and tried to explain in detail how and why they chose the consultant: because the fees were low and he had good references. After much discussion and apologies from SPs, the group decided to abandon the consultant and go it on their own. They began crafting their rating criteria for the intervention model review, and conducted their own reviews of the literature to empirically support their identified priority need. In essence, this ended up being a much better collaborative process than hiring out of house, and gave SUs and SPs opportunities to showcase their own knowledge and experience on various subjects. Ultimately, when they finally came together to review their three selected interventions, they easily developed joint recommendations for their priority intervention. They also congratulated themselves on solving what could have been an insurmountable barrier to working together. Their completion of this planning step gave them momentum and enthusiasm for more trustful, open, and respectful collaboration for working together on the next step in the process: choosing a sponsor and funder for their agreed-on recommended model.

SUMMARY AND EVALUATION OF PLANNING STEP 6: PLAN SERVICE USING EID

Summary of Planning Step 6: Plan Service Using EID

The macro practitioner/consultant hired by the SU/SP planning group takes on an important role in ensuring that the applicable intervention models in the research literature are brought for review. Additionally, the macro practitioner/consultant is critical to helping SUs and SPs develop joint rating criteria for intervention model review. More importantly, SUs and SPs need to bring the EID from the previous steps into the planning process to guide the choice of the prospective intervention model. It is here where the rubber hits the road for EI planning. The ability to overcome the politics of planning and to ensure that data drive the decision-making requires technical support from the macro practitioner/consultant who are working collaboratively with the joint SU/SP planning group. When reviewing the optional intervention models, SUs and SPs may decide that one can be adapted, amended, or implemented as designed. As well, they will review interventions for their community suitability for implementation in the local context, and critique the theoretical framework that grounds various intervention models. In this step, both cohorts will have opportunities to systematically explore how using EID for program development and evaluation can improve service delivery to clients in their local community.

Evaluation of Planning Step 6: Plan Service Using EID

Evaluation Form: Circle one number only for each question listed below.

Action Step 6.1. SU/SP Examine and Propose Intervention Models

a. How confident were you about achieving this goal?	Not confident	Somewhat confident	Very confident	Extremely confident
	1	2	3	4

b. What was the most important thing you learned about this step?

Action Step 6.2. SU/SP Rate Intervention Models

a. How confident were you about achieving this goal?	Not confident	Somewhat confident	Very confident	Extremely confident
	1	2	3	4

b. What was the most important thing you learned about this step?

Action Step 6.3. SU/SP Develop Web-based Summary and Joint Recommendations for Priority Intervention Model

a. How confident were you about achieving this goal?	Not confident	Somewhat confident	Very confident	Extremely confident
	1	2	3	4

b. What was the most important thing you learned about this step?

Your Total Score? _____

Group Discussion Notes:

(continue on back as needed)

REFERENCES

Beresford, P. (2007). The role of service user research in generating knowledge-based health and social care: From conflict to contribution. *Evidence & Policy: A Journal of Research, Debate and Practice, 3*(3), 329–341. doi:10.1332/174426407781738074

Carey, M. (2009). Happy shopper? The problem with service user and carer participation. *British Journal of Social Work, 39*(1), 179–188. doi:10.1093/bjsw/bcn166

Chaffin, M., & Friedrich, B. (2004). Evidence-based treatments in child abuse and neglect. *Children and Youth Services Review, 26*(11), 1097–1113. doi:10.1016/j.childyouth.2004.08.008

Chamberlin, J. (2005). User/consumer involvement in mental health service delivery. *Epidemiologia e Psichiatria Sociale, 14*(1), 10–14.

Cotterell, P., Harlow, G., Morris, C., Beresford, P., Hanley, B., Sargeant, A., . . . Staley, K. (2011). Service user involvement in cancer care: The impact on SUs. *Health Expectations, 14*(2), 159–169. doi:10.1111/j.1369-7625.2010.00627.x

Da Silva, D. (2012). *Evidence: Helping people share decision making: A review of the evidence considering whether shared decision making is worthwhile.* The Health Foundation.

Daykin, N., Sanidas, M., Tritter, J., Rimmer, J., & Evans, S. (2004). Developing user involvement in a UK cancer network: Professionals and users' perspectives. *Critical Public Health, 14*(3), 277–294. doi:10.1080/09581590400004402

Dill, K., & Shera, W. (2009). Designing for success: The development of a child welfare research utilization initiative. *Evidence and Policy: A Journal of Research and Debate, 5*(2), 155–166. doi:10.1332/174426409X437900

Dowding, K., & John, P. (2011). Voice and choice in health care in England: Understanding citizen responses to dissatisfaction. *Public Administration, 89*(4), 1403–1418. doi:10.1111/j.1467-9299.2011.01960.x

McDaid, S. (2009). An equality of condition framework for user involvement in mental health policy and planning: Evidence from participatory action research. *Disability & Society, 24*(4), 461–474. doi:10.1080/09687590902879064

McLaughlin, H. (2009). What's in a name: "Client," "patient," "customer," "consumer," "expert by experience," "service user"—What's next? *British Journal of Social Work, 39*(6), 1101–1117. doi:10.1093/bjsw/bcm155

Minkler, M., Thompson, M., Bell, J., & Rose, K. (2001). Contributions of community involvement to organizational-level empowerment: The Federal Healthy Start Experience. *Health Education and Behavior, 28*(6), 783–807. doi:10.1177/109019810102800609

Morrow, E., Ross, F., Grocott, P., & Bennett, J. (2010). A model and measure for quality service user involvement in health research. *International Journal of Consumers Studies, 34*(5), 532–539. doi:10.1111/j.1470-6431.2010.00901.x

National Association of County and City Health Officials. (2005). *Mobilizing for action through planning and partnerships (MAPP).* Retrieved from http://archived.naccho.org/topics/infrastructure/mapp

Public Health Ontario, 2011. *Priority setting process checklist.* Toronto, ON, Canada.

Sackett, D. L., Strauss, S. E., Richardson, W. S., Rosenberg, W., & Haynes, R. B. (2000). *Evidence-based medicine: How to practice and teach EBM* (2nd ed.). Edinburgh: Churchill Livingstone.

Welsh Assembly Government. (2004a). *Service user involvement framework.* Appendix 1 Checklist for Service User Involvement. Cardiff.

Welsh Assembly Government. (2004b). *Stronger in partnership: Involving SUs and carers in the design, planning, delivery and evaluation of mental health services in Wales.* Cardiff.

INTERNET REFERENCES

National Collaborating Centre for Methods and Tools: Building Capacity for Evidence-informed Public Health: A Planning Tool for Priority Setting. http://www.nccmt.ca/resources/search/106

This site presents a priority setting process checklist (PSPC) that demonstrates a structured way to carry out priority setting planning exercises. The PSPC addresses five domains of priority setting: (1) data gathering, (2) participation by stakeholders, (3) resources, (4) time, and (5) decision-making.

University of Kansas Community Toolbox: Developing and Using Criteria and Processes to Set Priorities. http://ctb.ku.edu/en/table-of-contents/assessment/assessing-community-needs-and -resources/criteria-and-processes-to-set-priorities/checklist

This Web site offers a definition of criteria as standards for making a judgment. In addition, it offers a definition of priority as the order of importance in which one thing falls in relation to another. It articulates clearly why a community planning group should develop and use criteria and processes to set priorities.

Government of Canada, Canadian Institutes of Health Research. Deliberative Priority Setting: A CIHR KT Module (2010)

This Web site offers a comprehensive online information base on priority-setting models and strategies. It is a thirty-two-page document that covers a vast array of priority-setting elements such as developing a plan and a timeline for the priority-setting process. The document clearly identifies that there are two major types of priority-setting processes: (1) priority setting for research, and (2) priority setting for service delivery.

Centers for Disease Control and Prevention: Setting HIV Prevention Priorities. http://stacks.cdc.gov/view/cdc/5184/

A Guide for Community Planning Groups: This Web site provides a guide to priority setting in community planning that includes chapters on (1) getting ready to set priorities, (2) steps for choosing interventions, and (3) managing the work. It also provides a large number of appendices that are sample conflict-of-interest forms and sample ground rules for planning groups. The guide is available as a PDF file on the CDC Web site.

POWERPOINT RESOURCES

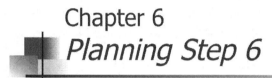

Chapter 6
Planning Step 6

Plan Service Using EID

Why is this planning step important?

- It increases our understanding of how we use evidence to direct our practice, the organizational and cultural context where we work, and how to incorporate SU perspectives.
- It creates new roles for SUs in community planning that include deciding on needed services and increasing SU voice in establishing community needs and priority interventions.

What does the literature say?

- Unless multiple opportunities for open and ongoing dialogue between SUs and those applying interventions are sustained, authentic SU involvement will never truly occur.
- While shared decision-making is often incorporated, it is less common in day-to-day practice.
- The best examples of increasing and encouraging SU shared decision-making are witnessed in the medical field.

Planning Step 6. Plan Service Using EID

Activity Sheet 6.1.a. SU/SP Brief Summary of Intervention Models

NAME OF INTERVENTION	BRIEF DESCRIPTION	OBJECTIVES	ACTIVITIES	EI RESULTS

Planning Step 6. Plan Service Using EID

Activity Sheet 6.1.b. SU/SP Intervention Model Rating Criteria

RATING CRITERIA	INTERVENTION MODEL #1	INTERVENTION MODEL #2	INTERVENTION MODEL #3
Appropriateness 1. **Fit with mandate** 2. **Fit with desire of stakeholders** 3. **Fit with funders**			
Impact 1. **Number reached** 2. **Expected degree of change**			
Capacity 1. **Skills available** 2. **Financial cost**			

Planning Step 6. Plan Service Using EID

Activity Sheet 6.2.a. Building SU/SP Analysis Skills

NAME OF AGENCY	SERVICE PROVIDED	IDENTIFIED NEED	AGENCY PARTIALLY MEETING PRIORITY NEED?	AGENCY COMPLETELY MEETING PRIORITY NEED?	AGENCY MEETING PRIORITY SERVICE NEED?

Planning Step 6. Plan Service Using EID

Activity Sheet 6.2.b. Building SU/SP Planning Skills

SERVICES PARTIALLY MEETING PRIORITY NEED	GAPS IN SERVICE	DUPLICATIONS OF SERVICE	SERVICES TO BE AUGMENTED	SERVICES TO BE EXPANDED	SERVICES TO BE REPLACED

Planning Step 6. Plan Service Using EID

Activity Sheet 6.3.a. SU/SP Three-Round Voting Template

INTERVENTION MODEL	ROUND 1 VOTE	ROUND 2 VOTE	ROUND 3 VOTE

Source: Adapted from National Association of County and City Health Officials (2005).

Planning Step 6. Plan Service Using EID

Activity Sheet 6.3.b. SU/SP Summary of Recommended Intervention Model

1. Summary of the Planning Process
    1.1 Brief Description of Intervention Models Reviewed
    1.2 Brief Description of Rating Criteria and Voting Method
    1.3 Brief Description of Service User/Provider Review of Existing Services
2. Summary of the Recommended Intervention Model
    2.1 Description of the Intervention Model
    2.2 Objectives of the Intervention Model
    2.3 Activities of the Intervention Model
    2.4 Outcomes and Indicators of Effectiveness of Intervention Model
    2.5 Staffing Requirements for Intervention Model

Planning Step 7

Decide on Intervention and Sponsors

OVERVIEW AND RATIONALE

Shared decision-making between SUs and SPs requires that they go through all the phases of decision-making together in order to come to an understanding of what is the best outcome for their local community. The stages of decision-making can be categorized as follows: (1) identifying and reviewing the EID collected and deciding on a priority problem or need in the local community, (2) reviewing the intervention models relevant to the identified priority problem or need and deciding on a priority intervention model to meet that specific local need, and (3) reaching agreement on the priority intervention model, sponsor, and funder source with the result the development of a joint proposal for funding for the chosen intervention model. While this type of planning process appears straightforward, it is the level of understanding between SUs and SPs that is the critical element affecting their decision-making effectiveness. It is this category of decision-making and reaching agreement that is the substance of Planning Step 7. While each of the three action steps within Planning Step 7 addresses the mechanics of decision-making, and while each highlights SU/SP collaboration in decision-making, the action steps do not eliminate the problem of power issues that are a barrier to effective decision-making in local community planning initiatives. Despite considerable attention to decision-making stages and mechanisms within this manual, a more active role for the macro practitioner is required in order to facilitate democratic decision-making. In this chapter we will increase the reader's understanding of these power issues and their impact on decision-making in local planning through an exploration of how the territory of SU/SP partnerships has unfolded in the literature, and then to turn to the pragmatics of decision-making between SUs and SPs in the description of planning activities that compose the final sections of this chapter.

The idea of sharing power with SUs has historically not resonated well with providers (Dunlop 2002; Dunlop & Holosko, 2005). Despite mandated collaboration, SUs find little opportunity to share their views about improving services with providers. Recent literature suggests that tension often exists when SUs desire a transfer of power and seek increased decision-making over their own lives (Holosko, Leslie, & Cassano, 2001). Moreover, SUs themselves, although not a homogenous group, have reported that the term *service user* (SU) itself adds to their perceived marginalization and exclusion (Hernandez, Robson, & Sampson, 2010; McLaughlin, 2009; Smith et al., 2011). As a result, despite government policy agendas promoting democratic engagement and decision-making, SUP in the planning and delivery of health and social care services is replete with challenges at the local level (Holosko et al., 2001).

Taylor, Jones, O'Reilly, Oldfield, and Blackburn (2010) have identified contextual factors that support SU involvement in meaningful decision-making and planning as (1) support from key stakeholders, (2) legitimacy and support from local systems, and (3) administrative support for involvement in decision-making. Similarly, research on facilitators of SU involvement by Coney (2004), identified three areas of importance: (1) creation of common guidelines and protocols, (2) education for professionals on how to work with SUs, and (3) agreements on standards of practice to maintain **joint agreement** on standards. Barriers to genuine decision-making on services by SUs include (1) previous token SU experiences, (2) attitudes of SPs, and (3) lack of government leadership and commitment to decision-making partnerships between SUs and SPs (Coney, 2004).

Several factors have been identified in various studies as barriers to such involvement in community planning. Some professionals find it challenging to view SUs as "experts," and resist movement toward increased SU involvement. Although there is evidence to suggest that professionals are commonly supportive of SU involvement, there are also inconsistencies between expressed support for said involvement and the actual practice of involving SUs (Campbell, 2001). This could reflect professionals' perceptions of themselves as being more supportive than users actually perceive them to be (Peck, Gulliver, & Towell, 2002), resistance to the idea of sharing power with and transferring power to SUs, or a conflict of professionals' "scientific," and users' more "social" ways of thinking and working (Summers, 2003).

Some SUs also believe that the decision-making involved in the planning process is often too stressful and complex (Carnaby 1997). Some SPs also believe that it may be difficult for SUs to understand the discussion of abstract ideas during the planning process. Some SUs have noted that agency staff and government officials (Reid & Green, 2002; Smull & Lakin, 2002) lack the ability to appropriately engage clients due to communication difficulties, lack of detailed knowledge about the person's preferences and/or needs, lack of ability to effectively facilitate meetings, and lack of incentive giving for SU involvement. Furthermore, some service cultures may promote dependence, which in turn limits SUs' choices and decision-making opportunities, and stifles **self-determination** and involvement (Wehmeyer & Ward, 1995). Additionally, resource distribution and utilization may be counterproductive in enabling services, staff, clients, and clients' families to effectively engage in individual planning processes.

Some of the more facilitating factors identified to increase SU involvement in community planning include but are not limited to knowledge or previous experience with the topic or service area, access to the SU organization, utilization of multiple SU representatives, offering or providing content and process-related support to SU representatives regarding complex discussion materials, early involvement of SU representatives in the guideline formation process, and implementing the SUs' perspectives or opinions as an agenda item in community meetings and discussions (van der Ham, Shields, van der Horst, Broerse, & van Tulder, 2014).

SU groups have played important roles in mutual support, combating stigma, helping others to recover and stay out of services, and participating in local service planning and development (Wallcraft, 2003). Research has also shown that SUs have been successful when they have been placed in the role of the community expert, providing detailed information about how the client actually experiences the community problem. This lens provides service agencies an additional perspective (Barnes & Shardlow, 1997).

Recent research has identified that SUs are seeking the following extended decision-making capabilities: (1) the ability to work collectively for change and mutual support; and (2) the importance of making known their own experiences, views, and ideas. SUs highlighted the importance and benefits of being able to network with each other, as individuals and in user-controlled organizations, both in terms of improving their quality of life and in sustaining a more effective voice and presence to make a perceived difference.

RELATIONSHIPS WITH FUNDERS

While it is imperative to incorporate SUs throughout every planning step in community-based initiatives, there is another key group who cannot be ignored in intervention planning and service provision—the funders. It is obvious that funders are an integral component to any successful intervention—as how else would new programs get off the ground? However, there has been a shift in recognition that funders should be incorporated throughout this planning process, and that they should be invited or even expected to serve as a legitimate voice, from the initial research stage all the way to project evaluation. Currently, in many programs funders are more likely to meet with researchers, practitioners, and SUs before and throughout the intervention process than they are to meet with them afterwards. This needs to be the case for all SU interventions in order to create an expectation and relationship between the SUs and their funders. Researchers and practitioners do not necessarily have to serve as a liaison or middle man if the SU and funder are able to directly communicate and collaborate their needs and generate practical solutions for all parties involved in the planned initiative.

Generating and strengthening the relationship between funders and SUs can lead to SUs increasing their presence, their voice, and their overall confidence to make funding decisions. For example, SUs can adopt a more nonexecutive role, in which they ensure more transparency, public voice, and accountability. Additionally, SUs can contribute the perspectives of clients and patients in their community in order to help the research and funding team to prioritize their goals and efforts (Blackburn, Hanley, & Staley, 2010).

DESCRIPTION OF PLANNING ACTIVITIES FOR PLANNING STEP 7: DECIDE ON INTERVENTION AND SPONSORS

This planning step contains three action steps. Remember that any of the three action steps might use more than one activity sheet. Upon completion of each of these three action steps for Planning Step 7, please complete the appropriate evaluation form found at the end of the chapter. Evaluation is an important completion part of the overall planning process.

Action Step 7.1. SU/SP Define Intervention and Choose Sponsor
Action Step 7.2. SU/SP Map External Environment of Chosen Sponsor
Action Step 7.3. SU/SP Choose Appropriate Funding Source

Action Step 7.1 (SU/SP Define Intervention and Choose Sponsor) brings SUs and SPs together with their consultant to develop a more detailed description of their previously chosen intervention model. As they work toward more specificity about the proposed intervention, they are setting the stage for the next choice—that of host agency to sponsor the intervention. In Action Step 7.2 (SU/SP Map External Environment of Chosen Sponsor), SUs and SPs will be guided in their decision-making about the host agency by factors such as (1) acceptance by the community, and (2) the ability of the host agency to meet the identified gap. Once the SU/SP planning group has decided on the agency sponsor for the priority intervention, SUs and SPs will jointly conduct an external environment mapping exercise to assess the legitimacy of the agency within the local community using six criteria shown in Activity Sheet 7.2.a (SU/SP External Environment Map). Finally, Action Step 7.3 (SU/SP Choose Appropriate Funding Source) is a joint SU/SP review of relevant funding sources that have been researched by the consultant during the planning process. In this final action step, SUs and SPs must decide on the priority funding source for the proposed intervention and sponsor. Jointly, SUs and SPs will make a recommendation on the most relevant funder by taking into account the information on federal, regional, municipal, foundation, and corporate sponsorship that the consultant has prepared for their information, review, and decision-making. The major tasks of the planning are contained within the three action steps: (1) SUs and SPs jointly define intervention and choose sponsor, (2) SUs and SPs map external environment of chosen sponsor, and (3) SUs and SPs choose appropriate funding source for grant proposal.

Action Step 7.1. SU/SP Define Intervention and Choose Sponsor

a. List of Activity Sheet(s): SU/SP Define Intervention and Choose Sponsor

Action Step	Activity Sheet(s)
7.1. SU and SP Define Intervention and Choose Sponsor	7.1.a. SU/SP Intervention Model Description 7.1.b. SU/SP Intervention Model and Sponsor Matching

b. Introduction: SU/SP Define Intervention and Choose Sponsor

Action Step 7.1 consists of SUs and SPs working with the consultant to specifically describe the intervention so that there is a shared understanding of exactly how the priority intervention will be implemented. The SU/SP group in the previous action step reviewed three EI intervention models researched by the consultant. In Action Step 7.1 the SU/SP group members further refine their knowledge of the specific intervention model by examining the description of the program, objectives, activities, staffing, and outcome indicators of effectiveness using Activity Sheet 7.1.a (SU/SP Intervention Model Description).

c. Description: SU/SP Define Intervention and Choose Sponsor

SUs and SPs have an opportunity to systematically explore how using EID for program development and evaluation can improve service delivery in their local community. The planning issues in Action Step 7.1 are (1) analysis based on the EI effectiveness data for the joint SU/SP group's chosen intervention, and (2) consensus decision-making regarding the joint SU/SP group's chosen sponsoring agency. In

Action Step 7.1, SUs and SPs examine more closely the specifics of their chosen intervention model and how it is going to meet the priority need.

Activity Sheet 7.1.a provides SUs and SPs with the opportunity to question their consultant on specific elements of the model and to gain more information regarding the primary objectives, activities, outcome indicators, measurement instruments, and staff and volunteer roles; these are all potential components that would be necessary to implement the intervention at a local level. Although SUs and SPs have reviewed the intervention model in the previous action step, they did not necessarily have the chance to drill down to the details and study the data that were part of the consultant's research report. In Action Step 7.1, joint decision-making by SUs and SPs is brought back to the forefront as they choose a sponsor for their priority intervention. Activity Sheet 7.1.b (SU/SP Intervention Model and Sponsor Matching) is a planning activity that helps SUs and SPs explore what agency would be the best match for the proposed intervention model by examining decision criteria such as (1) intervention model and agency fit, (2) agency acceptance by the community, (3) agency ability to meet the identified gap or need, and (4) agency EI effectiveness data. The culmination of this action step is a joint SU/SP recommendation that encompasses an EI intervention model and a consensus decision on a proposed host agency to implement the intervention.

Action Step 7.2. SU/SP Map External Environment of Chosen Sponsor

a. List of Activity Sheet(s): SU/SP Map External Environment of Chosen Sponsor

Action Step	Activity Sheet(s)
7.2. SU/SP Map External Environment of Chosen Sponsor	7.2.a. SU/SP External Environment Map

b. Introduction: SU/SP Map External Environment of Chosen Sponsor

A recommendation for a host agency was made by the SU/SP planning group in Action Step 7.1. The group made this decision after an examination of decision criteria such as (1) model/agency fit, (2) community acceptance, (3) ability to meet need, and (4) demonstration of agency EI effectiveness (Activity Sheet 7.1.b). Action Step 7.2 provides an opportunity for the SU/SP planning group to carry out a more intensive assessment of the chosen sponsor's suitability to implement the intervention through a mapping exercise that assesses the host agency's legitimacy and status within the local community with regard to (1) SU/SP review of sponsor relationships, (2) recipients and consumers, (3) providers of complementary services, (4) providers of fiscal resources, (5) providers of authority and legitimation, and (6) competing organizations (Activity Sheet 7.2.a).

c. Description: SU/SP Map External Environment of Chosen Sponsor

While the choice of an agency sponsor is often a highly political planning activity, the use of EID collected through the planning process can offset that reality. A review of Planning Step 4 and Planning Step 5 demonstrates how the EID collection activities highlight the integrity of decision-making within the SU/SP planning group. Examples

Figure 7.1. External Environment Map

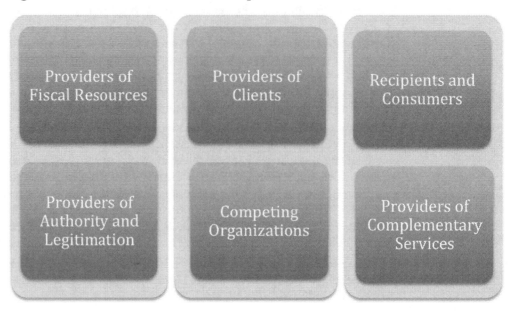

of data collection activities such as (1) needs assessments, (2) asset mapping, (3) inventory of services, (4) intervention model description, and (5) gap analysis document the research capacity of the SU/SP planning group and the group's consultants. Using specialist consultants to provide technical assistance in areas such as literature reviews, EID collection, intervention model review, priority-setting exercises, and budgeting adds to the credibility of the decision-making within the SU/SP planning process. Action Step 7.2 provides an opportunity for the SU/SP planning group to conduct an assessment of the chosen agency's legitimacy as a host agency. Activity Sheet 7.2.a outlines various constituents of importance in the local community: (1) recipients and consumers, (2) providers of complementary services, (3) providers of fiscal resources, (4) providers of authority and legitimation, (5) providers of clients, and (6) competing organizations (figure 7.1).

This external environmental mapping provides documentation of the agency's establishment as a legitimate and respected provider of services. If the agency is viewed by its constituents as having a stable, long-term organizational claim to provide services to a specific population, it likely has legitimacy within the local community (Hasenfeld, 1992). The SU/SP planning group uses Activity Sheet 7.2.a to assess the external environment of their chosen sponsor. Depending on the results of that assessment, a final recommendation on the chosen sponsor can be documented.

Action Step 7.3. SU/SP Choose Appropriate Funding Source

a. List of Activity Sheet(s): SU/SP Choose Appropriate Funding Source

Action Step	Activity Sheet(s)
7.3. SU/SP Choose Appropriate Funding Source	7.3.a. SU/SP Potential Funding Opportunities Chart

b. Introduction: SU/SP Choose Appropriate Funding Source

In Action Step 7.3 the SU/SP group will review funding sources that the consultant has researched and presented to the group in a graphic way to allow SUs and SPs to identify clearly whether the **funding priorities** of each granting agency are aligned with the priority needs and intervention model being proposed by SUs and SPs. This is a key action step, and is necessary to ensure that the grant proposal is targeted correctly to a funder who is interested in the chosen intervention model and target population. Hiring a specialist consultant to facilitate decision-making on funding sources is important here. Although the SU/SP planning group is responsible for making the decision on funders, it is important for the group to have as much information as possible before making a decision. Allowing the consultant to contact the program officers of funders to ascertain whether the priority intervention model is appropriate for their funding guidelines will strengthen the SU/SP funding opportunities review process. Once the funding source is chosen, then a decision needs to be made regarding how follow-up calls to the funding source will be carried out by the SU/SP planning group, and chosen host agency.

c. Description: SU/SP Choose Appropriate Funding Source

The consultant who is responsible for bringing forward specific funders for SU/SP review must have the sophistication and contacts to know that it is not just "all about the paperwork." SUs and SPs cannot assume that an EI outstanding grant proposal is necessarily the key to success. The SU/SP planning group (which will now include the chosen host agency) will have to decide who will contact the various funders' program officers, to gather information before they enter into the decision-making process using Activity Sheet 7.3.a (SU/SP Potential Funding Opportunities Chart). The consultant who is researching funding sources for the SU/SP planning group would be the obvious choice. Since it is the consultant's responsibility to ensure that he or she gives a comprehensive database of funding choices to the SU/SP planning group, it would be advantageous to allow the consultant to contact the program officer before the SU/SP review process to discuss the following: (1) appropriateness of the proposed intervention, (2) whether the proposed intervention fits with the goals of the funder, and (3) what, if any, reformulations might be necessary to meet the funding criteria. While researching funding sources, the consultant will be representing the SU/SP planning group and the chosen sponsoring agency. Notably, there may be multiple potential funding sources that need to be explored, such as (1) federal, regional, and municipal governments; (2) private foundations; (3) corporate sponsors; and (4) community nonprofits such as United Way. Action Step 7.3 requires additional research into funding sources and behind-the-scenes relationship development by the consultant in order to establish the credibility of the host agency and the proposed intervention. The SU/SP planning group will then review the potential funding opportunities utilizing Activity Sheet 7.3.a to collaboratively review and decide on the most favorable funding organization to receive the grant proposal. It will be important for the consultant to provide as much information on the various options available, as well as to bring the host agency into the discussions and decision-making to ensure that before the grant proposal is prepared all parties are in agreement about how to move forward with their proposed priority intervention. Realistically, although the budget has not yet been finalized and approved by the SU/SP planning group members, they have to assess the feasibility of implementing their chosen intervention model given available funding. The twenty-first century context of planning sometimes requires a "cart before the horse" approach where funding announcements drive decisions about local services. Consequently, budgets have to conform to the resources that are available to local SU/SP planning groups, and often interventions have to be scaled down due to these funder resource constraints.

CASE VIGNETTE: DECISIONS ON INTERVENTION AND SPONSORS

Rarely do decisions about intervention models and choice of local sponsor go smoothly. Inevitably, there will be disagreement about what specific intervention should be chosen to meet the priority community need. This case illustrates how intervention and sponsor discussions unearthed hidden agendas, and problematic relationship histories between SUs and SPs.

Although the SUs and SPs had been successful in carrying out a joint needs assessment, data became secondary to politics in Planning Step 7. Regrettably, the decision-making process about intervention and sponsor went awry at the last minute. At the outset, the SU/SP mission and goals were to plan a primary prevention strategy to educate adolescents on the dangers of drinking while pregnant. Although they did not declare a chosen sponsor, there was an understanding it would be the local health unit. When intervention models were presented for review and discussion, there was clearly no agreement between stakeholders.

Additionally, a clique had developed within the group made up of both SUs and SPs who had not supported primary prevention, but instead supported an early intervention strategy that would offer support services for parents of children with fetal alcohol spectrum disorder (FASD). A number of influential SUs and SPs caused a veering away from the original mission of primary prevention; this is known as mission drifting. Emotional arguments were presented about the demands of raising a child with FASD. Those stakeholders in the group who were passionate about providing services, but not education, were successful in changing the decision regarding intervention, and consequently changed their sponsor. Since it was not to be an educational initiative, public health was not the appropriate provider, because the new intervention model required that SUs and SPs choose a family service agency.

The most articulate and forceful group of SUs and SPs had already decided on a sponsor, and had already secured funding for this intervention from government using their well-developed political alliances. Members of the planning group, who were invested within the primary prevention agenda, were forced to argue against the need for support for families raising children with FASD—which was not a very enviable position. The ethical dilemma faced by SUs and SPs who supported the prevention end of the continuum was unexpected and forced planning group members to be pitted against each other. One side wanted planning to educate youth regarding how to prevent FASD, and the other side presented lived experiences of how FASD families were in need of respite care in order to cope with the demands of raising a family member with FASD. This case vignette tables two meaningful lessons: (1) the danger of cliques forming within the larger group who ultimately exercise considerable influence on other stakeholders and decision-making processes, and (2) the danger of the push–pull nature of planning prevention initiatives in a resource-scarce community environment.

SUMMARY AND EVALUATION OF PLANNING STEP 7: DECIDE ON INTERVENTIONS AND SPONSORS

Summary of Planning Step 7: Decide on Interventions and Sponsors

This planning step culminates in a Web-based summary and recommendations from the joint SU/SP provider group. SUs and SPs are no longer working in a parallel process but have joined their work together in a recommendation for a priority intervention based on collective EID. In this planning step, they have also assessed what local organization would be the best choice to host the priority intervention. While the choice of agency sponsor is in itself a highly political planning activity, the use of EID collected through the planning process can offset this reality. SUs and SPs together in this planning step will carry out an assessment of the agency's legitimacy as host agency and work with the consultant to identify the most appropriate funding source. Their final concern will be to upload their recommendations on (1) the priority intervention model, (2) the chosen sponsoring agency, and (3) the chosen funding source to the Web-based reporting system so that all SUs and SPs will have equal opportunities to review and comment on the proposed intervention model, host agency, and funding source sponsor before the draft proposal is presented for review to external stakeholders in Planning Step 8.

Evaluation of Planning Step 7: Decide on Interventions and Sponsors

Evaluation Form: Circle one number only for each question listed below.

Action Step 7.1. SU/SP Define Intervention and Choose Sponsor

a. How confident were you about achieving this goal?	Not confident	Somewhat confident	Very confident	Extremely confident
	1	2	3	4

b. What was the most important thing you learned about this step?

Action Step 7.2. SU/SP Map External Environment of Chosen Sponsor

a. How confident were you about achieving this goal?	Not confident	Somewhat confident	Very confident	Extremely confident
	1	2	3	4

b. What was the most important thing you learned about this step?

Action Step 7.3. SU/SP Choose Appropriate Funding Source

a. How confident were you about achieving this goal?	Not confident	Somewhat confident	Very confident	Extremely confident
	1	2	3	4

b. What was the most important thing you learned about this step?

Your Total Score? _____

Group Discussion Notes:

(continue on back as needed)

REFERENCES

Barnes, M., & Shardlow, P. (1997). From passive recipient to active citizen: Participation in mental health user groups. *Journal of Mental Health, 6*(3), 289–300. doi:10.1080/09638239718824

Blackburn, H., Hanley, B., & Staley, K. (2010). *Turning the pyramid upside down: Examples of public involvement in social care research.* Eastleigh, UK: INVOLVE.

Campbell, P. (2001) The role of users in psychiatric services in service development—influence not power. *The Psychiatrist, 25*(3), 87–88. doi:10.1192/pb.25.3.87

Carnaby, S. (1997). A comparative approach to evaluating individual planning for people with learning disabilities: Challenging the assumptions. *Disability & Society, 12*(3), 381–394. doi:10.1080/09687599727236

Coney, S. (2004). *Effective consumer voice and participation for New Zealand: A systematic review of the evidence.* Wellington, NZ: New Zealand Guidelines Group.

Dunlop, J. M. (2002). Managerial perceptions of local collaboration: The Ontario Healthy Babies/ Healthy Children example. *Dissertations Abstracts International, 64*(09), 3478.

Dunlop, J. M., & Holosko, M. (2005). The story behind the story of collaborative networks: Relationships do matter! *Journal of Health and Social Policy, 19*(3), 1–17. doi:10.1300/J045v19n03_01

Hasenfeld, Y. (1992). Theoretical approaches to human service organizations. In Y. Hasenfeld (Ed.), *Human services as complex organizations* (pp. 33–57). Newbury Park, CA: Sage.

Hernandez, L., Robson, P., & Sampson, A. (2010). Towards integrated participation: Involving seldom heard users of social care services. *British Journal of Social Work, 40*(3), 714–736. doi:10.1093/bjsw/bcn118

Holosko, M., Leslie, D., & Cassano, D. R. (2001). How service users become empowered in human service organizations: The empowerment model. *International Journal of Health Care Quality Assurance, 14*(3), 126–132.

McLaughlin, H. (2009). What's in a name: "Client," "patient," "customer," "consumer," "expert by experience," "service user"—What's next? *British Journal of Social Work, 39*(6), 1101–1117. doi:10.1093/bjsw/bcm155

Peck, E., Gulliver, P., & Towell, D. (2002) Information, consultation or control: User involvement in mental health services in England at the turn of the century. *Journal of Mental Health, 11*(4), 441–451.

Reid, D. H., & Green, C. W. (2002). Person-centered planning with people who have severe multiple disabilities: Validated practices and misapplications. In S. Holburn & P. Vietze (Eds.), *Person-centered planning: Research, practice and future directions* (pp. 183–202) Baltimore, MD: P. H. Brookes.

Smith, M., Gallagher, M., Wosu, H., Stewart, J., Cree, V. E., Hunter, S., & Wilkinson, H. (2011). Engaging with involuntary service users in social work: Findings from a knowledge exchange project. *British Journal of Social Work, 42*(8), 1460–1477. doi:10.1093/bjsw/bcr162

Smull, M. W., & Lakin, K. C. (2002). Public policy and person-centered planning. In S. Holburn & P. Vietze (Eds.), *Person-centered planning: Research, practice and future directions* (pp. 379–398). Baltimore, MD: P. H. Brookes.

Summers, A. (2003) Involving users in the development of mental health services: A study of psychiatrists' views. *Journal of Mental Health, 12*(2), 161–174. doi:10.1080/0963823031000103470

Taylor, J., Jones, R. M., O'Reilly, P. O., Oldfield, W., & Blackburn, A. (2010). The Station Community Mental Health Centre Inc.: Nurturing and empowering. *Rural and Remote Health, 10*(3), 1411.

van der Ham, A. J., Shields, L. S., van der Horst, R., Broerse, J. W., & van Tulder, M. W. (2014). Facilitators and barriers to service user involvement in mental health guidelines: Lessons from the Netherlands. *Administration and Policy in Mental Health and Mental Health Services Research, 41*(6), 712–723. doi:10.1007/s10488-013-0521-5

Wallcraft, J. (2003) *On our own terms: Users and survivors of mental health services working together for support and change.* London: Sainsbury Centre for Mental Health.

Wehmeyer, M., & Ward, M. (1995). The spirit of the IDEA mandate: Student involvement in transition planning. *Journal for Vocational Special Needs Education, 17*(3), 108–111.

INTERNET REFERENCES

University of Kansas, Community Tool Box: Participatory Approaches to Planning Interventions. http://ctb.ku.edu/en/table-of-contents/analyze/where-to-start/design-community-interventions/main

This section of the Community Tool Box elaborates on the advantages and disadvantages of using a participatory planning approach to select community interventions. It outlines who should be involved in the participatory planning process and discusses what level of participation is necessary for deciding on community interventions that will meet the community's needs.

University of Kansas, Community Tool Box: Criteria for Choosing Promising Practices and Community Interventions. http://ctb.ku.edu/en/table-of-contents/analyze/choose-and-adapt-community-interventions/criteria-for-selecting/main

This Web site provides information on choosing what interventions are appropriate for your community and promotes adapting the intervention to the specific community need identified. General characteristics of successful interventions are presented and advice is provided to community groups to find or create interventions that successfully address the community need in the way that works for the local community.

Public Health Agency of Canada, Canadian Best Practices Portal: Population Health Approach: The Organizing Framework. http://cbpp-pcpe.phac-aspc.gc.ca/population-health-approach-organizing-framework/key-element-3-base-decisions-evidence/

This site addresses the question of how EI decision-making can be accomplished at all stages of program development. It proposes that there are a number of online inventories of effective interventions and suggests that decision makers should use these sources of EI interventions.

What Works for Health: Policies and Programs to Improve Wisconsin's Health. http://whatworksforhealth.wisc.edu/

An interactive Web site provides choices of health factors and strategies to impact health outcomes in a variety of topic areas. The Web site provides communities with information to help select and implement EI interventions. For each intervention strategy, the Web site provides (1) an evidence rating, (2) expected outcomes, (3) implementation in Wisconsin and elsewhere, and (4) a link to helpful resources.

POWERPOINT RESOURCES

Chapter 7

Planning Step 7

Decide on Intervention and Sponsors

Why is this planning step important?

- It generates and strengthens the relationship between funders and SUs, leading to SUs increasing their presence, voice, and ability to make funding decisions.
- It delineates tasks and generates strategies for seeking, obtaining, and sustaining funding.
- It strengthens the relationship between funders and SUs, and so increases transparency.

What does the literature say?

- Research has shown that SUs have been successful when placed in community expert roles providing detailed information about how the client actually experiences the community problem.
- In fact, researchers and practitioners do not necessarily have to serve as liaisons with funders when SUs and funders collaborate.
- Barriers to SU decision-making on services include SP resistance and lack of government commitment.

Planning Step 7. Decide on Intervention and Sponsors

Activity Sheet 7.1.a. SU/SP Intervention Model Description

BRIEF DESCRIPTION OF INTERVENTION	PRIMARY OBJECTIVE	ACTIVITIES	OUTCOME INDICATORS	MEASUREMENT INSTRUMENTS	STAFF AND VOLUNTEER ROLES

Planning Step 7. Decide on Intervention and Sponsors

Activity Sheet 7.1.b. SU/SP Intervention Model and Sponsor Matching

NAME OF AGENCY	INTERVENTION MODEL AND AGENCY FIT	AGENCY ACCEPTANCE BY THE COMMUNITY	AGENCY ABILITY TO MEET THE IDENTIFIED GAP OR NEED	AGENCY EI EFFECTIVENESS DATA

Planning Step 7. Decide on Intervention and Sponsors

Activity Sheet 7.2.a. SU/SP External Environment Map

SU/SP REVIEW OF SPONSOR RELATIONSHIPS	RECIPIENTS AND CONSUMERS	PROVIDERS OF COMPLEMENTARY SERVICES	PROVIDERS OF FISCAL RESOURCES	PROVIDERS OF AUTHORITY AND LEGITIMATION	COMPETING ORGANIZATIONS

Planning Step 7. Decide on Intervention and Sponsors

Activity Sheet 7.3.a. SU/SP Potential Funding Opportunities Chart

NAME OF FUNDER	TYPE OF FUNDER*	WEB SITE	DESCRIPTION	DUE DATE

*Federal Government, Provincial/State Government, Municipal Government, Private Foundations, or Corporate Sponsors

Planning Step 8
Develop Joint Proposal

OVERVIEW AND RATIONALE

Congratulations! You have participated in and completed an eight-step planning process, achieved outcomes as a result of it, and evaluated each step in the process. As indicated in the introduction, we framed this manualized approach to planning based on a CD empowerment model. That is, we assumed that since you collaboratively worked together in this venture, your group would bond and galvanize into not just SUs and SPs, but also into one community planning group. The culminating proposal you are submitting to the funding body is a message to both the funder and the local community that you are no longer separate subgroups but are now united in one local community planning initiative. If your proposal is successful (and we hope that it is), it will make for a better community of care, as it will strengthen service delivery in your community through needs identification. This final step however, is a manageable but tall task, and we recommend that you find some community members to help who have experience in budgeting, proposal writing, and/or service delivery. As you read the details of proposal preparation in this chapter, you will learn that there are specialized skillsets needed to achieve success with this venture. The following describes what we refer to as the joint proposal that is your last planning step in this process.

Proposal writing may appear at first to be an arduous, daunting, and scary process. With effective planning and preparations, however, it becomes more manageable and less scary. To effectively write a proposal it is important to understand several key components associated with the process. These include (1) What is proposal writing and how is it different from academic writing? (2) Where and how can we search for Requests for Proposals (RFPs)? and (3) What are some do's and don'ts of proposal writing?

What is proposal writing? Generally defined, proposal writing is the process of completing an application request for a project funded through an institution such as the federal government, a public or a private corporation, or a foundation. While funding proposals are available through various sources, they all have a similar framework, which often includes the reason for the project, the project activities that are to be accomplished, the funding needed, strategies that will be used to evaluate the project, and any external organizational and/or community supports (Reese, 2005).

It is important to note that proposal writing is "an activity that is geared toward the future, oriented toward service, focused on a single project, written to persuade the reader using a personal and lay tone, team focused, and brief" (Walden & Bryan, 2010, p. 86). Likewise, Chung and Shauver (2008) and Parker (2007) defined proposal writing as the process of using shorter sentences, simpler phrases, bulleted points, and concrete, direct, and concise terms to inform a reviewer about the importance and significance of the proposed project. Proposal writing could be seen as "an essay contest with a budget" (Reese, 2005, p. 26). To compare proposal writing and academic writing, see figure 8.1.

Figure 8.1. Academic Writing vs. Proposal Writing: Contrasting Perspectives

ACADEMIC WRITING	PROPOSAL WRITING
Scholarly Pursuit	**Sponsor Goals**
Individual passion	*Service attitude*
Past Oriented	**Future Oriented**
Work that has been done	*Work that should be done*
Theme Centered	**Project Centered**
Theory and thesis	*Objectives and activities*
Expository Rhetoric	**Persuasive Rhetoric**
Explaining to the reader	*Selling to the reader*
Impersonal Tone	**Personal Tone**
Objective and dispassionate	*Conveys excitement*
Individualistic	**Team Focused**
Primarily a solo activity	*Feedback needed*
Few Length Constraints	**Strict Length Constraints**
Verbosity rewarded	*Brevity rewarded*
Specialized Terminology	**Accessible Language**
Insider jargon	*Easily understood*

Note. Adapted from Parker (2007).

Where to look for Requests for Proposals (RFPs)? There are various state, federal, and private funding agencies that have readily accessible proposal information. Boylan (2013, p. 26) described four common types of grants that are available: general operating support, program support, project support, and capital support.

1. General Operating Support: A grant given to an organization to use as it determines within the scope of its mission. A general operating (or gen op) grant is like an unrestricted gift from a donor. It is the best kind of funding to get, but it is also becoming the least common type of grant awarded.

2. Program Support: A grant given to continue or expand a specific set of activities done by the organization. Demonstrated effectiveness is key to a successful request (e.g., a grant for the summer reading program, with data to show that it helps children retain their reading skills during the summer months).

3. Project Support: A grant given to initiate a new activity or achieve a specific, time-limited goal. An example might be a grant to develop a curriculum for digital literacy, which includes staff training, a new laptop, and a digital projector and screen.

4. Capital Support: A grant given to build a new facility or improve an existing facility via redesign, furnishings, or structural/technology upgrades. These grants can be given to the project as a whole, or to an identifiable area. An example is a grant for the refurbishing for a specific library branch, or to create a new library area specifically for computer use.

After deciding the type of support that is needed, the next step is to find a funding source for the project. Reese (2005) points to three—although there are many more—popular sites that provide detailed grant information, which often includes grant contact information, deadlines, budgetary limits, and other details. These three U.S. sites are grants.gov (www.grants.gov), the Catalog of Federal Domestic Assistance (www.cfda.gov), and the Foundation Center (www.foundationcenter.org).

As indicated, these sites are targeted predominately to organizations within the United States. Finding the appropriate funding site was exemplified and made explicit in chapter 7.

Like most writing projects, proposal writing has certain rules—the do's and don'ts—that must be strictly followed. Failure to do so will surely result in the proposal being rejected. Below are a few do's and don'ts that should be considered when planning to submit a funding proposal.

1. Do read, reread, and have others reread the RFP. The RFP provides prospective grantees with specific contact information for the RFP, timelines for proposal submissions, whether or not to submit prework requirements such as a letter of intent (LOI) or to participate in selected workshops and/or Webinars, and most importantly to identify if there is a fit between the RFP and the agency's mission, vision, goals, and needs. As noted by Stokes (2012), proposals can be rejected simply because they did not follow all of the instructions given, or because they did not include the **key words** and phrases that tied the proposal to the needs of the organization. For instance, one example of a reason for a rejected funding proposal is simply nonadherence to pagination. As pointed out by Chung and Shauver (2008), 20 percent of funding proposals submitted to the National Institutes of Health had formatting errors, for which instructions were clearly outlined in the RFP.

2. Do be brief, yet very specific. After reading the RFP, it is important that proposal writers use direct, nonjargon language to relay their purpose to funders. Porter (2011) highlighted the fact that seasoned reviewers read multiple funding proposals; they often decide whether or not they want to fund a program based on the first page, and rarely change their mind as they read the rest of the proposal. Rejections occur as a result of great ideas that are unclear and/or unfocused, or proposals that are too broad in scope (Chung & Shauver, 2008).

3. Do be catchy, not cute. Proposal writing is completely different from academic writing, as indicated in figure 8.1. Therefore, it is important that proposal writing grabs and engages the reviewer's interest early. In other words, it is essentially an elegant sales pitch that must be used to catch the reader's attention. Porter (2011) provided three simple steps that can help with creating such a task: (1) Set the stage and lay out the problem (this is known as the "who cares" section). (2) State the theme (your proposed solution). (3) Create a vision that includes potential ways that your project or program will change the current situation, and/or bring about change (present the reader with the "so what" will happen if you fund me, and how this will serve the population).

4. Do plan ahead. A thoroughly and clearly articulated funding proposal can take about three to twelve months to craft and execute (Chung & Shauver, 2008). Most RFPs provide approximately forty-five days from opening until they are due, however. It is important to have preliminary information regard-

ing the populations served, the purpose for the proposal, and identified staff members to execute the grant. While staff do not have to be in place, it is important to have a plan for recruiting staff to fill the position(s) needed to fulfill the terms of the grant. In the planning phase, it is important to think about the long- and short-term goals of the program, with a small emphasis on whether or not the grant can be carried out if it is partially funded (Blanco & Lee, 2012). Finally, by planning ahead proposal writers provide themselves with adequate time to step away from proposal writing, and then return in four days to reread the proposal as a way of checking for errors and clarity (Blanco & Lee, 2012; Reese, 2005). While each funder will have its own format for proposal submission, all funding proposals have similar requirements for submission. The main elements are identified in the proposal checklist shown in figure 8.2 and include proposal components such as (1) proposal summary, (2) introduction of the sponsoring organization, (3) needs assessment data, (4) goals and objectives of the project proposed, (5) methodology, (6) evaluation design, (7) future funding plan for sustainability, (8) budget for the proposed project, and (9) appendices. These appendices will be specific to each funding organization; an itemized list would be provided by the funder, and may include components such as (1) certificate of incorporation and by-laws, (2) financial statements, (3) support letters or endorsements, and (4) resumes of key personnel.

Figure 8.2. Funding Proposal Checklist

This funding proposal checklist will help guide you in preparing and double-checking your proposal. As you write your proposal, go back to this checklist from time to time to make sure you are right on track. Check Yes, No, or N/A (not applicable).

PROPOSAL SUMMARY			
Clearly and concisely summarizes your project and request for funding	YES	NO	N/A
Background of your organization			
Your general objectives, especially if these are connected to your target grant-making agency's own objectives			
Brief summary of past projects and achievements (if applicable)			
Project overview			
Reasons for the grant request and target amount			
Specific objectives			
Details of the project activities to help achieve objectives			
Other factors that will show project is worthy of the grant			
Is your proposal summary brief, clear, and interesting enough to catch attention?			
INTRODUCTION OF THE SPONSORING ORGANIZATION			
Describes your organization and its qualifications for funding	YES	NO	N/A
Description of your organization's mission, accomplishments, and programs			

Description of members and clients			
Background on the management team and staff			
Past achievements of your organization			
Brief description of the area that will benefit your project			
Is your introduction brief and interesting?			
NEEDS ASSESSMENT DATA	**YES**	**NO**	**N/A**
Purposes and goals of the organization			
Statistical facts and figures			
Possible support and endorsement by credible agencies			
What benefits are there for members or beneficiaries?			
Are your assessments realistic and attainable?			
GOALS AND OBJECTIVES OF THE PROJECT PROPOSED			
Describes the outcome of the grant in measurable terms	**YES**	**NO**	**N/A**
Objectives describing the outcome of the grant program			
Goals should be related to the need and the target beneficiaries			
Backgrounder on the area that will benefit from the grant			
Target time table when objectives will be met			
Are your objectives specific and measurable?			
METHODOLOGY			
Describes the list of project activities	**YES**	**NO**	**N/A**
Activities related to problems and objectives			
Description of program activities			
List of activities			
List of people involved in the activities and their responsibilities			
Time table for each activity			
EVALUATION DESIGN			
Prepares measures on how objectives and methods will be evaluated	**YES**	**NO**	**N/A**
Procedures on how to evaluate the objectives			
Policies on how to modify methods used			
Personnel involved in the evaluation process			
Details of evaluation criteria			
Description of how data will be gathered and analyzed			
Instruments or questionnaires to be used			
Details on how evaluation will be used for program improvement			
FUTURE FUNDING PLAN FOR SUSTAINABILITY			
Presents future funding from other sources to implement the grant	**YES**	**NO**	**N/A**
List of other sources of funds and the amount of funds from each source			
Where will you get future funding to support the project if it is continued?			

Details on how other funds will be obtained, if necessary, to implement plan			
Note: Include a letter of commitment from funding source, if applicable			
BUDGET FOR THE PROPOSED PROJECT			
Clearly delineates costs of the project to be met by the funding source	YES	NO	N/A
Did you follow general accounting principles?			
Is your budget realistic and reflects the work plan?			
Is it specific, realistic, and detailed?			
Is it sufficient to cover the cost of the project as described in the narrative?			
Note: Do not forget to include computation of all figures and your assumptions of each cost.			
APPENDICES	YES	NO	N/A
Verification of tax-exempt status (IRS determination letter)			
Certificate of incorporation and by-laws			
List of officers and board of directors			
Financial statements for last completed fiscal year (audited, referred)			
Current general operating budget and special project budget (if applicable)			
List of clients served (if applicable)			
List of other current funding sources and uses			
Biographies of key personnel or resumes (if requested)			
Support letters or endorsements			
Commitment letters from project/program consultants or subcontractors (if applicable)			
Diagrams for equipment or schematics for building requests (if applicable)			

5. Do some preliminary research. Knowing your community, your audience, and your funder is of utmost importance. For example, if a foundation or grant calls for math and science, submitting a proposal for arts and craft is indicative that the proposal writer did not do his or her research, did not read the RFP, or expected to be the exception to the rule regarding the funding proposal (Flavin, 2014; Gitlin & Lyons, 2013). Proposals are forward thinking, and are indicative of the fact that proposal writers and SPs have an understanding regarding how long-term needs could bring about change. Truly knowing your community needs, like the ones you have described up until this point, provides solid evidence to reviewers regarding the community and how the project plans on servicing those needs (Keshavan, 2013). Additionally, researching other grants may also be beneficial in helping with the proposal-writing process. As novice or experienced proposal writers, reviewing grants that are funded provides information regarding items that reviewers are expecting in quality, and/or funded grants (Ludlow, 2014).

6. Do think and work collaboratively. Most agencies will provide variations of the service that the proposal writer is presenting, have access to the target population that the funding proposal is proposing to reach, or have other important assets (i.e., staff, experience) that may be beneficial to the grant. For example, Cambronero et al. (2012) underscored the fact that collaborating with others helps to create a think-tank of promising practices that may yield differing angles to viewing a problem, clarification of information, and an opportunity to build trust and relationships among organizations. Ultimately, this process helps to maximize the effectiveness of the proposal and shows community input. This is the precise rationale for this SU/SP planning manual, as we mentioned in the introduction.

7. Do establish a relationship with funders early in the planning process. Many funders have expectations that they will meet planning group members before and after the proposal submission. Creating a relationship between the planning group members and the funders helps to manage the proposal submission process, and builds relationships of trust and support that can be effective in funding proposal approval. Relationships with funders are often the deciding factor in receiving grants.

8. Do not oversell a service or product. Proposal reviewers are knowledgeable, yet skeptical about proposal requests that oversell the identified product or service. Reviewers evaluate multiple funding proposals in very limited time frames (Ludlow, 2014); therefore proposals that overpromise with limited resources impact a proposal score and/or review more negatively than positively.

9. Do not wait until the last minute to start writing. As stated earlier, to effectively complete a funding proposal from start to finish may range anywhere between three to twelve months (Chung & Shauver, 2008). Starting late will impact the clarity of the proposal and could result in errors in the proposal, could result in misunderstanding of the proposal, and could waste valuable resources. Most if not all funding proposals are time-consuming, and at times may require specific information that can take some time to get (i.e., letters of memorandum, letters of stakeholder support, etc.) (Boylan, 2013; Chung & Shauver, 2008; Ludlow, 2014)

10. Do not apply for RFPs that do not meet your clearly defined mission or vision. The fastest way to get a proposal rejected is to apply for RFPs that do not meet a granting agency's mission or vision. Flavin (2014) emphasized that applying for RFPs that do not meet the mission or vision of either party will most likely result in that proposal not being funded and may send the message that this proposal writer either did not read the RFP, is unclear of their agency's mission, or wanted to fit a proposal in where it should not be. Ludlow (2014) also explained that funding agencies are "focused on their priorities and what types of projects they want to fund" (p. 33); therefore, it is important to make sure that the plans of the agency are in line with the funding agency.

While proposal writing can be a scary process, it is not impossible. As pointed out by Reese (2005) it takes time, commitment, and knowledge about what works. Likewise, proposal writing is a process. And in the case of the eclipsed SU/SP group, this is the final step of the eight-stage planning process that has been going on for approximately six to twelve months already. The first few funding proposals may not get funded; however, they will provide the experience required to write others that will be funded in the future. It is important to remember that proposal writing, like any other skill, takes practice, patience, expertise, and time. Therefore, with continued practice succeeding at having your proposals awarded is possible.

DESCRIPTION OF PLANNING ACTIVITIES FOR PLANNING STEP 8: DEVELOP JOINT PROPOSAL

This planning step contains three action steps. Remember that any of the three action steps might use more than one activity sheet. Upon completion of each of these three action steps for Planning Step 8, please complete the appropriate evaluation form found at the end of the chapter to evaluate each action step. Evaluation is an important completion part of the overall planning process.

Action Step 8.1. SU/SP Develop Work Plan for Joint Proposal
Action Step 8.2. SU/SP Prepare Draft Proposal & Budget Summaries
Action Step 8.3. SU/SP Approve and Submit Final Proposal and Budget

Action Step 8.1 (SU/SP Develop Work Plan for Joint Proposal) describes the activities to be undertaken in this action step to develop the proposal and budget. From the first planning task of the work plan to review the funder's RFP to ensure a good fit for the priority intervention model, to the last planning task to prepare the proposal and budget, a clear pathway for action is established through Activity Sheet 8.1.a (SU/SP Work Plan for Joint Proposal).

Action Step 8.2 (SU/SP Prepare Draft Proposal & Budget Summaries) organizes the SU/SP approval process for both the joint proposal and the budget by using checklists that identify (1) proposal and budget components, (2) the specific responsibility of the SU/SP joint planning group and its consultants to submit the required components, and (3) documents that the SU/SP planning group has approved the submissions. In Action Step 8.2, the SU/SP planning group and its consultants are required to prepare a summary proposal and budget to be shared with external stakeholders in the next action step.

Action Step 8.3 (SU/SP Approve and Submit Final Proposal and Budget) contains planning activity sheets that document stakeholder feedback on the proposal and budget. Following the stakeholder meeting, the SU/SP planning group, with the advice of its consultants, jointly reviews the stakeholder feedback and decides whether they will incorporate the recommended changes. Action Step 8.3 finalizes the approved components for the joint proposal and budget and leads to the preparation of the final joint proposal and budget.

Action Step 8.1. SU/SP Develop Work Plan for Joint Proposal

a. List of Activity Sheet(s): SU/SP Develop Work Plan for Joint Proposal

Action Step	Activity Sheet(s)
8.1. SU/SP Develop Work Plan for Joint Proposal	8.1.a. SU/SP Work Plan for Joint Proposal
	8.1.b. SU/SP Proposal Responsibility Checklist
	8.1.c. SU/SP Develop Proposal Table of Contents

b. Introduction: SU/SP Develop Work Plan for Joint Proposal

Activity Sheet 8.1.a sets out clearly the roadmap that SUs and SPs and consultants will travel as they work their way toward their final joint proposal and budget submission. In this participatory planning model, proposal development is enhanced by the dialogue and decision-making that has already occurred throughout the planning process. The interaction among SUs and SPs and their consultants is critical to this empowerment model of planning where all knowledge and experience is valued and respected. That being said, it is clear that the consultants bring technical skills that the SUs and SPs may be missing. The consultants' expertise helps to facilitate the participatory process of proposal development. It is important to note that the choosing of consultants is also a shared responsibility between SUs and SPs with planning group members agreeing on the consultant who will be engaged in the SU/SP planning process. Action Step 8.1 further requires the SU/SP planning group to review the chosen funder's RFP, to see what is needed in the proposal, or to create their own table of contents for proposal components. Finally, in Action Step 8.1, the work plan offers clarity to the joint planning process through its well-defined and sequential planning activities to guide the SU/SP joint planning group and its chosen consultants.

c. Description: SU/SP Develop Work Plan for Joint Proposal

All of the planning activities for the work plan for joint proposal development in Action Step 8.1 are shown in the time lines for completion for the fifteen planning activities. Activity Sheet 8.1.a sets out clearly the pathway and responsibilities that SUs, SPs, and their consultants will have as they prepare the final proposal and budget. The clearly identified responsibilities identified in Activity Sheet 8.1.b (SU/SP Proposal Responsibility Checklist) help to ensure that the proposal and budget will be completed in time for the funder's critical submission dates. This work plan monitors the completion of activities by either the SU/SP planning group and/or the group's consultants, and identifies the dates that sections of the proposal have been completed. It is essentially a summary of the status of the proposal at specific points in time to ensure that all sections of the proposal will be completed in time for review and approval by the SU/SP planning group.

Action Step 8.1 further requires the SU/SP planning group to review the chosen funder's RFP to see what is needed in the proposal, or for the group to create its own table of contents for proposal submission. Action Step 8.1 requires the planning group to assign responsibility for joint proposal development and utilizes Activity Sheet 8.1.b to identify responsibility for proposal component completion and date of completion by either the SU/SP planning group or the consultants. In Activity Sheet 8.1.c (SU/SP Develop Proposal Table of Contents), the SU/SP planning group creates a table of contents that includes the following: (1) proposal summary, (2) introduction of the organization, (3) assessment of needs, (4) goals and objectives of the project, (5) methodology (program activities), (6) evaluation, (7) future funding, (8) budget, and (9) appendices. The table of contents outlined in Activity Sheet 8.1.c is a general template for proposal development; it should be noted, however, that funders may have a specific form for their proposal submission and the SU/SP planning group will utilize whatever proposal components are suggested by their identified funding source.

Action Step 8.2. SU/SP Prepare Draft Proposal and Budget Summaries

a. List of Activity Sheet(s): SU/SP Prepare Draft Proposal and Budget Summaries

Action Step	Activity Sheet(s)
8.2. SU/SP Prepare Draft Proposal and Budget Summaries	8.2.a. SU/SP Checklist of Proposal Submissions and Approvals 8.2.b. SU/SP Checklist of Budget Submissions and Approvals

b. Introduction: SU/SP Prepare Draft Proposal and Budget Summaries

Action Step 8.2 addresses specifically what proposal components have been completed in previous planning steps and what components are the responsibility of the SU/SP planning group and/or the group's consultants. Action Step 8.2 further identifies the responsibility of the budget consultant to prepare a budget summary using identified budget line items and to bring this forward for approval by the SU/SP planning group. Using the activity sheets designed for Action Step 8.2 allows the SU/SP planning group to manage the proposal development and budget development process in a structured and strategic way to ensure completion by the required date.

c. Description: SU/SP Prepare Draft Proposal and Budget Summaries

Activity Sheet 8.2.a (SU/SP Checklist of Proposal Submissions and Approvals) is used to identify the following proposal components: (1) proposal summary, (2) introduction to the host agency, (3) needs assessment data, (4) GIS map, (5) asset map, (6) goals/objectives, (7) literature review, (8) intervention model description, (9) intervention model evaluation, (10) future funding, (11) budget, (12) cover letter, and (13) appendices. In Action Step 8.2 the proposal checklist identifies clearly what sections of the proposal need to be completed and approved before the SU/SP planning group and its consultants can prepare summaries. Activity Sheet 8.2.a is a summary of the status of proposal components that have been reviewed and approved by the SU/SP planning group. This checklist allows the SU/SP planning group to monitor the timely submission and approval of proposal components to ensure that there is sufficient time for proposal development and submission. Since all components prepared by the SU/SP planning group and its consultants must be reviewed and approved, this checklist provides a visual monitoring system to ensure timely completion before the required deadline for submission to the funder.

Similarly, Activity Sheet 8.2.b (SU/SP Checklist of Budget Submissions and Approvals) is used to identify the following budget items: (1) personnel, (2) benefits, (3) travel, (4) equipment, (5) supplies, (6) contractual, (7) office space, and (8) other. In Action Step 8.2 the budget checklist identifies what sections of the budget need to be completed and approved before the SU/SP planning group and its consultants can complete the summaries of the proposal and budget. A sample budget plan for funding proposals is shown in figure 8.3.

The review of the summary proposal and budget is carried out by the SU/SP planning group with the assistance from the group's consultants, but the approval of both documents is the exclusive decision-making responsibility of the SUs and SPs.

Figure 8.3. Sample Budget Plan for Proposals

Budget Category	Amount of Request	In-Kind Donations	Project Total
(1) Personnel			
(2) Benefits			
(3) Travel			
(4) Equipment			
(5) Supplies			
(6) Contractual			
(7) Office Space			
(8) Other			

TOTAL EXPENSES

Source. Adapted from Yuen & Terao (2003).

Action Step 8.3. SU/SP Approve and Submit Final Joint Proposal and Budget

a. List of Activity Sheet(s): SU/SP Approve and Submit Final Joint Proposal and Budget

Action Step	Activity Sheet(s)
8.3. SU/SP Approve and Submit Final Joint Proposal and Budget	8.3.a. SU/SP Summary of Draft Proposal
	8.3.b. SU/SP Summary of Draft Budget
	8.3.c. Stakeholder Feedback Sheet: SU/SP Review of Draft Proposal by Component
	8.3.d. Stakeholder Feedback Sheet: SU/SP Review of Draft Budget by Section
	8.3.e. Checklist of Recommended Proposal Changes Approved by SU/SP Group
	8.3.f. Checklist of Recommended Budget Changes Approved by SU/SP Group
	8.3.g. SU/SP Approved Components for Joint Proposal

b. Introduction: SU/SP Approve and Submit Final Joint Proposal and Budget

Action Step 8.3 employs a number of activity sheets to assist the planning group and consultants to prepare their final joint proposal and budget. The SU/SP planning process has been designed to include external stakeholder feedback to engage and enrich community engagement in support of the funding proposal. Before the stakeholder meeting the SU/SP planning group and their consultants will have decided what should be included in the summary proposal and summary budget, and will have developed tables of contents for both the proposal summary and the draft budget. Additionally, the planning group will have developed stakeholder feedback sheets on both the proposal and budget, and a checklist of recommended changes to the proposal and budget that the group will review and potentially approve following the stakeholder meeting before finalizing the final joint proposal and budget.

c. Description: SU/SP Approve and Submit Final Joint Proposal and Budget

Before the stakeholder meeting the SU/SP planning group and consultants need to decide what should be included in the summary proposal and budget, and what will be shared. Activity Sheet 8.3.a (SU/SP Summary of Draft Proposal) contains the table of contents for the summary proposal: (1) list of appendices, (2) proposal summary, (3) brief introduction of sponsoring organization, (4) summary of needs assessment/asset map, (5) summary of goals, objectives, program activities, (6) overview of evaluation design, and (7) summary of sustainability plan and future funding. In a separate document (Activity Sheet 8.3.b), the table of contents for the budget summary contains the following items: (1) brief introduction to the draft budget preparation, (2) identification of draft budget categories, (3) draft budget and justifications, (4) draft budget worksheet, and (5) consultant recommendations on draft budget.

In order to document recommendations from the stakeholder meeting, the SU/SP planning group needs to utilize two stakeholder feedback sheets: (1) Activity Sheet 8.3.c and (2) Activity Sheet 8.3.d. Activity Sheet 8.3.c contains the following items: (1) proposal component, (2) stakeholder name, and (3) stakeholder draft proposal review comments. Activity Sheet 8.3.d contains the following items: (1) budget category, (2) stakeholder name, and (3) stakeholder draft budget review comments.

Following the stakeholder meeting, the SU/SP planning group, with the advice of the consultants, jointly reviews the stakeholder feedback sheets on the proposal and the budget. When reviewing the proposed proposal, the SU/SP planning group and consultants will utilize Activity Sheet 8.3.e. This activity sheet itemizes each proposal component and each recommended change to the proposal component; it also documents the SU/SP approval of recommended changes. Similarly, when reviewing the proposed budget, the planning group, with the advice of its consultants, jointly reviews the stakeholder feedback sheets on the proposed budget.

When reviewing the proposed budget, the planning group and consultants will utilize Activity Sheet 8.3.f. This activity sheet itemizes each budget category, and each recommended change to the proposed budget; it also documents the SU/SP approval of recommended changes. A detailed budget justification that provides specific information for each of the budget categories will be included with the budget to provide detailed information about expenditures for the final joint proposal to be submitted. Action Step 8.3 finalizes the approved components for the joint proposal and budget and leads to the preparation of the table of contents for the proposal, which includes (1) proposal summary, (2) introduction of the host organization, (3) assessment of needs, (4) goals, objectives of project, (5) methodology, (6) evaluation, (7) future funding, (8) budget, and (9) appendices (Activity Sheet 8.3.g). Action Step 8.3 culminates with the submission of the proposal, budget, and cover letter to the identified funding agency.

CASE VIGNETTE: IT'S NOT ALL ABOUT THE PAPER TRAIL

Given the importance of providing resources to local communities, it is somewhat perplexing that organizations forget the people factor in many funding opportunities. The community in this case was an example of how it is not all about "just filling out the funding proposal." The group in this vignette pored over large, comprehensive data sets, such as census data, social indicator data, crime statistics, and health status data in order to complete a fifteen-page application for funding for a housing initiative for new immigrants. The planning group was primarily made up of local ministers and clergy whose members were involved in supporting recent immigrants including their families. When they heard through the media that the government had issued an RFP to address housing needs of immigrant families, they immediately developed a coalition of faith-based organizations and members to begin their proposal development. In this coalition there were a number of members who had been involved previously in projects (although not specifically housing projects) that had received funding, so they were initially very confident that their proposal would have a favorable review. Here is where the story gets a bit more interesting.

After much hard work assessing massive amounts of data, researching the extant literature on immigrant housing, and preparing their proposal, they suddenly noticed that the RFP required letters of support from all other local agencies that provided housing and immigrant support services. It was hard to imagine that they had not contacted these agencies and asked for their participation at the beginning of their funding proposal application process. This lack of stakeholder engagement at the onset of the proposal process did not go unnoticed when their application was submitted without the requested and required letters of support. The government program manager responsible for the RFP had been contacted by another local community group in the same geographic region, and had consulted with them as they prepared their proposal that was complete with support letters from local community stakeholders, including a few local faith-based organizations.

In the end, the proposal reviewers viewed the inclusiveness of the coalition that included housing and immigrant services and other community stakeholders favorably: it not only contained the required letters of support, but also demonstrated that community engagement and commitment influences all funding sources, both public and private. The primary lesson in this vignette is that all funding sources have designated managers who oversee the funding process, and who are available for consultation on the proposal submission. Heeding the advice of these program managers regarding proposal requirements such as letters of support is necessary. Furthermore, heeding their advice about community inclusiveness is mandatory.

SUMMARY AND EVALUATION OF PLANNING STEP 8: DEVELOP JOINT PROPOSAL

Summary of Planning Step 8: Develop Joint Proposal

The final planning stage culminates the entire previous planning process of Planning Steps 1 to 8. After spending this interactive time in a parallel planning process targeted to both a community's assets and identified need, the issue of resourcing the intervention/program/service now requires formal joint proposal development. To achieve these action steps, the previously separate SU/SP groups now gather into a joint planning group that equally represents each subgroup. Early on in the planning process, the SUs and SPs recognized the need to hire consultants for specific tasks within the planning process. They now engage with those consultants in reviewing sections of the proposal and budget in order to achieve their goal of joint SU/SP proposal development and submission. In addition, they offer stakeholders opportunities to comment on the draft funding proposal and budget, and incorporate these comments into their approval process for the final proposal and budget submission to their identified funding agency.

Evaluation of Planning Step 8: Develop Joint Proposal

Evaluation Form: Circle one number only for each question listed below.

Action Step 8.1. SU/SP Develop Work Plan for Joint Proposal

a. How confident were you about achieving this goal?	Not confident	Somewhat confident	Very confident	Extremely confident
	1	2	3	4

b. What was the most important thing you learned about this step?

Action Step 8.2. SU/SP Prepare Draft Proposal & Budget Summaries

a. How confident were you about achieving this goal?	Not confident	Somewhat confident	Very confident	Extremely confident
	1	2	3	4

b. What was the most important thing you learned about this step?

Action Step 8.3. SU/SP Approve and Submit Final Proposal and Budget

a. How confident were you about achieving this goal?	Not confident	Somewhat confident	Very confident	Extremely confident
	1	2	3	4

b. What was the most important thing you learned about this step?

Your Total Score? _____

Group Discussion Notes:

(continue on back as needed)

POSTSCRIPT: SUNSETTING THE SU/SP PLANNING GROUP

When the SU/SP planning group chose a sponsor for the proposed intervention and submitted the funding proposal, the planning group will formally end with a mechanism called sunsetting, which allows planning group members to put their planning group to rest after months of working together. There are circumstances when some members of the planning group may be asked to sit on an advisory committee to the program within the sponsoring organization, but this is optional. The SU/SP planning group members were recruited and engaged in the planning process due to their importance as stakeholders within a specific social problem or target population in need in the local community. Once these stakeholders have completed the SU/SP planning process, have submitted their program proposal, and have hopefully attained funding for the recommended intervention, their responsibility is officially over. If the local community identifies another social problem or target population that is of importance, then a new group of stakeholders would be recruited for that specific planning initiative. The eight-step planning process model outlined in this manual is not designed to build a permanent planning infrastructure for local communities, but rather to target social problems and target populations of need in order to advocate for services in that particular problem and geographic area. It will be important for SU/SP planning group members to finalize their process by reviewing the evaluation data completed during each planning step, and to celebrate their work together on the specific social problem in their local community.

REFERENCES

Blanco, M. A., & Lee, M. Y. (2012). Twelve tips for writing educational research grant proposals. *Medical Teacher, 34*(6), 450–453. doi:10.3109/0142159X.2012.668246

Boylan, W. (2013). Why and when to turn to grant seeking: And a little bit of how. *Public Libraries, 52,* 26–28.

Cambronero, J. G., Allen, L. H., Cathcart, M. K., Jestement, L. B., Kovacs, E. J., McLeish, K. R., & Nauseef, W. M. (2012). Writing a first grant proposal. *Nature Immunology, 13*(2), 105–108. doi:10.1038/ni.2183

Chung, K. C., & Shauver, M. J. (2008). Fundamental principles of writing a successful grant proposal. *Journal Hand Surgery of America, 33*(4), 566–572. doi:10.1016/j.jhsa.2007.11.028

Flavin, R. (2014). Tips for writing a winning grant proposal. *Techdirections, 74*(1), 18–19.

Gitlin, L., & Lyons, K. (2013). *Successful grant writing: Strategies for health and human service professionals.* New York: Springer Publications.

Keshavan, M. S. (2013). How to write a grant and get it funded. *Asian Journal of Psychiatry, 6*(1), 78–79. doi:10.1016/j.ajp.2013.01.005

Ludlow, B. L. (2014). Secrets of successful grant writing to support rural special education programs. *Rural Special Education Quarterly, 33*(2), 29–37.

Parker, R. (2007). Why academics have a hard time writing good grant proposals. *Journal of Research Administration, 38*(2), 37–43.

Porter, R. (2011). Crafting a sales pitch for your grant proposal. *Research Management Review, 18*(2), 79–84.

Reese, S. (2005). Grant writing 101: Finding the funding for a great project often begins with the writing of a successful grant proposal. *Techniques, 80*(4), 24–27.

Stokes, K. (2012). Writing clear statements of needs and goals for grant proposals. *American Medical Writers Association Journal, 27,* 25–28.

Walden, P. R., & Bryan, V. C. (2010). Tenured and non-tenured college of education faculty motivators and barriers in grant writing: A public university in the south. *Journal of Research Administration, 41*(3), 85–98.

Yuen, F. K., & Terao, K. L. (2003). *Practical grant writing and program evaluation*: Pacific Grove, CA: Brooks/Cole.

INTERNET REFERENCES

Grant Writers Online: Components of a Grant Proposal. http://www.grantwritersonline.com

This site provides an explanation of each component of a grant proposal. The recommended project proposal components include (1) a brief overview of the grant seeker, (2) contact information, (3) overview of the project with reasons for funding assistance, (4) amount of grant money being requested, (5) brief summary of grant seeker's past projects, and (6) grant general objectives.

Grant Proposal Writing: Catalogue of Federal Government Assistance. http://researchguides.library.wisc.edu/proposalwriting/

This site offers assistance in two components. First, information is provided on developing a grant proposal; second, information is provided on writing a grant proposal. The site outlines clearly the expectations for applying for U.S. federal grants.

The Grantmanship Centre. https://www.tgci.com/

This site offers information and tools to write successful grant proposals. The site offers three articles: (1) Getting the Grant 101: The Essentials; (2) Where's the Money? Finding the Right Funding; and (3) Managing Your Grant: Nuts, Bolts, and Coffee. The site also offers a free resource entitled "Funding State-by-State" that provides information on top grant-making foundations, community foundations, and corporate giving programs.

Guide for Writing a Funding Proposal: Michigan State University. http://www.learnerassociates.net/proposal/

This site was created to help people be successful in gaining funds for projects. The site provides writing hints on a number of proposal sections and provides examples of each section. There is also an entire proposal example offered on the site, a selection of books on proposal writing, and links to other proposal writing resources.

POWERPOINT RESOURCES

Chapter 8
Planning Step 8

Develop Joint
Proposal

Why is this planning important?

- It helps community groups to establish their priorities and to effectively write a funding proposal that clearly defines:
    - The reason for project, project activities, funding needed, strategies used for evaluation, and any external organizational and/or community supports.
- It creates a roadmap for the funder of how the proposed program will change the current situation and make it better for people who live in the local community.

What does the literature say?

- There are four common types of grant support:
    - General operating support, program support, project support, and capital support.
- Do's of funding proposal writing
    - Read, reread, and have others reread; be brief but specific; be catchy, not cute; plan ahead; do preliminary research; think and work collaboratively.
- Don'ts of proposal writing
    - Oversell a service or product; wait until the last minute; apply for grants that don't meet your mission or vision.

Planning Step 8. Develop Joint Proposal

Activity Sheet 8.1.a. SU/SP Work Plan for Joint Proposal

Activity	Sep	Oct	Nov	Dec	Responsibility
(1) SU/SP Group: Review RFP from funder to insure relevance to your project.	▓				
(2) SU/SP Group: Contact program manager of funding agency to discuss your proposal and its suitability to the RFP.	▓				
(3) SU/SP Group: Review the preliminary needs assessment report.	▓				
(4) SU/SP Group: Identify responsibility for proposal sections and time lines for completion using Activity Sheet 8.1.b.	▓				
(5) SU/SP Group: Assign responsibility for drafting budget to consultants.	▓				
(6) SU/SP Group: Assign responsibility for drafting specific intervention model chart to consultants.	▓				
(7) SU/SP Group: Assign responsibility for drafting evaluation section to consultants.	▓				
(8) SU/SP Group: Using proposal components from Activity Sheet 8.1.b, identify which sections have been completed.	▓				
(9) SU/SP Group: Using proposal components from Activity Sheet 8.1.b, identify sections that have not been completed.	▓				
(10) SU/SP Group: Identify responsibility for incomplete sections and set time lines for completion.					
(11) SU/SP Group: Compile draft proposal/budget for review by stakeholders.		▓▓			
(12) SU/SP Group: Conduct stakeholder meeting and document stakeholder comments on draft proposal/budget.			▓		
(13) SU/SP Group: Discuss feedback from stakeholder meeting and decide on revision to draft proposal/budget.			▓		
(14) SU/SP Group: With consultant input, prepare final grant and budget for submission to funder.				▓	
(15) SU/SP Group: With inclusion of host agency, prepare cover letter for proposal and budget submission.				▓	

Planning Step 8. Develop Joint Proposal

Activity Sheet 8.1.b. SU/SP Proposal Responsibility Checklist

PROPOSAL COMPONENT	SERVICE USER/ PROVIDER GROUP	CONSULTANTS	DATE COMPLETED
Proposal summary	X		
Introduction to the host agency	X		
Needs assessment data	X	X	
GIS map		X	
Asset map	X		
Goals/objectives	X		
Literature review		X	
Intervention model description		X	
Intervention model evaluation		X	
Future funding	X		
Budget		X	
Cover Letter	X		
Appendices	X	X	

Planning Step 8. Develop Joint Proposal

Activity Sheet 8.1.c. SU/SP Develop Proposal Table of Contents

Table of Contents

1. Proposal Summary
2. Introduction of the Organization
3. Assessment of Need/s
4. Goals and Objectives of the Project
5. Methodology (Program Activities)
6. Evaluation
7. Future Funding
8. Budget
9. Appendices

Planning Step 8. Develop Joint Proposal

Activity Sheet 8.2.a. SU/SP Checklist of Proposal Submissions and Approvals

PROPOSAL COMPONENT	SERVICE USER/ PROVIDER GROUP	CONSULTANTS	SU/SP DATE APPROVED
Proposal Summary	X		
Introduction to the Host Agency	X		
Needs Assessment Data	X	X	
GIS Map		X	
Asset Map	X		
Goals/Objectives	X		
Literature Review		X	
Intervention Model Description		X	
Intervention Model Evaluation		X	
Future Funding	X		
Budget		X	
Cover Letter	X		
Appendices	X	X	

Planning Step 8. Develop Joint Proposal

Activity Sheet 8.2.b. SU/SP Checklist of Budget Submissions and Approvals

BUDGET ITEMS	SERVICE USER/ PROVIDER GROUP	CONSULTANTS	SU/SP DATE APPROVED
1. Personnel		X	
2. Benefits		X	
3. Travel		X	
4. Equipment		X	
5. Supplies		X	
6. Contractual		X	
7. Office Space		X	
8. Other		X	

Planning Step 8. Develop Joint Proposal

Activity Sheet 8.3.a. SU/SP Summary of Draft Proposal

Table of Contents: Proposal Summary

1. List of Appendices
2. Proposal Summary
3. Brief Introduction of Sponsoring Organization
4. Summary of Needs Assessment/Asset Map
5. Summary of Goals, Objectives, Program Activities
6. Overview of Evaluation Design
7. Summary of Sustainability Plan and Future Funding

Planning Step 8. Develop Joint Proposal

Activity Sheet 8.3.b. SU/SP Summary of Draft Budget

Table of Contents: Budget Summary

1. Brief Introduction to the Draft Budget Preparation
2. Identification of Draft Budget Categories
3. Draft Budget and Justifications
4. Draft Budget Worksheet
5. Consultant Recommendations on Draft Budget

Planning Step 8. Develop Joint Proposal

Activity Sheet 8.3.c. Stakeholder Feedback Sheet: SU/SP Review of Draft Proposal by Component

PROPOSAL COMPONENT	STAKEHOLDER NAME	STAKEHOLDER DRAFT PROPOSAL REVIEW COMMENTS
1. Proposal Summary		
2. Introduction to Host Agency		
3. Needs Assessment		
4. Goals/Objectives		
5. Methodology		
6. Evaluation		
7. Future Funding		
8. Appendices		

Planning Step 8. Develop Joint Proposal

Activity Sheet 8.3.d. Stakeholder Feedback Sheet: SU/SP Review of
Draft Budget by Section

BUDGET CATEGORY	STAKEHOLDER NAME	STAKEHOLDER DRAFT BUDGET REVIEW COMMENTS
1. Personnel		
2. Benefits		
3. Travel		
4. Equipment		
5. Supplies		
6. Contractual/Consultants		
7. Office Space		
8. Other		

Planning Step 8. Develop Joint Proposal

Activity Sheet 8.3.e. Checklist of Recommended Proposal Changes Approved by SU/SP Group

PROPOSAL COMPONENT	RECOMMENDED CHANGES	SU/SP GROUP APPROVAL
1. Proposal Summary		
2. Introduction to Host Agency		
3. Needs Assessment		
4. Goals/Objectives		
5. Methodology		
6. Evaluation		
7. Future Funding		
8. Budget	N/A	N/A
9. Appendices		

Planning Step 8. Develop Joint Proposal

Activity Sheet 8.3.f. Checklist of Recommended Budget Changes Approved by
SU/SP Group

BUDGET CATEGORY	RECOMMENDED CHANGES	SU/SP GROUP APPROVAL
1. Personnel		
2. Benefits		
3. Travel		
4. Equipment		
5. Supplies		
6. Contractual		
7. Office Space		
8. Other		

Planning Step 8. Develop Joint Proposal

Activity Sheet 8.3.g. SU/SP Approved Components for Joint Proposal

Table of Contents: Joint Proposal

1. Proposal Summary: Overview of project
2. Introduction of the Host Organization: Description of organization programs
3. Assessment of Needs: Report on data collection
4. Goals, Objectives of Project: Outcome of grant—measurable
5. Methodology: Description of program activities
6. Evaluation: Details of evaluation design
7. Future Funding: Sustainability plan for the future
8. Budget: Budget activity sheet showing costs of project
9. Appendices: Documents relevant to the grant proposal requested or voluntarily supplied

Supplementary Readings

Ager, W., Dow, J., & Gee, M. (2005). Grassroots networks: A model for promoting the influence of service users and carers in social work education. *Social Work Education, 24*(4), 467–476. doi:10.1080/02615470500097033

Agnew, A., & Duffy, J. (2010). Innovative approaches to involving service users in palliative care social work education. *Social Work Education, 29*(7), 744–759. doi:10.1080/02615471003657976

Allain, L., Brown, H. C., Danso, C., Dillon, J., Finnegan, P., Gadhoke, S., & Whittaker, F. (2006). User and carer involvement in social work education. A university case study: Manipulation or citizen control? *Social Work Education, 25*(4), 403–413. doi:10.1080/02615470600593790

Andreassen, T. (2008). Asymmetric mutuality: User involvement as a government-voluntary sector relationship in Norway. *Nonprofit and Voluntary Sector Quarterly, 37*(2), 281–299. doi:10.1177/0899764007310417

Arthur, A., Ryland, L. T., & Amundsen, K. (2012). The user perspective in performance auditing: A case study of Norway. *American Journal of Evaluation, 33*(1), 44–59. doi:10.1177/1098214011408283

Attree, P., Morris, S., Payne, S., Vaughn, S., & Hinder, S. (2010). Exploring the influence of service user involvement on health and social care services for cancer. *Health Expectations, 14*, 48–58.

Baines, D., Cunningham, I., & Fraser, H. (2011). Constrained by managerialism: Caring as participation in the voluntary social services. *Economic and Industrial Democracy, 32*(2), 329–352. doi:10.1177/0143831X10377808

Barker, J., & Thomson, L. (2014). Helpful relationships with service users: Linking social capital. *Australian Social Work, 68*(1), 130–145. doi:10.1080/0312407X.2014.905795

Barnes, M., & Cotterell, P. (Eds.). (2012). *Critical perspectives on user involvement.* Bristol, UK: Policy Press.

Bennett, S., & Sanderson, H. (2009). *Working together for change: Using person-centred information for commissioning.* UK: Department of Health.

Bennison, G. (2014). Engaging communities and service users: Context, themes and methods. *British Journal of Social Work, 44*(2), 473–474. doi:10.1093/bjsw/bcu008

Beresford, P. (2000). Service users' knowledges and social work theory: Conflict or collaboration? *British Journal of Social Work, 30*(4), 489–503.

Beresford, P. (2001a). Service users. *British Journal of Social Work, 31*(4), 629–630. doi:10.1093/bjsw/31.4.629

Beresford, P. (2001b). Service users, social policy and the future of welfare. *Critical Social Policy, 21*(4), 494–512. doi:10.1177/026101830102100404

Beresford, P. (2003). User involvement in research: Exploring the challenges. *Nursing Times Research, 8*(1), 36–46. doi:10.1177/136140960300800106

Beresford, P. (2006). Making the connections with direct experience: From the western front to user-controlled research. *Educational Action Research, 14*(2), 161–169. doi:10.1080/09650790600717987

Beresford, P. (2009). Control. In J. Wallcraft, B. Schrank, & M. Amering (Eds.), *Handbook of service user involvement in mental health research* (pp. 181–198). Chichester, UK: Wiley Blackwell.

Beresford, P., & Andrews, E. (2012). *Caring for our future: What service users say.* Joseph Rowntree Foundation.

Beresford, P., & Boxall, K. (2012). Service users, social work education and knowledge for social work practice. *Social Work Education: The International Journal, 31*(2), 155–167. doi:10.1080/02615479.2012.644944

Beresford, P., & Croft, S. (2001). Service users' knowledges and the social construction of social work. *Journal of Social Work, 1*(3), 295–316. doi:10.1177/146801730100100304

Beresford, P., & Croft, S. (2004). Service users and practitioners reunited: The key component for social work reform. *British Journal of Social Work, 34*(1), 53–68. doi:10.1093/bjsw/bch005

Beresford, P., & Croft, S. (2008). Democratising social work: A key element of innovation: From "client" as object, to service user as producer. *Innovation Journal, 13*(1), 3–24.

Beresford, P., Croft, S., & Adshead, L. (2008). "We don't see her as a social worker": A service user case study of the importance of the social worker's relationship and humanity. *British Journal of Social Work, 38*(7), 1388–1407. doi:10.1093/bjsw/bcm043

Beresford, P., & Hoban, M. (2005). *Participation in anti-poverty and regeneration work and research.* Joseph Rowntree Foundation.

Bornarova, S. (2009). User involvement in social work education: Macedonian perspective. *Ljetopis Socijalnog Rada, 16*(2), 279–298.

Botes, L., & van Rensburg, D. (2000). Community participation in development: Nine plagues and twelve commandments. *Community Development Journal, 35*(1), 41–68.

Bowl, R. (1996). Legislating for user involvement in the United Kingdom: Mental health services and the NHS and community care act 1990. *International Journal of Social Psychiatry, 42*(3), 165–180. doi:10.1177/002076409604200301

Branfield, F., & Beresford, P. (2006). *Making user involvement work: Supporting service user networking and knowledge.* Joseph Rowntree Foundation.

Brett, J., Staniszewska, S., Mockford, C., Herron-Marx, S., Hughes, J., Tysall, C., & Suleman, R. (2014). Mapping the impact of patient and public involvement on health and social care research: A systematic review. *Health Expectations, 17*(5), 637–650.

Brkic, M., & Jugovic, A. (2009). Experience of service user involvement in the education of social workers in Serbia. *Ljetopis Socijalnog Rada, 16*(2), 469–481.

Broer, T., Nieboer, A. P., & Bal, R. (2014). Mutual powerlessness in client participation practices in mental health care. *Health Expectations, 17*(2), 208–219.

Brown, K., & Young, N. (2008). Building capacity for service user and carer involvement in social work education. *Social Work Education, 27*(1), 84–96. doi:10.1080/02615470701381491

Burns, D., Heywood, F., Taylor, M., Wilde, P., & Wilson, M. (2004). *Making community participation meaningful: A handbook for development and assessment.* Bristol, UK: The Policy Press.

Callahan, R., & Gilbert, G. (2005). End-user satisfaction and design features of public agencies. *The American Review of Public Administration, 35*(1), 57–73. doi:10.1177/0275074004272620

Carey, M. (2010). Should I stay or should I go? Practical, ethical and political challenges to "service user" participation within social work research. *Qualitative Social Work, 10*(2), 224–243. doi:10.1177/1473325010362000

Carr, S. (2004). *SCIE Position Paper 3: Has service user participation made a difference to social care services?* Social Care Institute for Excellence.

Cook, T. (2012). Where participatory approaches meet pragmatism in funded (health) research: The challenge of finding meaningful spaces. *Forum: Qualitative Social Research, 13*(1), 1–23.

Cooper, H., & Spencer-Davis, E. (2006). Involving service users in inter-professional education narrowing the gap between theory and practice. *Journal of Interprofessional Care, 20*(6), 603–617.

Cornwall, A. (2008). Unpacking "Participation": Models, meanings and practices. *Community Development Journal, 43*(3), 269–283. doi:10.1093/cdj/bsn010

Cossar, J., & Neil, E. (2015). Service user involvement in social work research: Learning from an adoption research project. *British Journal of Social Work, 48*(1), 225–240. doi:10.1093/bjsw/bct1

Cotterell, P. (2008). Exploring the value of service user involvement in data analysis: "Our interpretation is about what lies below the surface." *Educational Action Research, 16*(1), 5–17. doi:10.1080/09650790701833063

Cowden, S., & Singh, G. (2007). The "user": Friend, foe or fetish? A critical exploration of user involvement in health and social care. *Critical Social Policy, 27*(1), 5–23. doi:10.1177/0261018307072205

Croft, S., & Beresford, P. (1989). User-involvement, citizenship and social policy. *Critical Social Policy, 9*(26), 5–18. doi:10.1177/026101838900902601

Croft, S., & Beresford, P. (1992). The politics of participation. *Critical Social Policy, 12*(35), 20–44. doi:10.1177/026101839201203502

D'Amour, D., Ferrada–Videla, M., San Martin Rodriguez, L., & Beaulieu, M. (2005). The conceptual basis for interprofessional collaboration: Core concepts and theoretical frameworks. *Journal of Interprofessional Care, 19*(1), 116–131. doi:10.1080/13561820500082529

Elliott, T., Frazer, T., Garrard, D., Hickinbotham, J., Horton, V., Mann, J., &Whiteford, A. (2005). Practice learning and assessment on BSc (hons) social work: "Service user conversations." *Social Work Education, 24*(4), 451–466. doi:10.1080/02615470500097009

Elstad, T. A., & Kristiansen, K. (2009). Mental health centres as "meeting-places" in the community: Exploring experiences of being service users and participants. *Scandinavian Journal of Disability Research, 11*(3), 195–205. doi:10.1080/15017410802622928

Eversole, R. (2012). Remaking participation: Challenges for community development practice. *Community Development Journal, 47*(1), 29–41. doi:10.1093/cdj/bsq033

Faulkner, A. (2009). Principles and motives for service user involvement in mental health research. In J. Wallcraft, B. Schrank, & M. Amering (Eds.), *The handbook of service user involvement in mental health research* (pp. 13–24). Chichester, UK: Wiley–Blackwell.

Felton, A., & Stickley, T. (2004). Pedagogy, power and service user involvement. *Journal of Psychiatric and Mental Health Nursing, 11*(1), 89–98. doi:10.1111/j.1365–2850.2004.00693.x

Ftanou, M. (2014). Evaluating the better access initiative: What do consumers have to say? *Australian Social Work, 67*(2), 162–178.

Giannakopoulou, C., Fakoya, A., Aina, C., & Campbell, T. (2006). User involvement in the provision of HIV services: Some lessons learned from a user group in an HIV treatment centre in London. *Journal of the Royal Society for the Promotion of Health, 126*(4), 178–182. doi:10.1177/1466424006066285

Glasby, J., & Beresford, P. (2006). Who knows best? Evidence-based practice and the service user contribution. *Critical Social Policy, 26*(1), 268–284. doi:10.1177/0261018306059775

Gordon, S. (2005). The role of the consumer in the leadership and management of mental health services. *Journal of Australasian Psychiatry, 13*(4), 362–365. doi:10.1111/j.1440-1665.2005.02215.x

Grant, J. (2007). The participation of mental health service users in Ontario, Canada: A Canadian application of the consumer participation questionnaire. *International Journal of Social Psychiatry, 53*(2), 148–158. doi:10.1177/0020764006074557

Gray, B. (2004). Strong opposition: Frame based resistance to collaboration. *Journal of Community and Applied Social Psychology, 14*(3), 166–176.

Green, L., & Wilks, T. (2009). Involving service users in a problem based model of teaching and learning. *Social Work Education, 28*(2), 190–203. doi:10.1080/02615470802112985

Greene, S. (2005). Including young mothers: Community based participation and the continuum of active citizenship. *Community Development Journal, 42*(2), 167–180.

Hague, J., & Mullender, A. (2006). Who listens? The voices of domestic violence survivors in service provision in the United Kingdom. *Violence Against Women, 12*(6), 568–587. doi:10.1177/1077801206289132

Hardina, D. (2014). The use of dialogue in community organization practice: Using theory values and skills to guide group decision-making. *Journal of Community Practice, 22*, 365–384.

Havlíková, J., & Hubíková, O. (2011). Implementation of active user principle: Learning from the Czech social services reform. *Journal of Social Service Research, 37*(2), 180–196. doi:10.1080/01488376.2011.547735

Heffernan, K. (2009). Responding to global shifts in social work through the language of service user and service user involvement. *International Journal of Social Welfare, 18*, 375–384. doi:10.1111/j.1468-2397.2008.00614.x

Hitchen, S., Watkins, M., Williamson, G. R., Ambury, S., Bemrose, G., Cook, D., & Taylor, M. (2011). Lone voices have an emotional content: Focusing on mental health service user and carer involvement. *International Journal of Health Care Quality Assurance, 24*(2), 164–177. doi:10.1108/09526861111105112

Hodge, S. (2005). Participation, discourse and power: A case study in service user involvement. *Critical Social Policy, 25*(2), 164–179. doi:10.1177/0261018305051324

Hopton, J. (1994). User involvement in the education of mental health nurses. An evaluation of possibilities. *Critical Social Policy, 14*(42), 47–60. doi:10.1177/026101839401404204

Hsieh, C. (2014). Beyond multiplication: Incorporating importance into client satisfaction measures. *Research on Social Work Practice, 24*(4), 470–476. doi:10.1177/1049731513511668

Humphreys, C. (2005). Service user involvement in social work education: A case example. *Social Work Education, 24*(7), 797–803. doi:10.1080/02615470500238710

Jones, N., Lyytikainen, M., Mukherjee, M., & Gopinath Reddy, M. (2007). Decentralization and participatory service delivery: Implications for tackling childhood poverty in Andhra Pradesh, India. *Journal of Children and Poverty, 13*(2), 207–229. doi:10.1080/10796120701520382

Kidd, M. (2011). A firsthand account of service user groups in the United Kingdom: An evaluation of their purpose, effectiveness, and place within the recovery movement. *Journal of Groups in Addiction & Recovery, 6*(1–2), 164–175. doi:10.1080/1556035X.2011.570562

King, A. (2011). Service user involvement in methadone maintenance programmes: The "philosophy, the ideal and the reality." *Drugs: Education, Prevention and Policy, 18*(4), 276–284. doi:10.3109/09687637.2010.495098

Kleintjes, S., Lund, C., Swartz, L., Flisher, A., & The MHAPP Research Programme Consortium. (2010). Mental health care user participation in mental health policy development and implementation in South Africa. *International Review of Psychiatry, 22*(6), 568–577. doi:10.3109/09540261.2010.536153

Kroner, D. G. (2012). Service user involvement in risk assessment and management: The transition inventory. *Criminal Behaviour and Mental Health, 22*(2), 136–147. doi:10.1002/cbm.1825

Langton, H., Barnes, M., Haslehurst, S., Rimmer, J., & Turton, P. (2003). Collaboration, user involvement and education: A systematic review of the literature and report of an educational initiative. *European Journal of Oncology Nursing, 7*(4), 242–252.

Law, J., Bunning, K., Byng, S., Farrelly, S., & Heyman, B. (2005). Making sense in primary care: Leveling the playing field for people with communication difficulties. *Disability & Society, 20*(2), 169–184. doi:10.1080/09687590500059267

Leathard, A. (2005). Evaluating inter-agency working in health and social care: Politics, policies and outcomes for service users. In D. Taylor & S. Balloch (Eds.), *The politics of evaluation: Participation and policy implementation* (pp. 135–149). Bristol, UK: The Policy Press.

Leppo, A., & Perälä, R. (2009). User involvement in Finland: The hybrid of control and emancipation. *Journal of Health Organization and Management, 23*(3), 359–371. doi:10.1108/14777260910966771

Leung, T. T. F. (2011). Client participation in managing social work service: An unfinished quest. *Social Work, 56*(1), 43–52. doi:10.1093/sw/56.1.43

Lloyd, M., & Carson, A. (2011). Making compassion count: Equal recognition and authentic involvement in mental health care. *International Journal of Consumer Studies, 35*(6), 616–621. doi:10.1111/j.1470-6431.2011.01018.x

Lombe, M., & Sherraden, M. (2008). Inclusion in the policy process: An agenda for participation of the marginalized. *Journal of Policy Practice, 7*(2–3), 199–213.

Loughran, H., & McCann, M. E. (2015). Employing community participative research methods to advance service user collaboration in social work research. *British Journal of Social Work, 45*(2), 705–723. doi:10.1093/bjsw/bct133

Martin, G. P. (2008). Representativeness, legitimacy and power in public involvement in health-service management. *Social Science & Medicine, 67*(11), 1757–1765. doi:10.1016/j.socscimed.2008.09.024

McKeown, M., Malihi–Shoja, L., Hogarth, R., Jones, F., Holt, K., Sullivan, P., & Mather, M. (2012). The value of involvement from the perspective of service users and carers engaged in practitioner education: Not just a cash nexus. *Nurse Education Today, 32*(2), 178–184. doi:10.1016/j.nedt.2011.07.012

McLaughlin, H. (2007). Ethical issues in the involvement of young service users in research. *Ethics and Social Welfare, 1*(2), 176–193. doi:10.1080/17496530701450364

McLaughlin, H. (2010). Keeping service user involvement in research honest. *British Journal of Social Work, 40*(5), 1591–1608. doi:10.1093/bjsw/bcp064

Milewa, T. (1997). User participation in service planning: A qualitative approach to gauging the impact of managerial attitudes. *Journal of Management in Medicine, 11*(4), 238–245. doi:10.1108/02689239710177350

Minogue, V., Boness, J., Brown, A., & Girdlestone, J. (2005). The impact of service user involvement in research. *International Journal of Health Care Quality Assurance, 18*(2), 103–112. doi:10.1108/09526860510588133

Minogue, V., & Girdlestone, J. (2010). Building capacity for service user and carer involvement in research: The implications and impact of best research for best health. *International Journal of Health Care Quality Assurance, 23*(4), 422–435. doi:10.1108/09526861011037470

Molyneux, J., & Irvine, J. (2004). Service user and carer involvement in social work training: A long and winding road? *Social Work Education, 23*(3), 293–308. doi:10.1080/0261547042000224047

Morgan-Trimmer, S. (2013). "It's who you know": Community empowerment through network brokers. *Community Development Journal, 49*(3), 458–472.

Morrison, C., & Dearden, A. (2014). Beyond tokenistic participation: Using representational artifacts to enable meaningful public participation in health service design. *Health Policy, 112*(3), 179–186. doi:10.1016/j.healthpol.2013.05.008

Moss, B., Boath, L., Buckley, S., & Colgan, A. (2009). The fount of all knowledge: Training required to involve service users and carers in health and social care education and training. *Social Work Education, 28*(5), 562–572. doi:10.1080/02615470802406510

Nathan, S., Harris, E., Kemp, L., & Harris–Roxas, B. (2006). Health service staff attitudes to community representatives on committees. *Journal of Health Organization and Management, 20*(6), 551–559. doi:10.1108/14777260610702299

Nathan, S., Johnston, L., & Braithwaite, J. (2011). The role of community representatives on health service committees: Staff expectations vs. reality. *Health Expectations, 14*(3), 272–284. doi:10.1111/j.1369–7625.2010.00628.x

Nilsen, E., Myrhaug, H., Johansen, M., Oliver, S., & Oxman, A. (2006). Methods of consumer involvement in developing health care policy and research, clinical practice guidelines and patient information material. *Cochrane Database of Systematic Review* (3). doi:10.1002/14651858.CD004563.pub2

Nolan, M., Hanson, E., Grant, G., Keady, J., & Lennart, M. (2007). "Introduction: What counts as knowledge, whose knowledge counts? Towards authentic participatory enquiry." In M. Nolan, E. Hanson, G. Grant, & J. Keady (Eds.), *User participation in health and social care research: Voices, values and evaluation* (pp. 1–13). Berkshire, UK: McGraw Hill Education.

Nordgren, L. (2008). The performativity of the service management discourse. "Value creating customers" in health care. *Journal of Health Organization and Management, 22*(5), 510–528. doi:10.1108/14777260810898723

Oliver, S., Rees, R., Clark-Jones, L., Milne, R., Oakley, A., Gabby, J., . . . Gyte, G. (2008). A multi-dimensional conceptual framework for analyzing public involvement in health services research. *Health Expectations, 11*(2), 72–84. doi:10.1111/j.1369–7625.2007.00476.x

Owens, C., Farrand, P., Darvill, R., Emmens, T., Hewis, E., & Aitken, P. (2011). Involving service users in intervention design: A participatory approach to developing a text-messaging intervention to reduce repetition of self-harm. *Health Expectations, 14*(3) 285–295. doi:10.111/j.1369-7625.2010.00623.x

Pagliari, C. (2007). Design and evaluation in eHealth: Challenges and implications for an interdisciplinary field. *Journal of Medical Internet Research, 9*(2). doi:10.2196/jmir.9.2.e15

Patterson, S., Weaver, T., & Crawford, M. (2010). Drug service user groups: Only a partial solution to the problem of developing user involvement. *Drugs: Education, Prevention, and Policy, 17*(1), 84–97. doi:10.3109/09687630802225495

Patterson, S., Weaver, T., Agath, K., Rutter, D., Albert, E., & Crawford, M. J. (2009). User involvement in efforts to improve the quality of drug misuse services in England: A national survey. *Drugs: Education, Prevention, and Policy, 16*(4), 364–377. doi:10.1080/09687630802061544

Petersen, K., Hounsgaard, L., Borg, T., & Nielsen, C. V. (2012). User involvement in mental health rehabilitation: A struggle for self-determination and recognition. *Scandinavian Journal of Occupational Therapy, 19*, 59–67. doi:10.3109/11038128

Purtell, R. A., & Wyatt, K. M. (2011). Measuring something real and useful in consumer involvement in health and social care research. *International Journal of Consumer Studies, 35*(6), 605–608. doi:10.1111/j.1470–6431.2011.01016

Putti, M. H., & Brady, B. (2011). From tea and sympathy to optimal matching of need: Developing a shared vision for a community-based family support service. *Child Care in Practice, 17*(3), 271–284. doi:10.1080/13575279.2011.581650

Pyle, N. R., Arthur, N., & Hurlock, D. (2009). Service user positioning in interprofessional practice. *Journal of Interprofessional Care, 23*(5), 531–533. doi:10/1080/13561820802565551

Read, S., & Maslin-Prothero, S. (2011). The involvement of users and carers in health and social research: The realities of inclusion and engagement. *Qualitative Health Research, 21*(5), 704–713. doi:10.1177/1049732310391273

Rhodes, P., Nocon, A., Booth, M., Chowdrey, M. Y., Fabian, A., Lambert, N., . . . Walgrove, T. (2002). A service user's research advisory group from the perspectives of both service users and researchers. *Health and Social Care in the Community, 10*(5), 402–409.

Rise, M. B., Solbjør, M., Lara, M. C., Westerlund, H., Grimstad, H., & Steinsbekk, A. (2013). Same description, different values. How service users and providers define patient and public involvement in health care. *Health Expectations, 16*(3), 266–276. doi:10.1111/j.1369-7625.2011.00713.x

Rose, D., Fleischmann, P., & Schofield, P. (2010). Perceptions of user involvement: A user-led study. *International Journal of Social Psychiatry, 56*(4), 389–401. doi:10.1177/0020764009106618

Ross, J. D., Copas, A., Stephenson, J., Fellows, L., & Gilleran, G. (2005). Public involvement in modernising genitourinary medicine clinics: Using general public and patient opinion to influence models of service delivery. *Sexually Transmitted Infections, 82*(6), 484–488. doi:10.1136/sti.2006.020750

Roulstone, A., & Hudson, V. (2007). Carer participation in England, Wales and Northern Ireland: A challenge for interprofessional working. *Journal of Interprofessional Care, 21*(3), 303–317. doi:10.1080/13561820701327822

Rummery, K. (2009). Healthy partnerships, healthy citizens? An international review of partnerships in health and social care and patient/user outcomes. *Social Science & Medicine, 69*(12), 1797–1804. doi:10.1016/j.socscimed.2009.09.004

Scott, J. B. (2008). The practice of usability: Teaching user engagement through service-learning. *Technical Communication Quarterly, 17*(4), 381–412. doi:10.1080/10572250802324929

Scottish Government. (2014). *A project to support more effective involvement of service users in adult support and protection activity.* Edinburgh.

Seden, J. (2008). Innovation still needed? Service user participation in social care services and practice-led management. *Innovation Journal, 13*(1), 53–61.

Seim, S., & Slettebø, T. (2011). Collective participation in child protection services: Partnership or tokenism? *European Journal of Social Work, 14*(4), 497–512. doi:10.1080/13691457.2010.500477

Serapioni, M., & Duxbury, N. (2014). Citizens' participation in the Italian health care system: The experience of mixed advisory committees. *Health Expectations, 17*(4), 488–499. doi:10.222/j.1369–7625.2012.00885.x

Simmons, R., & Birchall, J. (2007). Tenant participation and social housing in the UK: Applying a theoretical model. *Housing Studies, 22*(4), 573–595. doi:10.1080/02673030701408535

Simmons, R., Birchall, J., & Prout, A. (2011). User involvement in public services: "Choice about voice." *Public Policy and Administration, 27*(1), 3–29. doi:10.1177/0952076710384903

Simons, L., Tee, S., Lathlean, J., Burgess, A., Herbert, L., & Gibson, C. (2007). A socially inclusive approach to user participation in higher education. *Journal of Advanced Nursing, 58*(3), 246–255. doi:10.1111/j.1365-2648.2007.04216.x

Skokandić, S., & Urbanc, K. (2009). Participation of service users in social work education: Teachers' perspective. *Ljetopis Socijalnog Rada, 16*(2), 327–354.

Smith, E., Ross, F. M., Mackenzie, A., & Masterson, A. (2005). Developing a service-user framework to shape priorities for nursing and midwifery research. *Journal of Research in Nursing, 10*(1), 107–118. doi:10.1177/136140960501000101

Speed, E. (2006). Patients, consumers and survivors: A case study of mental health service user discourses. *Social Science & Medicine, 62*(1), 28–38. doi:10.1016/j.socscimed.2005.05.025

Staley, K., & Minogue, V. (2006). User involvement leads to more ethically sound research. *Clinical Ethics, 1*(2), 95–100.

Storm, M., Hausken, K., & Knudsen, K. (2011). In-patient service providers' perspectives on service user involvement in Norwegian community mental health centres. *International Journal of Social Psychiatry, 57*(6), 551–563. doi:10.1177/0020764010371270

Storm, M., Knudsen, K., Davidson, L., Hausken, K., & Johannessen, J. O. (2011). "Service user involvement in practice": The evaluation of an intervention program for service providers and in-patients in Norwegian community mental health centers. *Psychosis, 3*(1), 29–40. doi:10.1080/17522439.2010.501521

Treloar, C., Rance, J., Madden, A., & Liebelt, L. (2011). Evaluation of consumer participation demonstration projects in five Australian drug user treatment facilities: The impact of individual versus organizational stability in determining project progress. *Substance Use & Misuse, 46*(8), 969–979. doi:10.3109/10826084.2010.540289

Tritter, J. Q., & McCallum, A. (2006). The snakes and ladders of user involvement: Moving beyond Arnstein. *Health Policy, 76*(2), 156–168. doi:10.1016/j.healthpol.2005.05.008

Tunstall, R. (2001). Devolution and user participation in public services: How they work and what they do. *Urban Studies, 38*(13), 2495–2514. doi:10.1080/00420980120094632

Tyler, G. (2006). Addressing barriers to participation: Service user involvement in social work training. *Social Work Education, 25*(4), 385–392. doi:10.1080/02615470600593394

Warren, L., & Boxall, K. (2009). Service users in and out of the academy: Collusion in exclusion? *Social Work Education, 28*(3), 281–297. doi:10.1080/02615470802659464

Webb, S. (2008). Modeling service user participation in social care. *Journal of Social Work, 8*(3), 269–290. doi:10.1177/1468017808091040

Whiteford, M. (2011). Square pegs, round holes: Rough sleeping and service user involvement. *Practice: Social Work in Action, 23*(1), 45–58. doi:10.1080/09503153.2010.532547

Wilson, C., Llewellyn, P., & Moskowitz, H. (2011). Editorial. Measuring consumer involvement in health and social care: Dividing fact from fiction. *International Journal of Consumer Studies, 35*(6), 603–604. doi:10.1111/j.1470-6431.2011.01039.x

Wilson, G., & Daly, M. (2007). Shaping the future of mental health policy and legislation in Northern Ireland: The impact of service user and professional social work discourses. *British Journal of Social Work, 37*(3), 423–439. doi:10.1093/bjsw/bcm021

Yates, P. (2010). Guest editorial: Time to change consumer involvement in nursing research. *Journal of Cancer Nursing, 33*(3), 171–172.

Zubritsky, C., Mullahy, M., Allen, M., & Alfano, E. (2006). The state of the Olmsted decision and the impact of consumer participation in planning. *American Journal of Psychiatric Rehabilitation, 9*(2), 131–143. doi:10.1080/15487760600876345

Selected Abbreviations and Acronyms

CD: community development

CDPM: community development planning model

CEPD: community empowerment and program development

COE: code of ethics

HSO: human service organization

EI: evidence-informed

EID: evidence-informed data

EIP: evidence-informed practice

FASD: fetal alcohol spectrum disorder

GIS: geographical information system

LOI: letter of intent

MOU: memorandum of understanding

NGT: nominal group technique

PAR: participatory action research

RFP: request for proposal

SP: service provider

SU: service user

SUP: service user participation

SU/SP: service user/provider

SWOT: strengths, weaknesses, opportunities, and threats

Glossary: Commonly Used Terms for the CDPM

Action steps: Sequential steps that identify the process(es) that lead to intended learning outcomes. They must specify an action, be reasonable, be task-oriented, and provide clarification of the intended objectives.

Advanced generalist practice: A more inclusive paradigm of today's social work practice, building on the former generalist approach. In advanced generalist practice the practitioner uses a multisystem and multilevel framework and exercises increased specification and integration of theory research and methods to assessment and intervention in all practice situations.

Advocacy: Health and human service professional practice that assists clients in getting their voices heard and needs met by taking action to change negative conditions.

Availability sample: A method of sampling based on participants who are available and willing to participate in the study. This is a nonprobability-based sample.

Benchmark: A standard or point of reference against which program processes or outcomes can be compared. It is typically used in program evaluation studies.

Best practices: Interventions or programs that have been reviewed, researched, and promoted by independent sources, and determined to be effective in producing desired results.

Bottom-up planning approach: An approach that creates partnerships between community residents and professionals who offer technical expertise but share leadership of the planning process with community residents.

Budgeting: An estimate of income and expenditure for a set period of time.

Campbell Collaboration: A nonprofit organization in the United Kingdom that prepares, maintains, and promotes the accessibility of systematic reviews in areas such as health education, criminal justice, social policy, and social care. Randomized Clinical Trials (RCTs) are the gold standard for research studies used by Campbell.

Case series: A report on a series of participants with an outcome of interest, where no control or comparison group is being used.

Case study: An examination of a single individual, family, group, organization, community, or aspect of society using varying supportive evidence for that particular unit of analysis.

Client: The individual or family unit that receives services. The client is also known as the patient, consumer, service user, peer, resident, beneficiary, (service) recipient, customer, advocate, participant, or member. Social workers retain the use of the word client in their professional practice, although in health-care settings they are normally required to use the term *patient*.

Client outcomes: The short- and long-term benefits that people receive from services or interventions provided by human service organizations.

Close-ended questions: A question, or series of questions, that have answers that are definitive as in yes–no questions, or are part of a Likert scale (always, sometimes, never), or the like.

Cluster sampling: The selection of groups of individuals with similar characteristics from a larger population to be selected and included in a study as the unit of analysis.

Cochrane Collaboration: An international organization in the United Kingdom whose aim is to help people make well-informed decisions about health care by preparing, maintaining, and ensuring the accessibility of systematic reviews of professional literature.

Code of ethics (COE): The National Association of Social Workers (NASW) professional conduct expectations required of social workers. The COE identifies core values and establishes ethical principles and standards that guide social workers' decision-making and conduct when ethical issues and dilemmas arise.

Cohort study: A group of individuals sharing certain significant characteristics in common, such as sex, age, place of birth, and so on that researchers follow over time.

Collaborate/collaboration: The manner in which two or more people or groups work together to achieve a shared goal, often represented in a relational process that encourages sharing knowledge, reciprocal learning, and building consensus.

Collaborative leadership: A body of theory and management practice that focuses on cooperative and shared leadership to deliver results across organizational hierarchies and boundaries.

Collective efficacy: The shared belief of a group regarding its combined ability to organize and/or execute actions required to produce an expected outcome.

Community of care: The neoliberal policy of transferring responsibility for individuals in need from large, often isolated, state institutions to their families, local social support networks, and welfare agencies.

Community asset mapping: A way of illustrating identified dimensions of communities and their strengths that focus on their resources, needs, and problems to target efforts, promote relationships, and provide solutions for health and human service agencies. Often used in community development processes.

Community development (CD): Practices of civic activists, professionals, agencies, and involved citizens to build stronger and more-resilient local communities by providing necessary skills to empower individuals and groups to create positive change in a respective community.

Competing organizations: Organizations with similar goals, missions, and service outputs that vie against one another for clients, resources, productivity, or recognition in a friendly or rivalrous manner.

Confirmation bias: The inclination to search for, seek out, interpret, and prioritize information that serves as evidence for one's beliefs or hypotheses.

Consensual decision-making: A group decision-making process that seeks the input, consent, and/or approval of all participants and stakeholders.

Constituent: A voting, participatory member of an organization or group with the power to appoint, elect, or reject individuals.

Consumer voice: The tabling of expressed consumer concerns, needs, expectations, preferences, and/or aversions that is usually facilitated through a qualitative in-depth process of evidence-based research and/or market research techniques.

Convenience sampling: A sample that is easily accessible based on time, availability, financial constraints, and so on.

Cost-benefit analysis: A systematic process for calculating and comparing benefits and cost of a project, decision, or government policy to determine its feasibility and justification.

Counterfactual condition: Projecting or providing empirical evidence regarding incidence statistics if an intervention program was not offered.

Critical appraisal skills: The ability of assessing and interpreting research or evidence by systematically considering its validity, results, and relevance.

Cross contamination: The process of introducing individuals who have been through an intervention into a population that is currently going through that same intervention.

Cultural competency: The ability to make services respectful of clients' cultural beliefs and behaviors influenced by gender, ethnicity, poverty, language, disability, sexuality, age, or other cultural influences, so that services are sensitive, inclusive, and acceptable to clients.

Data: A collection of information and facts from which conclusions may be drawn. These may consist of numbers, words, or images, particularly as measurements of a set of events, behaviors, or variables.

Data sources: Documents, people, and observations that provide information for assessment, research, or evaluation.

Democratic decision-making: A type of decision-making that occurs when a leader gives up ownership and control of a decision and decision-making process, allowing the group to vote. It often includes and/or relies on majority vote, consensus, weighing pros and cons, and options.

Demographic data: Background information of statistical characteristics of human populations (age, gender, race, income, etc.). These data are typically used as independent variables to subgroup variables to compare cohorts in data analysis.

Dependent variable: The idea or concept under investigation in an experiment or the target behavior that is being affected during the experiment.

Descriptive statistics: Numbers used to describe the basic features (mean, median, mode, variance, or standard deviation) of sample data in a study.

Devolution: The statutory granting of authority, responsibility, and/or administration of services from higher levels of government (sovereign or national) power to subnational levels such as regional, state, or local levels.

Direct cost: The actual dollar costs associated with the operation of a program, including all operating and support costs noted in the program's budget.

Disempowerment: The deprivation of esteem, influence, or authority; the process of making an individual, group, or entity seem detached, ineffectual, or unimportant.

Effectiveness study: A study evaluating a treatment outcome conducted under clinically representative, or real-life, conditions. It is usually used in the later stages of evaluating a new intervention.

Efficiency: The degree to which outcomes are achieved in terms of input and resources allocated.

Eight-step model of evidence-informed planning: A structured method for accomplishing major community development planning tasks. Each step comprises prescribed action steps that when achieved in stepwise fashion, contribute to the equitable inclusion of service users in the planning process. The eight steps are (1) Define Stakeholder Participation, (2) Build Mission and Purpose, (3) Identify Community Strengths, (4) Identify Community Needs Using EID, (5) Identify Services and Set Priorities Using EID, (6) Plan Service Using EID, (7) Decide on Intervention and Sponsors, and (8) Develop Joint Proposal.

Empirical: Measurable outcomes that rely on the replication of findings and systematic observations gathered using certain standards of evidence.

Empowerment: An increase in perceived self-efficacy resulting from a belief in the ability to positively influence the environment and to improve personal circumstances.

Equitable distribution: The process of equally dividing something among groups of people.

Ethical practice dilemmas: A circumstance or instance in which different ethical or moral values are in conflict, particularly those related to one's particular professional code of ethics, such as in health and human services.

Evaluation assessment: A study of the options for conducting an evaluation of a program including the purpose, proposed methods, stakeholders, and dissemination.

Evaluation research: A systematic inquiry to describe or assess the intervention impact of a specific program of intervention on individuals by determining its activities and outcomes.

Evidence-informed planning: Planning and implementation that are influenced and guided by empirical research and data.

Evidence-informed practice (EIP): Interventions/treatments for which systematic empirical research has provided validation of statistically significant effectiveness such as treatment for specific problems.

External environment: The factors, influences, and other human service organizations outside of a specific health and human service agency that affect its exchange relationships, resources, decisions, and planning.

Facilitator: One who assists a group or individual to understand common objectives, and guides the group or individual to purposely plan and execute a particular action, behavior, or position.

Findings: The outcomes of research, or what the research found.

Focus group: An organized discussion group with specifically selected individuals targeted to gain unique information about a particular topic. Often used in qualitative or marketing research studies.

Focused interview: A discussion with research participants during data collection, organized around several predetermined questions or topics, but providing some flexibility in the sequencing of the questions, and with a predetermined set of responses or specific data elements to be obtained.

Formative program evaluation: An ongoing preliminary evaluation that reviews and describes in-depth implementation and progress of a program and produces data to refine its future development.

Funding priorities: The process of focusing a funding proposal on the service needs of clients that most require funding at a specific point in time.

Funding proposal: A mandated detailed written document aimed to request funding and financial assistance from stakeholders and other interested external parties, with minimally including a budget, goals, objectives, outputs, outcomes, and strategies.

Gap analysis: A comparison of actual performance indicators with potential performance that identifies noticeable areas between expected and/or desired utilizations of resources, and the actual use of resources that need to be addressed.

Garbage in, garbage out: A concept borrowed from computer information processing used primarily to call attention to the fact that computers will unquestioningly process the most nonsensical of input data and produce a nonsensical output.

Gatekeepers: People who can help and facilitate individuals to form connections with larger groups of community members.

Globalization: A process of cross-border interactions and integration between people, companies, and governments of different nations; a process driven by international trade and investment, and aided by information technology.

Goal: A broad statement of aims or intended outcomes for an intervention by an individual, organization, or government.

Gray literature: Research materials not published in easily accessible journals or databases. Such materials may include conference proceedings, abstracts, research presented at conferences, newsletters, unpublished theses, and so on.

Grounded theory methods: The systematic generation of data-based theory to develop explanations, hypotheses, concepts, typologies, meanings, and descriptions of phenomena under investigation.

Group-administered questionnaire: A written survey generally administered to a sample of respondents in a group setting (i.e., focus group participants, students in a classroom, etc.) in an effort to generate a high response rate from a specific group of people.

Guided discussion: An active learning technique in which, rather than asking direct or specific questions, a researcher asks general questions to get a sense of what the respondent knows or explores alternative ways of thinking about a topic.

Health disparity: The differences in health status between one population group and typically a more-advantaged group.

Hierarchies of evidence: The relative authority of various types of scientific evidence and research relating to health and human services. For instance, it is generally accepted that quantitative, randomized control trials (RCTs) rank above observational, qualitative studies in their accuracy and validity of date planning purposes.

Home interview: Asking a research participant a series of questions in a place where he or she resides rather than in an office or laboratory.

Identifying information: Personal information such as last name, social security number, home address, detailed family history, and so on, that may be used to identify a research participant.

In-depth interview: Use of a structured, unstructured, or open-ended interview guide that has standardized or nonstandardized questions, measurement scales, and so on to collect data in a research study.

Independent variable: The variable that affects or is presumed to affect the dependent variable under study and is included in the research design so that its effect can be determined.

Indigenous knowledge: The knowledge that is unique to a local group or culture.

Indirect cost: Administrative expenses or costs used to support the operation of the host organization that are added to a budget.

Indirect practice: Areas of social work practice—administration, supervision, research, evaluation, policy development, planning, community development, consulting, and education—that do not necessarily involve immediate face-to-face or personal contact with clients, but facilitate client change, often at meso and macro levels.

Intangible cost: Costs that are not easily expressed in actual dollar amounts; for example, the cost of one's quality of life is intangible.

Interorganizational exchanges: Open communication and an ongoing flow of reciprocal information and resources between organizations and agencies to reach a desired outcome. These form the lifeblood of effective health and human service organizations.

Intervention: A purposely planned course of treatment by human service professionals given to individuals or groups and targeted to specific client problems. An intervention aims to primarily promote cognitive and behavioral changes that optimize mental, physical, and psychological wellness and health, and discourage potentially averse and negative behaviors.

Inventory of existing services: A comprehensive listing of all services provided within health and human service agencies.

Joint agreements: A written, binding agreement in which all parties agree to collaboratively develop and implement a new entity, service, or agency by contributing agreed-on inputs, interventions, equity, and resources.

Joint partners: A collaboration of one or more individuals, groups, or agencies that mutually work together for a specified period of time and/or a particular purpose.

Key informant: An individual who is targeted for data collection because his or her information will provide an accurate and relatively wide perspective on the setting, as well as lead to other sources of information.

Key words: The main ideas contained within a published report or document; also known as key concepts.

Leadership: Involves a set of personal attributes, skill competencies, and leadership intuition. The five core attributes that define it in social work are (1) vision, (2) influencing others to act, (3) teamwork/collaboration, (4) problem-solving capacity, and (5) creating positive change.

Leading question: An inquiry that triggers the answer, or the information the examiner is seeking.

Local planning: Creating, organizing, and implementing functions to promote the needs and desires of a local community and achieve a desired goal. Often a local planning body/authority exists to facilitate this process.

Long-term objectives: The intended sustainable performance evaluative markers that an organization wants to achieve at some point in the future (usually five years or more).

Macro practice: Practice that focuses on facilitating changes in larger human systems that include organizations and communities, and that incorporates concepts and practices such as administration, program development, planning, research, organization, community development, evaluation, and policy analysis.

Management: The organization and coordination of tasks in an effort to reach a specific outcome.

Mean: The sum of the scores in a distribution divided by the number of scores in that same distribution. It is the arithmetic average.

Median: The midpoint (central number) that evenly divides the number in two, with 50 percent of all numbers above the median and 50 percent of the numbers below the median.

Mentoring: The process of creating and sustaining a learning relationship between a student and an expert in a specific role or domain in which direction, support, and guidance is provided for the purpose of increasing knowledge and experience in particular areas of interest.

Micro practice: Face-to-face practice with individuals, families, and groups. This is the lifeblood of most social work practice.

Mode: The number that appears the most frequently in a distribution of scores or numbers.

Narrative data: Information gained by listening to a study participant's descriptions of an event or story and recording them verbatim.

Needs assessment: A systematic planning process that addresses and determines needs or gaps between current conditions and desired conditions.

Negative leadership: Inappropriate or unethical leadership that is destructive to the morale and/or productivity of the unit or organization.

Neoliberalism: An economic doctrine and shift from liberalism that focuses on and promotes a freer movement of goods, resources, and enterprises to locate cheaper labor and resources and maximize profits, outputs, and efficiencies.

Net social value: The economic value of a project or program once net present (discounted) costs have been subtracted from net present (discounted) benefits.

Neutral location: A place where power distribution is relatively equal between the people who meet there (e.g., meeting a professor at a coffee shop or park instead of at a classroom or in the professor's office).

Nonprobability-based sample: A subgroup of study participants is selected by the researcher, and it is uncertain if they represent the larger population. These samples can be divided into five main types: availability, convenience, quota, judgment, and purposive.

Objective: A statement of intended outcomes of an intervention that are measurable and time framed.

Open-ended questions: Questions that give the responder complete freedom for any response. For example, what is your favorite thing about smoking?

Oppression: The exercise of power and authority in a purposeful, harmful, unjust, or burdensome manner against people in a mental, physical, social, or economic way.

Organization as a unit of analysis: This refers to the organization or agency being the primary lens through which those within it (e.g., clients, staff, administrators, etc.) and those outside it (e.g., funding bodies, government, etc.) are viewed and appraised.

Organization output: Measurable products or profits that are produced by an agency. In terms of health and human services, organizational outputs can include the number of clients treated/ served, the amount and quality of services given, and so on.

Organizational domain: The immediate task and general environments surrounding the focal organization that it exchanges goods, services, and resources with in order to survive (e.g., competing, legitimizing, or referring organizations in the organizational domain).

Organizational mission: A broadly defined but enduring statement of purpose that distinguishes the organization from others of its type and identifies the scope of its operations in product (or service) and market terms. Organizations should routinely review their statements to ensure alignment of their program goals and objectives.

Organizational outcomes: The intended results of planned positive changes that will help the organization achieve its mission and goals while working in tandem with other organizations, the community, and the service users.

Organizational task environment: The ability of forces from suppliers, funders, consumers, and competitors that pressure and influence ongoing changes within an organization's ability to obtain specific tasks and results.

Organizational values: The stated standards that anchor and guide an organization's conduct, ethics, and operations. These values are often considered the moral compass for all regulations, policies, procedures, and governance. All interventions offered are ideally aligned with the organization's values.

Outcome: The short- or long-term results and consequences of planned interventions. A positive outcome is a favorable result that achieves an expected goal. It may be due to care received or not received. It often represents the cumulative effects of one or more conditions or processes on a client at a defined point in time.

Outcome measurement: Assessing specific and identified data points of change over time, typically as the result of a planned intervention.

Outreach: A process of creating proactive awareness in the professional community and in the general public about the availability of services in order to identify and establish contact with those who are deemed appropriate for specified services.

Panel group: A defined group of persons who provide information or feedback to the researchers at different points of the study.

Participatory action research (PAR): Identifies a social problem or concern and seeks information about it by planned collaborations with individuals or organizations. This is one of the main methods of qualitative research.

Participatory evaluation: An evaluation model organized as a team project in which the evaluator and representatives of one or more stakeholder groups work collaboratively in developing the evaluation plan, conducting the evaluation, or disseminating and using the result.

Participatory relationships: Relationships in which a service user acts as both a consumer and a producer, and works with a service provider to create and maintain an effective reciprocal two-way relationship.

Partnership: An arrangement, usually written and legal, in which parties agree to cooperate to advance their mutual interests, such as an MOU (memorandum of understanding).

Performance measure: The process of designing and implementing quantitative and qualitative measures of program results, including short- and long-term outputs and outcomes.

Phenomenology: The study of reports of structures of consciousness, such as thoughts as experienced from the first person point of view.

Pilot study: A small-scale study administered in order to identify limitations within the research design or to amend the intervention to create better measures or outcomes before the actual study is implemented.

Plan: A written list of steps or a schematic diagram that incorporates planning tasks, responsibilities, and time frames that direct the ability to achieve desired goals, objectives, and/or outcomes.

Planning process: Determining goals, specific objectives, and interventions designed to meet a client or community need. The process should be cooperative, collaborative, action-oriented, measurable, and time-specific.

Policy advocacy: Conscious efforts to change and/or develop legislative, agency, and community policies for the purpose of improving powerless and oppressed groups' access to resources and opportunities in an effort to improve its quality of life and well-being.

Policy skills: The analytic skills, political skills, interactional skills, and value-clarifying skills needed to effectively set policy agendas, analyze problems, make proposals, and enact, implement, and assess policy.

Politics: Normally refers to the governing process of countries or organizations that set policies, laws, and procedures that health and human service agencies must comply with.

Postmodernism: The skeptical interpretations and understandings of culture, literature, art, philosophy, history, economics, architecture, fiction, and literary criticism.

Power transfer: The ability to control and shift authority from one place or person to another.

Practice evaluations: To access the impact of a specific intervention on a target and outcome of a participant or participant group. These evaluations are normally conducted in partnership with participants, and promote ethical and clinical practice.

Practice guidelines: Systematically developed statements, best practices, laws, and/or policy recommendations that are typically about health or mental health practices, to assist a practitioner to make evidence-informed decisions about how to effectively practice.

Practice wisdom: An integrative process for blending the strengths and minimizing the limitations of empirical practice with more-subjective, more-intuitive, and case comparison approaches, in order to develop knowledge about one's professional practice or effectiveness.

Practitioner-researcher: A professional who conducts investigations and at the same time works in the field that she or he is researching. These individuals often utilize this research approach to direct and inform their own practice and benefit clients.

Primary data: Information collected directly or first hand by the researcher for the study through surveys, observations, tests, interviews, and so on.

Probability sampling: The use of random sampling techniques that allow a researcher to make relatively few observations and generalize from those observations to the larger population.

Program: A large or small intervention or purposive activity intended to achieve specific goals with particular target populations of individuals.

Program activity: An intervention or the work done in any program that produces outputs and outcomes.

Program drift: When a program or its mission, goals, interventions, or processes deviate over time from the original intent.

Program evaluation: Using research and evaluation methods to assess the needs, effectiveness, efficiency, or legitimacy of a health or human service to ensure that goals and objectives are being met and that targeted problems are being addressed.

Program implementation: The process of converting program inputs into specific activities needed to produce outputs.

Program inputs: Any resources used by the program's activities to produce outputs.

Program logic models: A model developed by the R. J. Kellogg Foundation utilized to evaluate the effectiveness of a program that graphically depicts the logical relationship among resources, activities, outputs, and outcomes of a specific program.

Program recipient characteristics: A list of details describing the nature or quality belonging to a person who is receiving or participating in a series of events within an agency or institution.

Program objectives: A statement of intended outcomes of programs written in a measurable form to stipulate a target group, size, and direction of the specified outcomes, and the time frame for achieving these outcomes.

Program outcomes: The achieved results for which a program was designed.

Program output: A targeted goal of a program that shows its effectiveness.

Promising practices: A strengths-based term recently applied to best practices.

Providers of authority and legitimation: Individuals, groups, and organizations that provide agencies with legal representation, auspices, and parameters to affect their mission.

Providers of clients: Health and human service organizations in the organization's domain that refer and provide clients to the host organizations.

Providers of complementary services: Health and human service organizations in the organization's domain who provide services that assist the agency to deliver their own services in their communities of care.

Providers of fiscal resources: Health and human service organizations in the organization's domain that provide monetary or fiscal support to the host agency. Many agencies rely on numerous fiscal agencies for their support.

Putting a face to a problem: The ability to recognize individuals as persons rather than as concepts, ideas, or theories that are affected by a particular social problem.

Qualitative research: The systematic (focus on natural quality, reliance on the researcher as the instrument of the data, and a report style focusing more on narrative data than on numbers), first-hand observation of real-world phenomena explained through ethnography, phenomenology, case studies, and so on.

Quality assurances: A planned and systematic process that provides confidence in a product's or program's ability to serve its intended purpose.

Quantitative research: Research that systematically explores, describes, or tests variables in numerical or statistical forms.

Quota sampling: Probability or nonprobability sampling based on specified and required quotas from particular subgroups needed for a research study.

Rationale: A logical statement given to justify the purpose of a study or a particular research approach, design, and methodology.

Recall bias: Similar to a threat to an internal validity, recall bias is when people have differing interpretations of an event, behavior, intervention, or interaction. For example, if there was a contentious board meeting at a community agency that occurred a year ago and no minutes were taken to record it, different people who attended the meeting are likely to recall only the things that most affected them.

Recipient inclusion: The process of proactively including individuals/clients to receive a particular service.

Recipients and consumers: Health and human service organizations in the organization's domain that receive clients from a host organization and move them to the next phase of intervention in their community of care.

Reciprocity: A situation or practice in which individuals exchange things that are mutually beneficial for each individual.

Representative sample: A group being studied whose members are measured to have demographic characteristics (e.g., sex, age, race, etc.) that match the population at large. For example, if females make up 51 percent of the population, a representative sample would also be made up of 51 percent females.

Resource availability: Analyzing a project's demand for a resource relative to the availability of the resource across the organization.

Results-based management: A philosophy of management that emphasizes the importance of intentional program or organizational results in managing the organization, its programs, and its people.

Secondary data sources: Databases or sources in which information, statistics, or data have been collected for a different purpose, and often by someone other than the user. Common sources include censuses, annual reports, technical reports, files/charts of service users, organizational data, and so on.

Self-awareness: The insight, understanding, knowledge, and personal awareness of one's own personality and character, and the ability to see oneself as an individual, separate from others and the environment.

Self-determination: An ethical approach to social work and care management that supports clients fully in determining their own futures, by designing their own care plans and choosing the assistance that they desire to affect them.

Service coordination: A process through which the social worker assesses and arranges and/or authorizes services and then implements and monitors the service plan using various providers necessary to meet the client's needs.

Service delivery: Sets of principles, policies, standards, and constraints used to guide the development, design, deployment, operation, and intervention or services delivered by a service provider.

Service duplication: Duplication of specific services within the health and human service agency or community. Such duplication is currently discouraged by funding bodies.

Service integration: A method or model of incorporating and managing a number of coordinated services, agencies, or organizations for programs/interventions to help users, clients, and patients.

Service provider (SP): An employee, department, or treatment process of a health and human service agency (or private practitioner) that provides specified interventions to patients, clients, and service users.

Service user (SU): Any client/patient or recipient affiliated with a health and/or human service agency who receives services and/or assists the agency in offering service through providing advocacy, planning, providing feedback, helping with governance, and so on.

Short-term objective: An immediate outcome or desirable milestone that an agency wants to achieve that is focused, time framed, and measurable

Shared decision-making: A collaborative decision-making approach between patients and service providers that allows for decisions—taking into consideration the best scientific evidence available—to be made.

Snowball sampling: A nonprobability technique that asks current research participants to ask other people whom they know to participate in a study so that what is at first a small group of participants becomes a larger group.

Social capital: The collective benefits of social assets and networks based on trust, reciprocity, information, and cooperation that allow individuals to do things for each other.

Social justice: A more equal distribution of societal rights and economic resources to all members of society, including the allocation of social benefits and opportunities, as well as provision of basic citizen rights and protection of those rights.

Social work values: The core values and principles that guide the practice and purpose of social work, including minimally service, social justice, dignity and worth, valuing human relationships, integrity, and competence.

Sponsor: An individual, group, or business who supports an event, activity, person, or organization/agency financially, wholly or partially, through the provision of services or products. A sponsor is similar to a benefactor.

Stakeholder: Any individual, group, or organization with a vested interest in an identified issue, cause, aegis, organizational mandate, person, or group.

Strengths perspective: A perspective promoted by social work that focuses on clients' positive attributes, abilities, and potential rather than on their problems, deficits, or discrepancies.

Summary: A brief overview (abstract, synopsis, executive summary) of a research project or document.

Summative program evaluation: A systematic assessment of a program at a specified time period that determines the success of the program, the ability to meet its intended goals, participant satisfaction, overall outcome effectiveness, the cost benefit measures, and the possibility of replication.

Support costs: Costs that accrue to a program due to the support services and facilities used.

Survey questionnaire: A research tool or inventory used to gather information regarding a particular idea, concept, trait, and so on.

Sustainable objectives: Specific results that a person or system wants to achieve and maintain at a certain level within longer specific time frames and with available resources.

System navigators: Individuals responsible for identifying specific agencies for service users in need and who currently know the range of possible services and agencies that are available and realistic for service users. Often used interchangeably with the term *case managers*.

Systematic reviews: An in-depth overview of many primary research studies on a specific research question that tries to identify, appraise, and synthesize all relevant research evidence to answer questions or ask new questions about empirical problems/phenomena.

Task environment: This refers to the immediate external organizational domain or those organizations/agencies in the community that a health and human service organization regularly interacts and transacts with in order to fulfill its mission.

Theory: A coherent group of general and testable assumptions or propositions used to develop explanations for social and behavioral phenomena.

Transparency: Purposely operating in a manner that is easy for others to notice, see, and understand what, where, and how actions are typically performed in a governance or therapeutic relationship.

Treatment group: Persons in a study who receive the independent variable that is being given to see if it makes a difference.

Treatment intervention: Planned care provided to improve a situation in a positive way.

Uniqueness of social work practice: Social work practice is uniquely client-centered in that it takes the client where she or he is at and assists the client in facilitating his or her own personal growth and development. It involves knowledge, values, and skills that focus on the strengths of clients and their systems. Interventions of social work are targeted at the intersection between the individual and his or her environment.

Unit of analysis: The primary unit (families, individuals, objects, groups, classrooms, organizations, communities) used in perspective, data reduction, and analysis.

Upper-level management: Teams and individuals responsible for making primary decisions within a company or agency who are of higher-tier authority status on the organizational ladder and normally possess more power within an agency or organization than middle- or lower-level managers.

Value for money: An important goal for public officials and other stakeholders who are concerned with whether taxpayers and citizens are receiving efficient and effective programs and services for their tax dollars.

Variable: An entity that can take on different variables. While some variables are numerical, others are qualitative in nature and consist of more-interpretive variables, for example, one's overall affect.

Vulnerable populations: Groups of people who, as a result of life conditions and circumstances, are at increased risk of being harmed by specific social, environmental, and/or health problems, making them more susceptible to disempowerment, social injustice, and a lower quality of life.

Work plan: A written outline of a set of goals and processes in which an individual or group can accomplish specific tasks, objectives, targets, or outcomes. Ideally, work plans are developed in a collaborative and consensual way with all stakeholders of interest.

Index

About the Authors

Judith M. Dunlop, PhD, MSW, is Professor Emerita in the School of Social Work, Kings University College at Western University in London, Ontario, Canada. She is a part-time faculty member in interdisciplinary studies at Kings University College. She has taught macrolevel social work courses at both undergraduate and graduate levels across Canada and the United States with a particular focus on community organization and development. Over the past twenty-seven years, she has also worked as a community planner, community development worker, and research consultant on projects in public health, long-term care, family violence, developmental disabilities, child welfare, neighborhood regeneration, service user/service provider planning groups, and rural populations. Her cross-cultural work includes community development training with indigenous community health workers in Canada and participatory action research (PAR) with South Asian women in Canada. She has been a health and social services planner for local and regional community planning groups in the areas of child abuse prevention, prevention of developmental disabilities, and development of a long-term care facility. Her research on service user participation was conducted in the United States, Canada, and Scotland, and the findings from these studies have been presented over the past four years at international conferences in Ireland and Scotland. She has published book chapters and articles in the areas of interorganizational collaboration, community social work practice, social policy, health promotion, participatory action research (PAR), and the use of information technology in social work. She has been a member of the Association for Community Organization and Social Administration (ACOSA) since 1995 and is also now a member of the International Association for Community Development (IACD).

Michael J. Holosko, PhD, MSW, holds an endowed chair as the Pauline M. Berger Professor of Family and Child Welfare at The University of Georgia, School of Social Work. He is also currently a Visiting Professor at City University of Hong Kong. He has taught across the undergraduate and graduate curriculum in schools of social work (primarily), nursing, public administration, and applied social science in Canada, the United States, Hong Kong, Sweden, Australia, and the U.S. Virgin Islands. For the past thirty-eight years he has been a consultant to a variety of large and small health and human service organizations and industries in the areas of program evaluation, outcomes, accreditation, organizational development, communication, leadership, visioning, organizational alignment, and stress management. He has published numerous monographs, chapters, articles, and texts in the areas of evaluation, health care, social work practice, curricula, administration, technology, gerontology, leadership, family and child welfare, social policy, research, music intervention, and spirituality. His most-recent text is J. Wodarski, M. Holosko, and M. Felt, M. D. (2015). *Evidence-Informed Assessment and Practice in Child Welfare*, Springer Publications. He serves on the editorial boards of: *Research on Social Work Practice, Child and Adolescent Social Work Journal, Social Work in Public Health, Journal of Human Behavior and Social Environment, Hong Kong Journal of Social Work, Journal of Social Service Research,* and *Journal of Evidence-based Social Work Practice.* For a number of years, he has had both radio and television shows advocating for social justice in North America.